Co-Creation and Capitalism

John Paul II's
Laborem Exercens

Edited by
John W. Houck
and
Oliver F. Williams, C.S.C.

106882

University Press of America
LANHAM • NEW YORK • LONDON

Library of Congress Cataloging in Publication Data
Main entry under title:

Co-creation and capitalism.

"Co-published by arrangement with the Notre Dame
Center for Ethics and Religious Values in Business"—T.p.
verso.
Includes bibliographical references and index.
1. Catholic Church. Pope (1978-   : John Paul II).
Laborem exercens—Addresses, essays, lectures.
2. Church and labor—Addresses, essays, lectures.
3. Christianity and capitalism—Addresses, essays,
lectures. I. Houck, John W. II. Williams, Oliver F.
HD6338.C57 1983   261.8'5   83-10247
ISBN 0-8191-3358-2 (alk. paper)
ISBN 0-8191-3359-0 (pbk. : alk. paper)

Cover design/**Ann E. Mercer**

to

Monsignor John J. Egan

A MAN FOR ALL SEASONS

*The word of God's revelation
is profoundly marked by the
fundamental truth that man,
created in the image of God,
shares by his work in the
activity of the creator . . .*

John Paul II

Contents

letter, *Laborem Exercens.* The meeting brought together eighteen distinguished scholars and corporate and labor leaders. In a lively and fruitful three days, some 150 persons shared in the discussions, which *Newsweek* characterized as a "free marketplace of ideas" exploring a religious vision of business power. This volume enables that experience to be shared in the wider community.

Other resources developed by the Center which may be of interest are: *Full Value: Cases in Christian Business Ethics; Matter of Dignity: Inquiries Into the Humanization of Work;* and *The Judeo-Christian Vision and the Modern Corporation.*

We are most grateful for the encouragement and financial support provided by the Indiana Committee for the Humanities, The National Endowment for the Humanities, and the General Electric Educational Foundation; and at the University of Notre Dame: the Center for the Study of Man in Contemporary Society, the Center for Pastoral and Social Ministry, *Notre Dame Magazine*, the Center for Continuing Education, and the College of Business Administration.

We wish to thank Barry B. Burr, Deborah K. Buscoe, Janice Coffield, Mary Dooley Houck, Peggy Roach, Phyllis Sandfort, David E. Schlaver, C.S.C., Kristina Strom, Suzanne VanGoey, Dale T. Wolberg, and Kelly Lee Zellers for their help. For guidance and support, we wish to recognize our dean, Frank K. Reilly, our associate dean, Yusaku Furuhashi, and our chairman, William P. Sexton. Our special gratitude goes to the executive coordinator of the conference, Mary M. Tavis, and our copy editor, Katharine Terry Dooley; both of these good friends, it should be noted, served in a voluntary capacity.

Finally, it is our pleasure to dedicate this book to Monsignor John J. Egan, Special Assistant to the President, Father Theodore M. Hesburgh, C.S.C., and Director of the Center for Pastoral and Social Ministry of the University of Notre Dame. Monsignor Egan, better known as Jack, has been untiring in his generosity for the cause of the poor, and he has been a great inspiration to his colleagues, near and far, in pursuing social justice. He is indeed "A Man For All Seasons."

> John W. Houck
> Oliver F. Williams, C.S.C.
> Co-directors, Center for Ethics
>   and Religious Values in Business
> University of Notre Dame, Notre Dame, IN
> 1983

Introduction

Oliver F. Williams, C.S.C.

R. H. TAWNEY, IN *RELIGION AND THE RISE OF CAPITALISM*, SUCCINCTLY STATES THE continuing challenge for the church:

> Granted that I should love my neighbor as myself, the questions which, under modern conditions of large-scale organizations remain for solution are, Who precisely *is* my neighbor? and, How exactly am I to make my love for him effective in practice? . . . Traditional social doctrines had no specific to offer, and were merely repeated, when, in order to be effective, they should have been thought out again from the beginning and formulated in new and living terms.[1]

This task of rethinking the social teaching of the church is an ongoing one, for as circumstances change, new and different threats to human dignity come to light. On September 4, 1981, Pope John Paul II, issued a new statement of the social concerns of the church, *Laborem Exercens* (On Human Work). He affirms that modern technological, economic and political conditions demand a fresh emphasis in church teaching. His unique focus resounds throughout the document: "Human work is a key, probably the essential key, to the whole social question."[2]

It is John Paul's hope that a renewed understanding of the role of work in human life will provide a way through the tangle of problems presently facing the modern world. He notes some of these thorny issues:

> the widespread introduction of automation into many spheres of production, the increase in the cost of energy and raw materials,

1

working for a better and a more just social order. More precisely, these two tasks are not mutually exclusive but are intertwined. It must be acknowledged that this emphasis on working for more just social structures is a relatively new one, and that secular progress was not always linked so intimately with the Kingdom of God. Indeed, the meaning of the term "Kingdom of God" has been slowly emerging over the centuries. The notion of the Kingdom of God was a familiar one to the Jews of Jesus' time. They read in their scripture that the Kingdom was experienced in the historical acts of God (cf. 2 Samuel 7:12-16), and yet that it was also present beyond history (cf. Judges 8:23). It was localized in the ark of the covenant, and yet it was universally present in heaven itself. It was spoken of as present and yet future. In short, there were dialectical aspects of the Kingdom, and the Hebrew people longed for its fullness.

Jesus came into the world and preached: "Take heart, the Kingdom of God is at hand" (Mark 1:15). Where people are changing their way of life to conform to the will of God, there the Kingdom is coming (Matthew 6:9-13). Jesus made little attempt to spell out the details of the Kingdom; it was a manifestation of the Father's love and this is ultimately beyond the pale of human understanding. In the Hebrew Scriptures the prophets allude to the Kingdom with the image of the lion resting peaceably with the lamb. The stories of Jesus point to some of the qualities of the Kingdom – peace, harmony, justice and brotherhood.

After the resurrection of Jesus, his followers recognized that the Kingdom of God had come into the world in the very person of Jesus, the Christ. They awaited the fulfillment of the Kingdom in the second coming of Christ. The first generation of Christians seemed to think that the world would end in their lifetime and that they would be ushered into a new world, the fullness of the Kingdom of God. Gradually, Christians in the West identified the Kingdom of God with the church. St. Augustine in the *City of God* speaks of the Kingdom as totally God's work, and as present in the church.

Until recently, most Christians understood the Kingdom of God to be present in the institutional church. To be sure, this presence was not thought to be in its fullness, but rather it was imaged more like a seed that would blossom forth in God's good time at the second coming of Christ. The church was the place of the Kingdom "between the times." Between the first coming of Christ and his second coming, men and women could grow in Christian virtue – charity, forgiveness, generosity, and so on — by living and worshipping together in the church animated by the Spirit.

The architect who fashioned the intellectual underpinnings for the Church's view of what constitutes a good life on this earth was, for the most part, Thomas Aquinas (1225-1274). St. Thomas appropriated the Aristotelian principle that all things have a "nature," an essence, and that the goal is to do whatever it takes to bring that nature to perfection. Reflecting the prevailing wisdom of his time, Aquinas viewed the task of Christian life as one of becoming a virtuous person, holding that the purpose (end) of human life is ultimately to become suited for union with God in the next life. "Man's ultimate happiness consists solely in the contemplation of God. . . ."[8] As a result of a supernatural gift of grace, the person is enabled to develop virtue, and thus be in harmony with God's plan of creation. Aquinas focused on the virtues emphasized in the Bible — faith, hope and charity — and Aristotle's four cardinal virtues — wisdom, justice, fortitude and temperance. The stress in Aquinas is on *personal* morality; the contemporary emphasis on changing social structures to make the world a better place was not a great concern for the medieval religious scholars.

There was a gradual development in understanding what constitutes the vocation of Christians in the world. While the personal morality emphasis of Aquinas was never slighted, this standpoint has been expanded to include an equally important social dimension. The social dimension was fully appropriated into the Christian life in the documents of the Second Vatican Council. It is significant that John Paul quotes Vatican II's "The Church in the Modern World" eleven times in *Laborem Exercens*. The point of most of these citations is to stress the fact that the proclamation of the Kingdom of God entails working for socio-political changes which are aimed at bringing about a better life for the poor. For example, from paragraph 34 of "The Church in the Modern World," the Pope quotes as follows:

> Far from thinking that works produced by man's own talent and energy are in opposition to God's power, and that the rational creature exists as a kind of rival to the Creator, Christians are convinced that the triumphs of the human race are a sign of God's greatness and the flowering of his own mysterious design. For the greater man's power becomes, the farther his individual and community responsibility extends. . . . People are not deterred by the Christian message from building up the world, or impelled to

neglect the welfare of their fellows. They are, rather, more stringently bound to do these very things.[9]

The Person as a Co-Creator

The key theme of *Laborem Exercens* is that the person is actually sharing in the work of creation by labor.

> . . . Man ought to imitate God, his creator, in working, because man alone has the unique characteristic of likeness to God.[10]

> Man shares by his work in the activity of the creator.[11]

To call the creature a "co-creator" is a preposterous claim according to one school of Christian theology. Karl Barth argued that this title runs the risk of trivializing the unique character of God's creative action; the sovereignty of God seems to diminish, and the arrogance of the creature is a likely result. One theologian put the criticism this way:

> The cognizance of this increase of human powers has led some writers to refer to humanity as a "co-creator" with God. It is a flattering and awesome notion, but an outrageous one, on roughly the same plane with the notion that anyone could be "Miss Universe"![12]

Many, agreeing with the thrust of *Laborem Exercens*, see no serious problem with this term, assuming all the qualifications regarding human sinfulness and weakness are noted. Chapter One by Michael Novak champions the notion of the person sharing in the work of creation – the encyclical itself never uses the term "co-creation." Chapter Three, authored by David Hollenbach, probes some of the weak points in the way *Laborem Exercens* relates human work and God's creative activity. Stanley Hauerwas, in Chapter Two, serves as our devil's advocate, and dismisses the whole idea of co-creation. Later chapters assume there is value in the co-creation theme and explore its implications in various dimensions of business life.

John Paul, relying on his theological interpretation of the Book of Genesis, argues that the most important purpose of work is to develop one's humanity, to become a virtuous person; he calls this "the subjective dimension of labor." The human "dominance" over nature spoken of in the Book of Genesis is taken to mean that the person shares in the activity of the creator, and hence is of superior value. With this theological interpretation, the pope is trying to move the discussion of the worker beyond the concept of the "hired hand," of labor as a commodity. When labor is treated as a commodity, whether in national economic systems or by transnational corporations, it is to be challenged, argues the encyclical. The "development of the Kingdom of God" entails not only the transformation of the world by human labor (the *objective* dimension of work), but also, and more importantly, the transformation of the person (the *subjective* dimension of work). Forming virtuous persons according to God's intentions remains primary, yet advances in the social sciences have provided insight into the importance of a humane environment. The challenge is one of discerning the best way of fashioning an environment attuned to fostering the growth of individual character and creativity.

The pope is suggesting that a crucial task of the church is to educate men and women so that they realize their co-creator roles. This knowledge will not only bring them in harmony with God's intentions, but will also provide an enormous source of motivation for doing work with pride and fulfillment. All this effort will also be seen in the larger context of the Kingdom of God.

Laborem Exercens: Socialist Economics?

An expert in Catholic social thought, Monsignor George C. Higgins, warns us away from the rocky shoals of the debate between capitalism and socialism. "It would be regrettable if Americans were to get bogged down in an ivory-tower, theoretical debate about the relative merits of capitalism and socialism. . . ."[13] What is needed, he wisely counsels, is a discussion of the reform, both of capitalism and socialism, where appropriate. The fact is, however, that some have identified *Laborem Exercens* with socialist economics, and have therefore dismissed it as irrelevant to the situation of the United States. For example, an editor of *Fortune* magazine writes that the encyclical

> displays once again the evidently invincible determination of the Church not to understand capitalism. Judging from the general tenor of *Laborem Exercens*, the Church remains wedded to socialist economics. . . . The capitalist alternative, which has markets allocating resources more rationally than planners and moralists, is never described fairly.[14]

While it is true that church teaching since the 1971 document of Pope Paul VI, *Octogesima Adveniens*, has in principle accepted a form of socialism as *one* viable way of organizing economic affairs, the teaching has never indicated a preference for "socialist economics."

In my judgment it is not correct to say that church social teaching misunderstands the wisdom—and even the morality—of a market economy. The best moral argument for the market economy is that it allocates resources and promotes economic growth so as to foster a humane community and improve the quality of life. This argument, advanced in 1776 by Adam Smith in his *Wealth of Nations*, is valid today as it was two hundred years ago. Smith writes of the dynamic that channels individual self-interest to the common good.

> In civilized society he stands at all times in need of the co-operation and assistance of great multitudes, while his whole life is scarce sufficient to gain the friendship of a few persons. . . . Man has almost constant occasion for the help of his brethren, and it is in vain for him to expect it from their benevolence only. He will be more likely to prevail if he can interest their self-love in his favour, and show them that it is for their own advantage to do for him what he requires of them. Whoever offers to another a bargain of any kind proposes to do this. . . . It is not from the benevolence of the butcher, the brewer, or the baker, that we expect our dinner, but from their regard to their own interest.[15]

Church teaching accepts this mechanism but with a key qualification. A summary statement of the church's social teaching in this area was given by John XXIII:

> At the outset it should be affirmed that in economic affairs first place is to be given to the private initiative of individual men who, either working by themselves, or with others in one fashion or another, pursue their common interests.

> But in this matter . . . it is necessary that public authorities take active interest, the better to increase output of goods and to further social progress for the benefit of all citizens.[16]

This framework underpins the suggestions of *Laborem Exercens*. While accepting the value of a market economy, religious social thought argues that one must have a conscious concern for the common good of all, and not depend on unconscious workings of the market, the "hidden

hand" to solve all problems. Smith believed in God's providence working to insure the common good, a self-regulating economy. Religious
social thought says, in effect, that we must make God's work our own,
that we must have a conscious care for the common good. This sometimes requires government regulation of the market. To be sure, regulation is tricky business and the good consequences sought are often
elusive. A failure in a particular regulation is no argument against
regulation, however, but rather one for better regulation. We must
learn how to do it right![17]

Church social teaching recognizes that participation in market economy can be a great aid toward developing character. The habits and virtues required to participate in the market—honesty, industriousness,
patience, deferred gratification, for example—are ones extolled by the
church. *Laborem Exercens* reiterates this point:

> The church's teaching has always expressed the strong and deep
> conviction that man's work concerns not only the economy but
> also, and especially, personal values. The economic system itself
> and the production process benefit precisely when these personal
> values are fully respected. In the mind of St. Thomas Aquinas,
> this is the principal reason in favor of private ownership of the
> means of production.[18]

Another way of indicating where church social teaching departs from
Adam Smith, or at least from some of his contemporary interpreters,
is to point to the church's concern that competition or self-interest
always be in the context of cooperation. *Laborem Exercens* makes the
point many times:

> In the final analysis, both those who work and those who manage
> the means of production or who own them must in some way be
> united in this community. . . . Just efforts to secure the rights of
> workers who are united by the same profession should always
> take into account the limitations imposed by the general economic
> situation of the country. Union demands cannot be turned into a
> kind of group or class "egoism," although they can and should
> also aim at correcting—with a view to the common good of the
> whole society—everything defective in the system of ownership
> of the means of production or in the way these are managed.[19]

There is growing evidence that competition is increasingly seen in the
context of cooperation. For example, the crisis of productivity is one

that concerns all of American business and is the subject of considerable research. Whether the answer is discussed in terms of Theory Z, quality circles, or quality of work life, the research points to a growing consensus that we must move beyond the concept of labor as a commodity. When people are given an opportunity to use their initiative at an appropriate level, to share in the decisions that affect them, in short, when they are treated in accord with their dignity, the quality of work rises and absenteeism declines; people find fulfillment in their work. More and more U.S. firms are involving their employees in aspects of the design and control of work, and indications are that this moral policy is yielding dividends for all.

Consider labor-management strife. The history of American labor-management relations is perhaps best characterized by the image of a battlefield. Each party comes to the bargaining table to face the other as an adversary and hammer out a contract. In recent years, however, often spurred on by international competition from Asia and Europe, unions and management have been moving from contractual to consensual relationships. Emphasis is on building community in the workplace. Terms such as team building, organizational development and job enrichment have become commonplace in more progressive unions and firms. These strategies are designed to unlock the full potential of the person by treating workers as persons with dignity. Much remains to be done in this area, for the adversarial posture will not die easily, either with union leaders who have made their reputation as tough bargainers, or with managers who see their sole task as maximizing short-term profits. However, there is hope American labor-management relations are in the dawn of a new era.

Laborem Exercens teaches us that human fulfillment requires the exercise of creativity. The moral mandate is to structure the society, its economic system and productive process, so that personal creativity is nourished. Today we see a growing recognition that management must be enabled to be more creative. The focus is on hard work, human initiative, indeed entrepreneurship. Innovative companies are taking the lead in establishing a work environment that will enhance creativity. Much remains to be done, not only in the industrial world, but especially in developing countries. The hope is that the following essays might play a small part in paving the way for further progress.

NOTES

1. R. H. Tawney, *Religion and the Rise of Capitalism* (New York: New American Library, 1958), p. 156.
2. *Laborem Exercens,* Para. 3. All citations are to the text published by the United States Catholic Conference: Publication No 825, Office of Publishing Services.
3. Para. 1.
4. Cf. G. Weigel, "The Significance of Papal Pronouncements," *The Papal Encyclicals in Their Historical Context*, ed. A. Fremantle (New York, 1956).
5. For an analysis of the importance of the historical context of papal social encyclicals, see John Coleman, S.J., "What is an Encyclical? Development of Church Social Teaching,"*Origins*, June 4, 1981, pp. 33-41.
6. Richard John Neuhaus, "The Mind of the Most Powerful Man in the World," *Worldview*, September 1981, pp. 11-13.
7. Para. 27.
8. Aquinas, *Summa Contra Gentiles*, III, 37.
9. Para. 25.
10. *Ibid.*
11. *Ibid.*
12. Bruce C. Birch and Larry L. Rasmussen, *The Predicament of the Prosperous* (Philadelphia: The Westminster Press, 1978), p. 184.
13. Msgr. George C. Higgins, "Foreward," *On Human Work: A Resource Book*, (Washington D.C.: United States Catholic Conference, 1982), p. 3.
14. Daniel Seligman, "Keeping Up," *Fortune*, November 2, 1981, p. 63. Gregory Baum celebrates that *Laborem Exercens* "advocates. . . . a particular form of socialism." Cf. *The Priority of Labor* (New York: Paulist Press, 1982), p. 81.
15. Adam Smith, *The Wealth of Nations*, ed. Edwin Cannan (Chicago: University of Chicago Press, 1976), p. 18.
16. "Mater et Magistra," *The Gospel of Peace and Justice: Catholic Social Teaching Since Pope John*, ed. Joseph Gremillon (Maryknoll, N.Y.: Orbis Books, 1976), p. 154.
17. For example, see Charles L. Schultze, *The Public Use of Private Interest* (Washington, D.C.: Brookings Institution, 1977).
18. Para. 15.
19. Para. 20.

PART ONE

The Theology
of Co-Creation

The word of God's revelation is profoundly marked by the fundamental truth that man, created in the image of God, shares by his work in the activity of the creator and that, within the limits of his own human capabilities, man in a sense continues to develop that activity, and perfects it as he advances further and further in the discovery of the resources and values contained in the whole of creation.

Laborem Exercens, Para. 25

Through his labor and his native endowments man has ceaselessly striven to better his life. Today, however, especially with the help of science and technology, he has extended his mastery over nearly the whole of nature and continues to do so . . . In the face of these immense efforts which already preoccupy the whole human race, men raise numerous questions among themselves. What is the meaning and value of this feverish activity? How should all these things be used? To the achievement of what goal are the strivings of individuals and societies heading?

Gaudium et Spes, Para. 33

. . . the Church has always had the duty of scrutinizing the signs of the times and of interpreting them in the light of the gospel.

Gaudium et Spes, Para. 4

. . . the modern world shows itself at once powerful and weak, capable of the noblest deeds or the foulest. Before it lies the path to freedom or to slavery, to progress or retreat, to brotherhood or hatred. Moreover, man is becoming aware that it is his responsibility to guide aright the forces which he has unleashed and which can enslave him or minister to him.

Gaudium et Spes, Para. 9

What are we to make of the modern world which we humans have *fabricated*? Our answer goes a long way toward determining whether we accept or reject a theology of co-creation.

Pope John Paul II, in powerful and direct language, argued that we share by our work, both physically and intellectually, in "the activity of the Creator." And while he does not use the words *co-creator* or *co-creation* in *Laborem Exercens*, there does not seem to be among the scholars in this volume any controversy about the appropriateness of either *co-creator* or *co-creation* as descriptive of John Paul's position.

Capitalism as a system, and corporations as the system's operating units, are today great centers of human power, ingenuity, and creativity. This was equally true in 1848 when Marx and Engels observed in the *Manifesto*:

> The bourgeoisie (industrialists), during its rule of scarcely one hundred years, has created more massive and more colossal productive forces than have all preceding generations together. The subjection of nature's forces to man and machinery; the application of chemistry to industry and agriculture; (the development of) steam navigation, railways and electric telegraphs; the clearing of whole continents for cultivation; the canalization of rivers and the conjuring of whole populations out of the ground (off the land?) — what earlier century had even a presentiment that such productive forces slumbered.

An important difference today from the time of the *Manifesto* is the systematic use of science and technology, with the contemporary corporation becoming often a huge knowledge factory filled with specialists pursuing information bits and technical competence. Tracy Kidder describes all of this in the brilliant book, *The Soul of the New Machine*, as a team of computer engineers beat out rival companies and the Japanese competitors in creating an advanced computer. It is intriguing that the process represents a sporting event, "the thrill of victory, the agony of defeat," where one team wins the contest but will soon be reconstituted with different specialists to work on the next generation of the state of the art.

To comprehend the power possessed, often unconsciously, by these managers and engineers, one only has to walk the corridors of universities, high schools and even grade schools to observe students hunched over their computer screens or to observe television commercials telling us that "if we really care for our children we'll buy a home computer." This process of research, invention, production, and marketing, in the words of the *Manifesto*, truly "creates a world after its own image."

Three theologians in Part One examine the appropriateness of co-creation as an acceptable concept in theological discourse. Michael Novak sees Pope John Paul II calling us to be co-creators with God in fashioning a new and more just world.

> The human person is a creator and nowhere more so than at his daily ecomonic tasks . . . the human person is made in the image of God. Each has the vocation to work and to create. Creation theology does not set person against person, class against class, nation against nation. It calls forth the human capacity to create a new world . . .

For Novak, a theology of co-creation deals with the fundamental issue: how do we humans exercise our power and creativity? And Novak believes that corporate capitalism, or to use his term—Democratic Capitalism, is inextricably a part of God's empowerment of humans.

For Stanley Hauerwas, there are grave questions about a theology of co-creation being faithful to the religious tradition which, he argues, has humankind as a *representative* of God: "A representative is not a co-creator. A representative does not 'share by his work in the activity of the creator,' but instead reflects what that activity has already accomplished." There are in Hauerwas' view no theological warrants for co-creation, and religious groups run the risk of upsetting the critical creator-human ecology by this "remarkably bad idea." David Hollenbach, S.J., takes another tack on the matter: the Christian faith must rebut the presupposition that the sabbath precludes interest in what our powerful and creative corporations like IBM, Bell Labs, and Genetech are doing. He calls for an "adequate" theology:

> An adequate theology of work and human creativity needs *both* a deep sensitivity to the capacity of human beings to be co-creators with God *and* a ruthlessly realistic assessment of the conflicts and oppressions which human freedom can and does create. Without the first the theology has no basis for hope and thus cannot be Christian. Without the second the theology will not be capable of generating an ethic that is usable in human history — the time between Paradise and the coming of the Kingdom of God.

CHAPTER 1

Creation Theology

by Michael Novak

THIS PAPER MARKS THE THIRD TIME IN RECENT YEARS THAT I HAVE LECTURED AT Notre Dame on the theology of work. In 1979, I argued that an adequate theology of the laity for our era would have to begin with a theology of work and, therefore, with a theology of economic systems and particularly of democratic capitalism.[1] Lay Catholics have a special obligation to come to a theological understanding of our own distinctive American system, the first modern nation in the *novus ordo seclorum*. In 1980, the subject assigned me was the theology of the corporation which, I argued, should begin with the theological category of creation: or, more precisely, of human co-creation with God.[2]

In the meantime, Pope John Paul II's brilliant encyclical *Laborem Exercens* has appeared, and the Pontiff has highlighted, "perhaps more than has been done before—the fact that human work is a key, probably the essential key, to the whole social question."[3] He has also squarely rooted the "elements for a spirituality of work" in the biblical category of creation or, more precisely, co-creation. The Pope has highlighted the crucial role played by *invention* and *discovery* in the human vocation "to subdue the earth." In short, Pope John Paul II has illustrated a remarkably "American" way of approaching the nature and the destiny of man, the role of capital and labor, private property and com-

17

munity. Without doubt, *Laborem Exercens* is a remarkable manifesto for the future. It calls us both to continue on the path we have been following, but also to change, in order to do some things better, and more justly, than they have ever been done before.

Thus, in this my third lecture in this sequence, I would like to develop some of Pope John Paul II's main insights in *Laborem Exercens*, especially as they apply to democratic capitalism. I wish to stress: (1) his conception of the subjective character of labor; (2) the priority he assigns to labor over capital; (3) his failure to reflect fully upon capital; (4) his emphasis on private property; and (5) his stress on discovery and invention. In my judgment, *Laborem Exercens* brings Catholic social teaching toward a more realistic grasp of the effective principles of development than any other ecclesiastical document. There remain a few gaps in what Pope John Paul II has attempted, and these I mean to address. First, however, it may be useful to summarize the structure of his thought.

Laborem Exercens is divided into five parts. The introduction (1-3) situates the discussion of work, "the key to the social question," in the tradition of Catholic social teaching since *Rerum Novarum*, ninety years ago. Part II, "Work and Man," will surely become a *locus classicus* in the theology of work in several dimensions, including reflections on various historical eras and various conceptions of work (4-10). Part III (11-15) is an historical excursus on "The Conflict between Labor and Capital in the Present Phase of History." It is here that the Pope treats the priority of labor, economism and materialism, work and ownership, and his own "personalist" argument. Part IV (16-23) considers the rights of workers, and is remarkable for its novel distinction between the direct and indirect employer. Part V turns to "Elements for a Spirtuality of Work" (24-27). Here the theology of creation and the theology of toil and suffering receive their fullest treatment.

It is obvious that this encyclical is unusually rich in intellectual construction. It has the ring of modernity, even of the future, while it also offers a daring interpretation of the nineteenth and twentieth centuries. In its grasp, it intends to include Africa and Asia, Latin America as well as North America, and the Soviet socialist nations as well as Western Europe. Its style often suggests the precise personal imprint of the Pope, for there are in the text many echoes of his scholarly writings, particularly on personalism in conflict with Soviet socialism.

Man as the Subject of Work

Animals do not work, only man works, the Pope asserts. Work bears "the mark of a person operating within a community of persons."[4] Work has an interior dimension, a dimension of spirit and intentionality, of intellect and will. "Man is the image of God partly through the mandate received from his creator to subdue, to dominate, the earth. In carrying out this mandate, man, every human being, reflects the very action of the creator of the universe."[5] Again: "The expression 'subdue the earth' has an immense range. It means all the resources that the earth (and indirectly the visible world) contains and which, through the conscious activity of man, can be discovered and used for his ends." Thus, the Pope imagines that the Creator has hidden many resources in his creation, which it is the task of humans to discover through conscious labor. He envisages "future phases of development, which are perhaps already to some extent beginning to take shape, though for the most part they are still almost unknown to man and hidden from him." The Pope sees technology as "the fruit of the work of the human intellect and a historical confirmation of man's dominion over nature."[6]

Yet technology can also become man's enemy, and so the Pope turns to the *subject* of work, the human person: "In fact, in the final analysis it is always man who is the purpose of the work, whatever work it is that is done by man—even if the common scale of values rates it as the merest 'service,' as the most monotonous, even the most alienating work."[7] Anyone who has worked in any field knows the toil and suffering always involved in it—the teacher grading papers, the dentist probing mouths, the digger in a gravel pit, the miner, the preacher, the political leader on the telephone. The Pope quotes from Ecclesiastes (2:11): "Then I considered all that my hands had done and the toil I had spent in doing it," and he adds: "There is no one on earth who could not apply these words to himself."[8] In short, the Pope wishes to place the consideration of work upon the plane of human dignity, beyond all considerations of a merely material or merely economic nature. Work is made for man, not man for work—as Jesus had earlier said even of the sabbath.

From the beginning of the industrial age, the Pope asserts, "various trends of materialistic and economistic thought" posed a danger to this Christian understanding.[9] Here is how Pope John Paul II describes this historical problem:

For certain supporters of such ideas, work was understood and treated as a sort of "merchandise" that the worker—especially the industrial worker—sells to the employer, who at the same time is the possessor of the capital, that is to say, of all the working tools and means that make production possible. This way of looking at work was widespread especially in the first half of the 19th century. Since then explicit expressions of this sort have almost disappeared and have given way to more human ways of thinking about work and evaluating it.[10]

The Pope opposes any:

> . . . onesidedly materialistic civilization, which gives prime importance to the objective dimension of work, while the subjective dimension—everything in direct or indirect relationship with the subject of work—remains on a secondary level. In all cases of this sort, in every social situation of this type, there is a confusion or even a reversal of the order laid down from the beginning by the words of the Book of Genesis: Man is treated as an instrument of production, whereas he—he alone, independent of the work he does—ought to be treated as the effective subject of work and its true maker and creator. Precisely this reversal of order, whatever the program or name under which it occurs, should rightly be called "capitalism"—in the sense more fully explained below. Everybody knows that capitalism has a definite historical meaning as a system, an economic and social system, opposed to "socialism" or "communism." But in light of the analysis of the fundamental reality of the whole economic process—first and foremost of the production structure that work is—it should be recognized that the error of early capitalism can be repeated wherever man is in a way treated on the same level as the whole complex of the material means of production, as an instrument and not in accordance with the true dignity of his work—that is to say, where he is not treated as subject and maker, and for this very reason as the true purpose of the whole process of production.[11]

In accepting a Marxist view of early capitalism and, in particular, in accepting as a *definition* of capitalism the reversal of right order, the Pope seems to have committed an historical injustice. This point may be sharply illustrated by the contrast which appeared in the United States in the early nineteenth-century in the conflict between slave labor and free labor. To assert, as the Pope does, that under capitalism free labor is regarded as "merchandise" is to go too far. Merchandise can be bought; it is not hired. The hired laborer retains an independence and a dignity lacking both to the peasants and serfs of the central European lands and to slaves in America. The hired laborer accepts a contract for a time, for his purposes. An especially good illustration of this reality appears in Abraham Lincoln's address at the Wisconsin State Fair in 1859. In many ways, Lincoln's entire address anticipates the central themes of *Laborem Exercens*. If I quote from him at length, it is to give a concrete sense of how the world of labor looked to fairgoers in Wisconsin in 1859:

> The world is agreed that labor is the source from which human wants are mainly supplied. There is no dispute upon this point. From this point, however, men immediately diverge. Much disputation is maintained as to the best way of applying and controlling the labor element. By some it is assumed that labor is available only in connection with capital — that nobody labors, unless somebody else, owning capital, somehow, by the use of that capital, induces him to do it. Having assumed this, they proceed to consider whether it is best that capital shall hire laborers, and thus induce them to work by their own consent; or buy them, and drive them to it without their consent. Having proceeded so far they naturally conclude that all laborers are necessarily either hired laborers, or slaves. They further assume that whoever is once a hired laborer, is fatally fixed in that condition for life; and thence again that his condition is as bad as, or worse than, that of a slave. . . .
>
> But another class of reasoners hold the opinion that there is no such relation between capital and labor, as assumed; and that there is no such thing as a freeman being fatally fixed for life, in the condition of a hired laborer, that both these assumptions are false, and all inferences from them groundless. They hold that labor is prior to, and independent of, capital; that, in fact, capital is the fruit of labor, and could never have existed if labor had not first existed — that labor can exist without capital, but that capital could never have existed without labor. Hence they hold that labor is the superior — greatly the superior — of capital. . . .[12]

In Lincoln's experience, free labor is different from slavery or serfdom. The free laborer retains his dignity and his liberty. He feels the undercurrent of upward mobility. He does not necessarily move with this undercurrent (Lincoln's letters to his own unambitious, dependent brother attest poignantly to those who take no advantage of their opportunities).[13] In a word, it is emphatically *not* the case that capitalism can be *defined* as a reversal of the subjective dimension of work, in which the hired laborer is treated merely as an instrument of production. Such a reversal is a sin against capitalism, not its inward dynamic. There are many texts in Adam Smith, particularly in his reflections on the reasons why colonies prosper,[14] in Alexander Hamilton's "Report on Manufactures,"[15] and in other central documents of democratic capitalism which take, in effect, the same view of the moral question as does Pope John Paul II.

The Priority of Labor over Capital

Pope John Paul II goes on to "recall a principle that has always been taught by the church: the principle of the priority of labor over capital."[16] In the process of production, "labor is always a primary efficient cause, while capital, the whole collection of means of production, remains a mere instrument or instrumental cause." This very idea, which the Pope describes as "an evident truth that emerges from the whole of man's historical experience," was also given testimony before the Congress of the United States in Abraham Lincoln's First Annual Message to Congress, on December 3, 1861. Re-phrasing some of the very words he had used at the Wisconsin State Fair in 1859, Lincoln declared:

> Labor is prior to, and independent of, capital. Capital is only the fruit of labor, and could never have existed if labor had not first existed. Labor is the superior of capital, and deserves much the higher consideration. Capital has its rights, which are as worthy of protection as any other rights. Nor is it denied that there is, and probably always will be, a relation between labor and capital, producing mutual benefits. The error is in assuming that the whole labor of community exists within that relation.[17]

Moreover, Lincoln attached a very great importance to the principle of free labor and its superiority to capital. He himself had been a hired laborer. He valued the system of liberty, political and economic. He saw its importance for the entire human race:

> This is the just, and generous, and prosperous system, which opens the way to all — gives hope to all, and consequent energy,

and progress, and improvement of condition to all. No men living are more worthy to be trusted than those who toil up from poverty — none less inclined to take, or touch, aught which they have not honestly earned. Let them beware of surrendering a political power which they already possess, and which, if surrendered, will surely be used to close the door of advancement against such as they, and to fix new disabilities and burdens upon them, till all of liberty shall be lost.

From the first taking of our national census to the last are seventy years; and we find our population at the end of the period eight times as great as it was at the beginning. The increase of those other things which men deem desirable has been even greater. We thus have at one view what the popular principle applied to government, through the machinery of the States and the Union, has produced in a given time; and also what, if firmly maintained, it promises for the future. There are already among us those, who, if the Union be preserved, will live to see it contain two hundred and fifty millions. The struggle of to-day, is not altogether for to-day — it is for a vast future also. With a reliance on Providence, all the more firm and earnest, let us proceed in the great task which events have devolved upon us.[18]

On the priority of labor over capital, both Abraham Lincoln and Pope John Paul II share the same principle, and expect from it common fruitfulness.

The Meaning of Capital

The definition which Pope John Paul II gives to capital, as we have seen, is pejorative; the definition he gives to capital is severely limited. He writes: "Everything contained in the concept of capital in the strict sense is only a collection of things."[19] "Man alone is a person," the Pope adds. He includes in this "collection of things" both "the natural resources placed at man's disposal, but also the whole collection of means by which man appropriates natural resources and transforms them in accordance with his needs (and thus in a sense humanizes them) . . ." One might argue that the Pope's definition of capital is too narrow, since it excludes the persons whose investments in the discovery and transformation of natural resources, and in the means of production, go beyond the mere self-centered indulgence in material luxuries such as have characterized the wealthy aristocracy of most cultures at most times.

Still, Pope John Paul II actually uses this narrow definition to creative effect. For his central intention is to show that both capital and labor are centered in one same purpose: the primacy of man.

Thus, for the Pope, "capital cannot be separated from labor; in no way can labor be opposed to capital or capital to labor, and still less can the people behind these concepts be opposed to each other . . ."[20] "A labor system can be right"—that is, "intrinsically true and also morally legitimate"—"if in its very basis it overcomes the opposition between labor and capital . . ." He continues: "Opposition between labor and capital does not spring from the structure of the production process or from the structure of the economic process." This is a remarkably anti-Marxist view. In general, the Pope goes on, the economic process "demonstrates that labor and what we are accustomed to call capital are intermingled; it shows that they are inseparably linked." His thought here is quite rich, and he presses on: "All that we can say of everything in the production process which constitutes a whole collection of 'things,' the instruments, the capital, is that it conditions man's work; we cannot say that it constitutes as it were an impersonal 'subject' putting man and man's work into a position of dependence."

The Pope attributes the break between capital and labor, as though both were two impersonal forces, to the error of considering human labor solely according to its economic purpose. He calls this error "economism." Its fundamental error he attributes to materialism, that is, a belief in the primacy or superiority of the material over the personal and the spiritual. The Pope argues that dialectical materialism pursued this line of thought rigorously, but that "economism influenced this non-humanistic way of stating the issue before the materialist philosophical system did."

Here, perhaps, the Pope fails to note that, as a scientific discipline, economic thought necessarily abstracts from the full tissue of humanistic discourse in order to concentrate upon one aspect of reality only, under its own proper formal light. This is true of any science. In this case, the error would lie, not in the science itself, or in legitimate abstraction, but in employing such a science as if it were a full vision of human life. In this sense, economism is to economics what scientism is to science.

However, the Pope does implicitly recognize this point, for he sees clearly that "the antinomy between labor and capital . . . did not originate merely in the philosophy and economic theories of the 18th century; rather it originated in the whole of the economic and social practice of that time, the time of the birth and rapid development of in-dustrialization . . ." Too much attention went to the means, the creation of wealth, too little to the end: man himself. "It was this practical error that struck a blow first and foremost against human labor, against the working man . . ." He then notes that this "same error, which is now part of history and which was connected with the period of primitive capitalism and liberalism" can nevertheless be repeated whenever similar premises recur.

From the point of view of democratic capitalism, one can have few objections to the Pope's argument at this point. Abraham Lincoln justified the system on similar grounds. It is, however, a little odd to think of labor in subjective, personalist terms, without thinking of capital in equally humanistic terms. For the use to which wealth is put by human beings does have large moral consequences for entire societies. If the wealthy live in luxury and spend their money solely for their own amusement, they create an atmosphere throughout the body politic. At the end of the 18th century, Adam Smith directed attention to those cities in Europe which did live from the luxury of courts and governments.[21] In all cases, the citizenry of such cities, depending on moneys so spent, lived in considerable indolence and dissipation. In those relatively few cities, however, in which the wealthy were begin-ning to invest, instead, in commerce and industry, quite different habits of life were visible among their citizenry. In short, it makes a moral difference whether the wealthy simply consume their wealth or save and invest it. Capital, too, has its subjective, moral, and humanistic dimension. Indeed, some humanists today speak of the habits and skills appropriated by individuals or peoples as a form of "human capital," a sort of natural resource developed to its potential. Unlike material possessions, internalized skills are inalienable; once acquired, they are part of a person forever.

Ownership

The Pope seems, in para. 14, on ownership, to concede the very point I have just been making, for he hastens to point out that in speak-ing of labor and capital he does not mean to be dealing with abstract

The Pope calls for "associating labor with the ownership of capital, as far as possible," and for "producing a wide range of intermediate bodies with economic, social and cultural purposes. . . ." Here the emphasis on mediating structures and the associative principle strikes very close to the heart of the genius of American life, as described by Tocqueville and many since.

Finally, the Pope summarizes his "personalist" argument. "Labor is in a sense inseparable from capital," and the worker "wishes to be able to take part in the very work process as a sharer in responsibility and creativity."[25] He does not wish to be caught "in a system of excessive bureaucratic centralization, which makes the worker feel that he is just a cog in a huge machine moved from above . . ." for "man's work concerns not only the economy but also, and especially, personal values." This is "the principle reason in favor of private ownership of the means of production." For the personalist argument holds that "the human person can preserve his awareness of working 'for himself.' " Private property is the secret both to personalism and to creativity.

Invention and Discovery

By choosing the biblical category of creation as his fundamental metaphor for the social order, Pope John Paul II goes beyond "liberation theology" to something rather deeper and more promising. "Since work in its subjective aspect is always a personal action, an *actus personae*, it follows that the whole person, body and spirit, participates in it, whether it is manual or intellectual work."[26] Being faithful to his own person, the human being "shares by his work in the activity of the Creator." Moreover, he "develops that activity and perfects it as he advances further and further in the discovery of the resources and values contained in the whole of creation."[27]

The Creator, in Pope John Paul II's vision, has hidden within creation untold riches, resources, and possibilities which it is the vocation of humans to discover and to realize, for the common good of all. He, therefore, places great emphasis upon invention and discovery. This is the golden thread he sees down the epochs of history, as humans through their labor discover more and more of the Creator's secrets and bring them to human use. It is through such discovery that man "subdues the earth:"

Man dominates the earth by the very fact of domesticating animals, rearing them and obtaining from them the food and clothing he needs, and by the fact of being able to extract various natural resources from the earth and the seas. But man "subdues the earth" much more when he begins to cultivate it and then to transform its products, adapting them to his own use. Thus agriculture constitutes through human work a primary field of economic activity and an indispensable factor of production. Industry in its turn will always consist in linking the earth's riches—whether nature's living resources, or the products of agriculture, or the mineral or chemical resources—with man's work, whether physical or intellectual. This is also in a sense true in the sphere of what are called service industries and also in the sphere of research, pure or applied.[28]

This passage tempts me once again to return to the vision of Abraham Lincoln, who was commending a similar message to the people of Wisconsin in 1859. Lincoln called attention to how rich this earth is, when its secrets are finally penetrated by human intelligence; how productive intellect might be applied to every aspect of the work experience. Lincoln, in effect, called upon the farmers of Wisconsin to be what Pope John Paul II asks us to be: co-creators with God.

No other human occupation opens so wide a field for the profitable and agreeable combination of labor with cultivated thought, as agriculture. I know of nothing so pleasant to the mind, as the discovery of anything which is at once new and valuable—nothing which so lightens and sweetens toil, as the hopeful pursuit of such discovery. And how vast, and how varied a field is agriculture, for such discovery. The mind, already trained to thought, in the country school, or higher school, cannot fail to find there an exhaustless source of profitable enjoyment. Every blade of grass is a study; and to produce two, where there was but one, is both a profit and a pleasure. And not grass alone; but soils, seeds, and seasons—hedges, ditches, and fences, draining, droughts, and irrigation—plowing, hoeing, and harrowing—reaping, mowing, and threshing—saving crops, pests of crops, diseases of crops, and what will prevent or cure them—implements, utensils, and machines, their relative merits, and [how] to improve them—hogs, horses, and cattle—sheep, goats, and poultry—trees, shrubs, fruits, plants, and flowers—the thousand things of which these are specimens—each a world of study within itself.[29]

The Response of the Right and the Left

One of the most interesting features of *Laborem Exercens* is that both the right and the left have acclaimed it. Writing in the *Ecumenist*, Gregory Baum says that "Catholics who have followed the recent shift to the left in Church teaching and have therefore acquired socialist sympathies are delighted with the encyclical and understand it as a confirmation of the direction in which they have moved."[30] Simultaneously, under the editorship of Philip Lawler, the Heritage Foundation published four highly respectful and sympathetic lectures on the encyclical, in which the lecturers also found their views confirmed.[31] Baum reads the encyclical for its "extended, critical and creative dialogue with Marxism." The Heritage lecturers believe that it confirms the basic principles and practices of liberal capitalist democracies, which they as Catholic scholars have come to cherish.

In some sense, both these readings seem correct. More than most Western Marxists, Pope John Paul II came to intellectual maturity fighting against pervasive Marxist catechetics. His own writings record the intellectual battles he has fought to express contemporary Catholic values against the domination of Marxism. There are evidences in this encyclical of this continued opposition to Marx. To call the Pope's dealings with Marxism "dialogue" is surely euphemism. Yet it is clearly true that his own thought has been shaped more by the living experience of Marxism than by the living experience of the liberal capitalist democracies.

There is one decisive feature in Pope John Paul II's encyclical, however, which seems to tip the balance. Whereas Gregory Baum stresses those aspects of the encyclical which seem to encourage "collectivism" (the Pope actually uses the word "socialization") and "planning," the greatest single stress of the encyclical falls upon the human person, the concrete individual, the *subject* of human labor. This concept comes closer than any other in the tradition of papal documents to emphasizing, although in a traditional Catholic context, the role of the *individual*. As we have seen, it is this stress which gives Pope John Paul II a new "personalist" defence of the traditional Catholic teaching on private property. This emphasis also correlates strongly with Vatican Council II's teachings on religious liberty and individual conscience.

For over a century, the Popes have spoken of the Anglo-American philosophical and cultural tradition in almost exclusively pejorative terms. "Liberalism" has been scorned. So also has "individualism." To be sure, there are elements in the Anglo-American tradition, both in the meaning of liberalism and in the meaning of individualism, widely criticized by many scholars in many traditions. Furthermore, Anglo-American scholars as diverse as John Dewey and Josiah Royce have written powerfully and beautifully about community, in ways that make corrections both to the traditions of Thomism and to those of European phenomenology, existentialism and personalism.[32] Thus, in condemning "liberalism" and "individualism," the Popes have, on the one hand, been far less than specific regarding authors and doctrines and, on the other hand, have not always clearly expressed the ways in which the church itself has adopted certain liberal values (like religious liberty, the "open church," *aggiornamento*, and others) as its own. Finally, if there are some notions of liberalism and individualism to be rejected, Catholics nourished by a liberal and individualistic culture have a right to expect some clarity about a specifically *Catholic* form of liberalism and individualism. It is not likely that everything about liberalism is to be condemned. Nor is it likely that every form of individualism must be condemned.

Indeed, without a strong theory about individual responsibility, how could one defend liberty of conscience? Or respect dissent? Or endorse solitude, hermitage, the interior life, personal vocation, or other traditional Catholic forms of nourishing brave and strong individuals? Again, not all forms of community are healthy or consistent with Catholicism. Familism of certain kinds, for example, has injured many traditional Catholic cultures by imposing upon individual family members constraints which damage conscience. "He who is not willing to leave wife, brother, sister, or parents in My name's sake is not worthy of me." (Matthew 10:37). Nationalism, too, must be distinguished from patriotism. Mere conformity, mindless group think, emotionally crippling cliques, and partisanship of various sorts can easily corrupt genuine Catholic community. In any truly admirable form of Catholic community built upon the ideal of charity, there is an exquisite interplay between the twin values of the inimitable person and the common good.[33] Indeed, personalism itself offers a specific theory of individualism whose practical expressions in different cultures deserve attention. Concepts like "individualism" and "community" are realized in practice quite differently in different Catholic cultures. Contrasts between Catholic Ireland and Catholic Italy, Catholic Austria and Catholic Britain, Catholic Spain and Catholic Poland, might easily be drawn, more perhaps in the sphere of actual living than in the sphere of speculative theory.

Furthermore, the experience of those two polarities—the person and the community—seems to be rather different for different generations even within the living memory of present-day families. In some senses, I believe my own great-grandparents in Slovakia, a region quite close to those from which Pope John Paul II's family has its roots, were stronger, bolder, more ornery individuals, on the one hand, and yet lived within rather closed village communities, on the other, than any of their descendents in succeeding generations. In the course of family history, in our case as in millions of others, it seems that great changes have taken place precisely around these two polar realities. From generation to generation, the liberties and hopes of individuals have changed, and so have the character of the communities in which they live. I, for one, would not judge all these changes as negative, nor all as positive. In all these various circumstances, nonetheless, our families have been nourished by the Eucharist and by Catholic faith in its many dimensions.

The task which lies ahead of Catholic theology, therefore, and particularly before that of the Catholic layman, is to give more consideration to theological conceptions of the person and the community. These realities differ in different historical eras and different cultural locations. It is possible (although not probable) that the life forms of Catholic clergy and religious have changed less than those of Catholic lay persons. In any case, good theology ought to touch the ground it covers. In this respect, much is yet to be learned about the specific life-forms of personhood and community in Anglo-American cultures. These cultures are perhaps less known to sophisticated theology than any other. They are certainly more differentiated and complex than the life-forms of simpler times and simpler cultures.

Without question, economic relationships affect the life-forms of personhood and community. But economic relationships are far from exhausting the texture of our lives. We live within various political institutions, too, as well as within various cultural institutions (family, church, neighborhood, intellectual networks, and the rest). There have been philosophers who assiduously resisted becoming professors on the ground that the life-form of the academy would affect their reflection in ways they did not wish to choose. So it is with the vocation of each of us. A pluralistic society invites us to choose among many possible life-forms. Some change their vocations (professions or occupations) more than once, in order to experience new horizons. Some change their political commitments. Some experience dramatic religious changes. In a free and open society, it is not easy to generalize about the inner life of individuals. Furthermore, a society with a vast variety of commercial, industrial, and non-profit enterprises generates ever new activities for the human mind. Wholly new fields of inquiry and invention occur: television, computers, microcomputers. Some ninety percent of chemicals used today were scarcely even known twenty years ago. No single person can possibly learn the techniques and processes of all the complex fields which touch contemporary life, from aeronautics to satellite communications, automobile engineering to medical drugs. Indeed, it is extremely difficult even for an expert within one field to keep up with all the developments within that field alone.

In a word, the Catholic lay person has experienced a tremendous explosion in human creativity during the past two hundred years. Virtually all the innovations and inventions of this sudden historic outburst of creativity spring from democratic capitalist lands. Such societies have been designed precisely to stimulate individual and corporate creativity. Jacques Servan-Schreiber observed in *The American Challenge* that social organization aiming at innovation is the genius of America and that Europe would have to learn it—as, since that time, both Europe and Japan have.[34] Sometimes one hears the argument that modern creativity was not caused by a capitalist economy but by technology. Yet one must also ask under which economic arrangements are technological breakthroughs nourished and promoted? The British Royal Society long awarded prizes for scientific and practical inventions. More significant, the law of patents protected inventors and their royalties as copyright laws protected authors. Financial incentives justified years of expense and sacrifice in practical research. Native intelligence comes alive under such a system. A system which bases itself upon human creativity reaps many rewards.

Creation Theology

Man the maker—*homo faber*—is not entirely determined by forces outside himself; his own capacities for self-reflection, invention and innovation constitute in him *imago Dei*: the image of God the Creator. The human person acts in a self-planned, creative, intelligent way. He makes his own decisions about himself. This is the radical theology which Pope John Paul II propounds. It is in sharing in the creativity of the Creator that the human subject fulfills his vocation. It is in using his own creative talents that the human person follows "the will of the Creator that work should enable man to achieve that 'dominion' in the visible world that is proper to him."[35] In this vocation, the human person gains "dominion" over every force of mere determinism. "Man has to subdue the earth and dominate it, because as 'the image of God' he is a person, that is to say, a subjective being capable of acting in a planned and rational way, capable of deciding about himself and with a tendency to self-realization."[36] The human person is *not* entirely the creature of nature and of society. The person is capable of standing against society, of dissent, of heroism, of fidelity to his own individual calling, and that same human person expresses the will of God in self-realization. This is a profound theory of individualism—perhaps better to be called personalism (in the spirit in which Jacques Maritain distinguishes between the person and the individual.[37])

The creation theology of Pope John Paul II is clearly different from the liberation theology of recent years, although its aims for peace, justice, and liberty remain the same. Creation theology differs from liberation theology, first, in rejecting the thesis of class struggle; second, in justifying capital as the material embodiment of human labor down the ages, while stressing the priority of labor; third, in rejecting the primacy of the contrast between oppression and liberation, in favor of the contrast between the absence and the presence of creativity; fourth, in its emphasis upon the strict connection between the human person as the subject of labor and his right to the fruits of his labor, including the right of ownership; fifth, in highlighting the danger of nationalization, collectivization, and socialization in which a "new class" of government administration comes to power, "claiming for itself a monopoly of the administration and disposal of the means of production and not refraining even from offending basic human rights;"[38] sixth, in interpreting the meaning of "socialization" more exactly than ever before, so as to preserve in it respect for the individual human person and his rights to private property:

> We can speak of socializing only when the subject character of society is ensured, that is to say, when on the basis of his work each person is fully entitled to consider himself a part owner of the great workbench at which he is working with everyone else.[39]

As means to this end, the Pope recommends several techniques not only entirely compatible with democratic capitalist practice but already far advanced beyond the experimental stage. In particular, he emphasizes "associating labor with the ownership of capital, as far as possible" and "producing a wide range of intermediate bodies with economic, social, and cultural purposes."[40] The latter is an invitation to the associative principle which Tocqueville found so striking in American life,[41] the "mediating structures" about which Peter Berger and Richard Neuhaus have written so well.[42] The former is practised—but not nearly so broadly as it ought to be—not only in the rapidly growing ESOPs, or employee stock option plans, but also in pension fund investments, profit-sharing plans, and corporative worker-ownership.[43] (Practical difficulties arise when workers financially either cannot or prefer not to accept the risks of profit-sharing, which in some years entails loss-sharing. But writers like Mortimer Adler consider employee-ownership the highest ideal of fully developed capitalism.)[44]

The Pope adds in an important paragraph:

> . . . the person who works desires not only due remuneration for his work; he also wishes that within the production process provision be made for him to be able to know that in his work, even on something that is owned in common, he is working "for himself." This awareness is extinquished within him in a system of excessive bureaucratic centralization, which makes the worker feel that he is just a cog in a huge machine moved from above, that he is for more reasons than one a mere production instrument rather than a true subject of work with an initiative of his own . . . In the mind of St. Thomas Aquinas, this is the principal reason in favor of private ownership of the means of production. While we accept that for certain well-founded reasons exceptions can be made to the principle of private ownership—in our own time we even see that the system of "socialized ownership" has been introduced—nevertheless the personalist argument still holds good both on the level of principles and on the practical level. If it is to be rational and fruitful, any socialization of the means of production must take this argument into consideration. Every effort must be made to ensure that in this kind of system also the human person can preserve his awareness of working "for himself."[45]

Finally, creation theology aims actually to *improve* the lot of the poor. In this way it overcomes a nagging difficulty in liberation theology, which rhetorically announces an "option for the poor" without in any way conceiving of an economic system creative enough actually to raise up the economic standing of the poor. In rejecting an economic theory based entirely upon "growth," without due emphasis upon the need to *distribute* the fruits of growth, liberation theology is on sound ground. But by depending upon tried-and-failed socialist experiments in economics during the past forty years, liberation theology offers the poor hardly more than a stone. "The economic system and the production process benefit precisely when these personal values are respected," the Pope writes, when ". . . the human person can preserve his awareness of working 'for himself.' "[46]

The human person is a creator and nowhere more so than at his daily economic tasks. Entire economies must become creative. Subsistence living is no longer enough. Subsistence living does not afford the sort of health care, education, leisure, and communications of which the human race is now capable. In virtually every nation of the world, huge tracts of arable land now go uncultivated. There is virtually no nation which could not be self-reliant in agriculture.[47] Yet a great many nations are not able now to feed themselves. This lack cannot fairly be ascribed to nature or to human persons. It can be ascribed to national *systems* of political economy. Nations like India have shown during the past decade how formerly food-dependent nations can, by making systemic changes (especially in incentive structures) and by popular use of agricultural science, move not only to self-reliance in foodstuffs but even to the exportation of foods. In a word, the possibilities of human creativity must be tapped.

The Creator did not treat all nations equally in their natural endowments. Culture differs from culture. Each person is incarnated in a particular setting of nature and a particular national history, "the great society to which man belongs on the basis of particular cultural and historical links." Each such particular culture "is not only the great 'educator' of every man, even though an indirect one (because each individual absorbs within the family the contents and values that go to make up the culture of a given nation); it is also a great historical and social incarnation of the work of all generations."[48] Yet in each of these national locations, in each of these historical cultures, the human person is made in the image of God. Each has the vocation to work and to create. Creation theology does not set person against person, class against class, nation against nation. It calls forth the human capacity to create a new world, *novus ordo seclorum* (to use the traditional phrase in a way which transcends its parochial limits).

As a pioneer in the creativity which every nation of the world may express, the United States has a special role to play in the task of development in which the world is now engaged. It is true that, at present, some experts estimate that some 800 million persons on this planet are living in abject hunger. Yet just 200 years ago, the entire population of the earth—mostly living lives aptly described as "solitary, poor, nasty, brutish and short"—also numbered 800 millions. It is the tremendous creativity of modern work which has allowed the population of the earth to rise to 4.4 billion persons, some 3.6 billion of whom have escaped the most abject poverty. The task before us, a task demanding all the creativity we possess, is to improve the lot of our poorest brothers and sisters. That is our "option for the poor." Pope John Paul II calls us to it, not in the mode of resentment and hostility, in the fashion of worldly ideologies, but in the mode of a theology of creation, in faith and in love. His is authentic Christian teaching, rooted both in centuries of reflection upon the Word of God and in reflection upon the experience of our time. It, too, is a theology of *praxis*: of what works—works for the human person in his subjectivity, and for "the economic system itself and the production process." What works is social organization for personal creativity. A society so constructed is in the image of the Blessed Trinity, the Creator of all things, Lord of history, Spirit brooding over dark creation.

NOTES

1. "What the Laity Can Teach the Church," ed. Russell Barta, *Challenge to the Laity* (Huntington, Ind.: Our Sunday Visitor, 1980).
2. "Can a Christian Work for a Corporation?" in *The Judeo-Christian Vision and the Modern Corporation*, ed. Oliver F. Williams, C.S.C. and John W. Houck (Notre Dame, Ind.: University of Notre Dame Press, 1982).
3. Para. 3. All citations to *Laborem Exercens* are to the text published in *Origins* 11 (September 24, 1981): 225-44. To reduce the number of footnotes referring to the encyclical, one note below frequently covers sequential citations from the same paragraph.
4. Preamble.
5. Para. 4.
6. Para. 5.

7. Para. 6.

8. Para. 27.

9. Para. 7.

10. Para. 7.

11. Para. 7.

12. Richard N. Current, ed., *The Political Thought of Abraham Lincoln* (Indianapolis, Ind.: Bobbs-Merrill, 1967), pp. 133-34.

13. The text of Lincoln's letter, written in 1951, runs as follows: "Your request for eighty dollars I do not think it best to comply with now. At the various times when I have helped you a little you have said to me, 'We can get along very well now'; but in a very short time I find you in the same difficulty again. Now, this can only happen by some defect in your conduct. What that defect is, I think I know. You are not lazy, and still you are an idler. I doubt whether, since I saw you, you have done a good whole day's work in any one day. You do not very much dislike to work, and still you do not work much, merely because it does not seem to you that you could get much for it. This habit of uselessly wasting time is the whole difficulty; it is vastly important to you, and still more so to your children, that you should break the habit. It is more important to them, because they have longer to live, and can keep out of an idle habit before they are in it, easier than they can get out after they are in." Ida M. Tarbell, ed., *Selections from the Letters, Speeches, and State Papers of Abraham Lincoln* (Boston: Ginn and Co., 1911), p. 13.

14. Smith writes, for example: "Every colonist gets more land than he can possibly cultivate. He has no rent, and scarce any taxes to pay. No landlord shares with him in its produce, and the share of the sovereign is commonly but a trifle. He has every motive to render as great as possible a produce, which is thus to be almost entirely his own. But his land is commonly so extensive, that with all his own industry, and with all the industry of other people whom he can get to employ, he can seldom make it produce the tenth part of what it is capable of producing. He is eager, therefore, to collect labourers from all quarters, and to reward them with the most liberal wages. But those liberal wages, joined to the plenty and cheapness of land, soon make those labourers leave him, in order to become landlords themselves, and to reward, with equal liberality, other labourers, who soon leave them for the same reason that they left their first master. The liberal reward of labour encourages marriage. The children, during the tender years of infancy, are well fed and properly taken care of, and when they are grown up, the value of their labour greatly overpays their maintenance. When arrived at maturity, the high price of labour, and the low price of land, enable them to establish themselves in the same manner as their fathers did before them." Adam Smilth, *An Inquiry into the Nature and Causes of the Wealth of Nations*, ed. Edwin Cannan (New York: Modern Library, 1937), p. 532.

15. Hamilton writes that when commerce and manufacturing are encouraged "each individual can find his proper element, and can call into activity the whole vigour of his nature." He observed that "to cherish and stimulate the activity

of the human mind, by multiplying the objects of enterprise, is not among the least considerable of the expedients, by which the wealth of a nation may be promoted." Alexander Hamilton, "Report on Manufacturers," in *The Papers of Alexander Hamilton*, ed. Harold C. Syrett, 25 vols. (New York: Columbia University Press, (1960-77), X: pp. 255-56.

16. Para. 12

17. Roy P. Basler, ed., *Abraham Lincoln: His Speeches and Writings* (Cleveland and New York: World Pub. Co., 1946), p. 633.

18. Ibid., p. 634. On July 4, 1976, during the bicentennial parade in Cresco, Iowa, the author had occasion to see a woman, age 101, born 15 years after Lincoln uttered these words. During her lifetime the U.S. had increased its population to 232 million. And Iowa had ceased being an "underdeveloped country."

19. Para. 12.

20. Para. 13. The many following citations are also from Para. 13.

21. Distinguishing between the wealthy who invest in productive labor and those who invest in unproductive hands (like the retainers near them), Smith wrote: "The proportion between those different funds necessarily determines in every country the general character of the inhabitants as to industry or idleness. We are more industrious than our forefathers; because in the present times the funds destined for the maintenance of industry, are much greater in proportion to those which are likely to be employed in the maintenance of idleness, than they were two or three centuries ago. Our ancestors were idle for want of a sufficient encouragement to industry. It is better, says the proverb, to play for nothing, than to work for nothing. In mercantile and manufacturing towns, where the inferior ranks of people are chiefly maintained by the employment of capital, they are in general industrious, sober, and thriving; as in many English, and in most Dutch towns. In those towns which are principally supported by the constant or occasional residence of a court, and in which the inferior ranks of people are chiefly maintained by the spending of revenue, they are in general idle, dissolute, and poor; as at Rome, Versailles, Compiegne, and Fontainbleau. If you except Rouen and Bourdeaux, there is little trade or industry in any of the parliament towns of France; and the inferior ranks of people, being chiefly maintained by the expence of the members of the courts of justice, and of those who come to plead before them, are in general idle and poor. . . . Wherever capital predominates, industry prevails: wherever revenue, idleness. Every increase or diminution of capital, therefore, naturally tends to increase or diminish the real quantity of industry, the number of productive hands, and consequently the exchangeable value of the annual produce of the land and labour of the country, the real wealth and revenue of all its inhabitants. . . . That portion of his revenue which a rich man annually spends, is in most cases consumed by idle guests, and menial servants, who leave nothing behind them in return for their consumption. That portion which he annually saves, as for the sake of the profit it is immediately employed as a capital, is consumed in the same manner, and nearly in the same time too, but

by a different set of people, by labourers, manufacturers, and artificers, who re-produce with a profit the value of their annual consumption." Smith, *Wealth of Nations*, pp. 319, 321.

22. Para. 14. The many following citations are also from Para 14.

23. Anticipating the Pope's point here, Theodore Roosevelt wrote: "Every man holds his property subject to the general right of the community to regulate it to whatever degree the public welfare may require it." *The New Nationalism* (New York: 1910), pp. 23-24.

24. These and the following quotations are from Para. 14.

25. Para. 15.

26. Para. 24.

27. Para. 25.

28. Para. 5.

29. Current, ed., *The Political Thought of Abraham Lincoln*, p. 136.

30. Gregory Baum, "John Paul II's Encyclical on Labor," *The Ecumenist* 20 (November-December, 1981): 3.

31. Philip F. Lawler, ed., *Papal Economics*, The Heritage Lectures #6 (Washington, D.C.: Heritage Foundation, 1982).

32. See John Dewey, *The Public and its Problems* (New York: Henry Holt & Co., 1927), chap. V: "Search for the Great Community." The idea of community is a major theme in Josiah Royce's later works. See especially *The Problem of Christianity*, 2 Vols. (New York: Macmillan, 1913); and *The Hope of the Great Community* (New York: Macmillan, 1916).

33. Jacques Maritain, *The Person and the Common Good*, trans. John J. Fitzgerald (Notre Dame, Ind.: University of Notre Dame Press, 1966), p. 49ff.

34. Jean-Jacques Servan-Schreiber, *The American Challenge*, trans. Ronald Steel (New York: Avon, 1969), chaps. 5 and 6.

35. Para 9.

36. Para 6.

37. See Maritain, *The Person and the Common Good*, chap. III: "Individuality and Personality."

38. Para 14.

39. Para 14.

40. Para 14.

41. ". . . private citizens, by combining together, may constitute bodies of great wealth, influence, and strength. . . . An association for political, commercial, or manufacturing purposes, or even for those of science and literature, is a powerful and enlightened member of the community, which cannot be disposed of at pleasure or oppressed without remonstrance, and which, by defending its own rights against the encroachments of the government, saves the common liberties of the country." Alexis de Tocqueville, *Democracy in America*, 2 Vols., Phillips Bradley ed., (New York: Vintage Books, 1945), 2: 342.

42. Peter L. Berger and Richard J. Neuhaus, *To Empower People: The Role of Mediating Structures in Public Policy* (Washington, D.C.: American Enterprise Institute, 1977).

43. See Peter F. Drucker, *The Unseen Revolution: How Pension Fund Socialism Came to America* (New York: Harper and Row, 1976).

44. Mortimer Adler and Louis O. Kelso, *The Capitalist Manifesto* (Westport, Conn.: Greenwood, 1975).

45. Para 15.

46. Para 15.

47. Ronald D. Nairn writes: ". . . the planet is not running out of resources. Particularly in agriculture, the capacity for abundance exists, awaiting its human activators." *Wealth of Nations in Crisis* (Houston: Bayland Publishing, 1979), p. 8.

48. Para 10.

CHAPTER 2

Work as Co-Creation: A Critique of A Remarkably Bad Idea

by Stanley Hauerwas

A GREAT CHORUS OF PRAISE HAS GREETED POPE JOHN PAUL II'S ENCYCLICAL *Laborem Exercens,* but I cannot join it. *Laborem Exercens* is a disaster both in the general perspective it takes toward work as well as its specific arguments. I wish I could find a way to interpret the encyclical in a positive manner, but I find I cannot. My dis-ease with this encyclical goes deeper, however, since the problems with *Laborem Exercens* may well signal the end of the social encyclical tradition that began with Leo XIII's *Rerum Novarum.* For it glaringly reveals the methodological shortcomings inherent in the encyclicals from their beginning.

Obviously this kind of broadside attack demands careful and detailed argument and that is exactly what I will try to provide. My concern with *Laborem Exercens* involves two interdependent arguments: (1) the theological analysis of work is deficient and (2) this results in a social and economic theory that systematically distorts the nature and significance of work in most people's lives. I will, therefore, try to show that John Paul II's understanding of work is theologically arbitrary, romantic, elitist, and certainly an insufficient basis for an adequate social theory or critique.

This document typifies Vatican encyclicals in the generality of its analysis. Concrete implications remain unclear or uncertain; when the encyclical tries to become concrete, it simply errs, or supports or condemns positions no one holds. That such stylistic deficiencies characterize the encyclicals no longer seems surprising, since they remain paradigmatic documents of a Constantinian church always wanting to mount social criticism while continuing to seem supportive of the powers that be.

To begin on a positive note it is interesting that *Laborem Exercens* does not appeal explicitly to natural law as the basis for its analysis of work or to determine the moral principles relevant for the evaluation of economic systems. Rather, more than in any past social encyclical, John Paul II attempts to ground his perspective directly in scripture. At least his intent is to avoid using scripture to buttress positions determined on other grounds. He employs an extensive discussion of scripture, in particular the creation account in the first three chapters of *Genesis*, to establish a theological perspective on work. He explicitly says "the Church's social teaching finds its source in sacred scripture, beginning with the Book of *Genesis* and especially in the Gospel and the writings of the apostles" (3).[1]

Yet I fear that John Paul II's use of scripture is highly selective and comes close to being dishonest. For example, why does he use *Genesis* when other texts of scripture might be equally relevant or even more appropriate? To be sure, the Gospel and apostolic writing are footnoted, but that never goes beyond very homiletic directives. Certainly scripture provides little support for the claim that work, no matter how interpreted, is the "key," even the "essential key," to the "whole social question" (3). Surely deserving at least an equal claim is the Pauline emphasis on the powers and/or the Johannine theme of church and world. Therefore one cannot help but feel that, in spite of claims to the contrary, John Paul II is only using scripture to buttress a theory arrived at on other grounds. Indeed his excerpting a narrow segment of *Genesis* reflects an implicit but continuing reliance upon the natural law presumption that creation *itself* furnishes sufficient grounds for universally relevant moral assessment. Such selective subordination of scripture and the Gospel to a fundamentally metaphysical perspective can only undermine the theological significance of Jesus' life for our discernment of God's creative activity and purpose.[2]

Some may feel that this kind of criticism is unfairly directed at a document like *Laborem Exercens*. After all, John Paul II is not writing a treatise that tries to do justice to every theological nuance. Rather he is trying to give moral and pastoral direction to people of good will as they are confronted by the complex and troubling economic realities of our day. Concern for theological fine points constitutes intellectual carping by those who lack the courage to take a position on anything — much less one concerning economic matters and based on scripture.

Such a response fails to recognize that *how* the encyclical argues is as important as what it says. For if the encyclical lacks the theological integrity which John Paul II wants to claim by his very use of scripture, then it compromises even some of the reasonable positive strategies he recommends. Therefore, while it is not necessary for John Paul II to touch all the theological bases to justify his position, he at least owes us an explanation why he has touched the ones he has.

In the Beginning

Yet, even if we give him his choice of *Genesis* as the key text his interpretation remains doubtful at best. In essence John Paul II argues that *Genesis* 1:27-28 entails the view that "work is a fundamental dimension of human existence on earth" (9). Even more, work is that activity provided through which man, created in God's image, is invited to share "by his work the activity of the Creator" (25). God means for man to continue perfecting or extending his creation through the advancement of "science and technology, and, above all, to elevating unceasingly the cultural and moral level of the society within which he lives in community with those who belong to the same family" (1). Thus, it seems, we are invited to think of ourselves as nothing less than co-creators with God.

The images are interesting which John Paul II uses to discuss how we became co-creators through our work. Drawing on the *Genesis* account, the Pope tells us our task is to subdue the earth (4), but our subduing is accomplished only as we "dominate" and each becomes "more and more the master of the earth" (4). We rightly "dominate" the earth through the domestication of animals, the cultivation of the earth, the extension of our powers through technology, but perhaps most of all through our creation of culture itself (5). Indeed the very meaning of rationality involves our power to dominate the earth (6) and that is why work is the characteristic unique to humanity as we alone have the power necessary to dominate. Only man can imitate God, because only man has the unique characteristic of likeness to God—i.e., to create through his work (25). Therefore work is not simply an opportunity for us, but a duty (16).

John Paul II's use of *Genesis* appears shockingly naive at best as he seems to assume that the meaning of these texts is clear if not self-interpreting. No attempt is made to substantiate his interpretations within their historical context or more importantly their place within the larger framework of *Genesis* and the Pentateuch. John Paul II works much like the preachers who write their sermons and then look for texts to support them.

There is, I think, little support for the way John Paul II construes these texts. This is particularly the case insofar as he legitimates the idea that work is the way mankind is invited to be a co-creator with God. For that is exactly opposite to what these texts are meant to convey. The good news of the creation account is that God completed his creation and that mankind needs do nothing more to see to its perfection. That is exactly why God could call it good and rest—and more importantly invite us to rest within his completed good creation. Indeed John Paul II's interpretation of the invitation to become co-creators is uncomfortably close to the view Eve accepted by allowing herself to be tempted by that subtle serpent.

Of course John Paul II is quite right that the terms "subdue" and "dominion" are in the text, but they certainly do not carry the strong implication that we are thus invited to be co-creators with God because we are made in his image. Indeed the force of those words in relation to our being God's image is meant to have a quite different effect. As Gerhard Von Rad argues:

> the distribution of weight in the Priestly account of man's creation speaks less of the nature of God's image than of its purpose. There is less said about the gift itself than about the task. This then is sketched most explicitly: domination in the world, especially over the animals. The commission to rule is not considered as belonging to the definition of God's image, but it is its

> consequence, i.e., that for which man is capable because of it.
> The close relation of the term for God's image with that for the
> commission to exercise dominion emerges quite clearly when we
> have understood *selem* or a plastic image. Just as powerful earth-
> ly kings, to indicate their claim to dominion, erect an image of
> themselves in the provinces of their empire where they do not
> personally appear, so man is placed upon earth in God's image
> as God's sovereign emblem. He is really only God's representa-
> tive, summoned to maintain and enforce God's claim to dominion
> over the earth.[3]

A representative is not a co-creator. A representative does not "share
by his work in the activity of the creator," but instead reflects what that
activity has already accomplished. Therefore, "subdue" and "dominion"
should not be interpreted, as John Paul II does, in terms of "dominate."
To be sure the Hebrew *rādā* is a strong expression meaning tread as
in a wine press.[4] But even so we see from the text that man does not
exercise this dominion by dominating, but rather by maintaining God's
good order.

Particularly significant in this respect are verses 29 and 30 in Chapter
1 of *Genesis*. For they clearly indicate that man's dominion did not extend to the domestication of animals to obtain his food. Rather for
nourishment man was graciously given "every plant yielding seed
which is upon the face of all the earth, and every tree with seed in its
fruit." And to the animals God has given "every green plant for food."
Therefore, perhaps the original paradigm of "domination"—i.e., the
human pretension that it is our right because of "special" rational nature
to kill and eat animals—is clearly seen in *Genesis* to be antithetical to
God's design and command.[5] John Paul II's underwriting the language
of domination by man of the animals is but another example of the long
history of human inability to accept that God's eschatological kingdom
is genuinely one of peace.

John Paul II's stress on "domination" seems particularly insensitive in
that we live at a time when many Christians and non-Christians alike
are recovering a sense of our unity with nature and the animal world.
We are learning that our task is not so much to dominate as it is to learn
to live in a covenant with God's good creation. As James Gustafson has
recently suggested, our task is not to control but to consent to God's
good order.[6] While I am certainly not suggesting that the Vatican
should underwrite the ecological romanticism so prevalent today, at the

very least the Pope should have felt some discomfort with any theological legitimation of the arrogance of our species' superiority and correlative assumption that we have the right to rape, or as John Paul II puts it, to "master" the world (4).

Equally troubling in this respect is the blessing of technology in *Laborem Exercens*. Of course he is certainly right to suggest that technology can be our ally as it "facilitates, perfects, accelerates, and augments" our work (5). Yet we are increasingly learning technology can just as easily become our master. Just to the extent we seek to control through technology we become controlled by it. For technology too often becomes a substitute for human cooperation and community; and if technology itself fails, then we cannot easily reclaim those forms of cooperation and community which have been replaced. I am certainly not suggesting that John Paul II should have taken a "small is beautiful" attitude, but at the very least he could have tried to help us understand more profoundly the ambiguity of technologically enhanced work.

Work and Idolatry

It may be objected that I have read far too much into John Paul's language of "share in the work of the creator," "dominate," and "master." After all, he is careful to limit man's mastery and dominion to the "visible world" (4,21). Yet this qualification is hardly sufficient since the "invisible world" simply seems to stand as an external limit to man's using this earth as the playground for the exercise of power. Such a limit does little to help us understand better the kind of dominion we ought to exercise in this world.

Or again it may be objected, I have overlooked John Paul II's clear understanding that sin has disordered work. As a result of sin, toil too often is an ever present aspect of work. Though John Paul II does not elaborate exactly what he means by toil, he seems to have in mind those aspects of work that are laborious in the sense they are physically tiring, dangerous, or unfulfilling (9). In short, toil is when work is no longer "for man," but man is defined as "for work" (6).

Yet this understanding of work and the effect of sin seems neither theologically or empirically warranted. John Paul II suggests that while sin may have affected work it has not changed its essential nature. Work still provides the means for us to participate in God's creative purposes. As he suggests, perhaps even because of the toilsome aspect of work it remains a good thing for us. Work is good because it is "something worthy, that is to say, something that corresponds to man's dignity, that expresses this dignity and increases it" (9). For it is through work that man "achieves fulfillment as a human being" and indeed in a sense becomes "more a human being" (9).

But in fact we know most of the work in which we engage does not promise that kind of fulfillment, and more importantly it is by no means clear that it should. Indeed, one must ask if scripture does not contain a much more realistic account of work and its status for human community than John Paul II's account. For by attributing such an extraordinarily high theological status to work he is led to describe work basically as a self-fulfilling activity. While it may be true that any kind of work may have periods of intrinsic pleasure and interest—i.e., bricklaying, running a punch press, writing, painting,—nonetheless most work is not intrinsically fulfilling, but a necessity for survival as well as contributing to our interdependence as social beings.

One of the interesting features of scripture's treatment of work is that work need not be regarded as ultimately significant. Work is simply common as it is the way most of us earn our living. Indeed if there is a grace to work it is that we do not need to attribute or find in our work any great significance or salvation. Our work does not have to have or contribute to some grand plan; its blessings are of a more mundane sort. Work gives us the means to survive, be of service to others, and, perhaps most of all, work gives us a way to stay busy. For while work may not be ultimately fulfilling, it is at least a great gift—a hedge against boredom. Attributing greater significance to work risks making it demonic as work then becomes an idolatrous activity through which we try to secure and guarantee our significance, to make "our mark" on history.

Therefore sin is not the lack of non-fulfillment that John Paul II seems to associate with toil. Rather sin is the corruption of work resulting from our rebellion against our status as creatures. John Paul II is quite right to remind us that work itself is not the result of sin—it was man's task to till and keep the garden prior to sin (*Genesis* 2:15)—but such tilling and keeping was still common work. Our sin was and is exactly to try to make it more than that.

No doubt John Paul II's account is motivated by an attempt to call attention to the dignity of the common man's labor. But in doing so he underwrites what can only be described as a romantic and elitist view of work. Thus he says, in perhaps the worst paragraph in *Laborem Exercens*:

> The ancient world introduced its own typical differentiation of people into classes according to the type of work done. Work which demanded from the worker the exercise of physical strength, work of muscles and hands, was considered unworthy of free men and was therefore given to slaves. By broadening certain aspects that already belonged to the Old Testament, Christianity brought about a fundamental change of ideas in this field, taking the whole content of the gospel message or its point of departure, especially the fact that the one who, while being God, became most like us in all things devoted most of the years of his life on earth to manual work at the carpenter's bench. This circumstance constitutes in itself the most eloquent Gospel of work, showing that the basis for determining the value of human work is not primarily the kind of work being done, but the fact that the one who is doing it is a person. The sources of the dignity of work are to be sought primarily in the subjective dimension, not in the objective one (6).

This may be the implication of a philosophy of personalism based on the work of Scheler, but it has precious little to do with the Gospel. It is ludicrous to assume that Jesus' occupation as a carpenter—an assumption for which there is no scriptural evidence—should suffice to raise work to a new status. I find such reasoning nothing less than embarrassing coming from a source that should know better. But even worse are the ethical assumptions supported by such reasoning for they in fact can legitimate some of the most inhumane forms of work as long as the person participating subjectively feels his "personhood" is being enhanced. Put more strongly, such a position virtually entails the view that we should be able to find work fulfilling no matter what its objective character. I am aware that John Paul II does not wish for such implications to follow, but I do not see how they can be avoided.

Of course it is possible to interpret his suggestion in a very radical manner so that any just economic system would require the elimination of all forms of unfulfilling work. Yet such a suggestion is utopian in the extreme. The issue is not that certain forms of work are not fulfilling but that they are improperly compensated by a society which fails to appreciate the need for someone to pick up the trash. Some of the passages in *Laborem Exercens* seem to suggest that John Paul II would prefer a society of happy peasants and self-initiating artists, but such a society is not only impossible, even more we should not desire it. The unpleasant and necessary character of work forces us to discover and enhance those aspects of our lives that are not work.[7]

Yet the story grows worse. For John Paul II is not content to use Jesus' life to underwrite romantic versions of the "dignity of labor." He goes further and suggests that through the toilsome aspect of work we are able to share in Christ's very work. "By enduring the toil of work in union with Christ crucified for us, man in a way collaborates with the son of God for the redemption of humanity. He shows himself a true disciple of Christ by carrying the cross in his turn every day in the activity he is called upon to perform" (27). Such a claim comes very close to trivializing the cross of Christ by identifying every kind of suffering or onerous task with Jesus' cross.

John Howard Yoder has argued that the cross is not some general symbol of life's difficulties. Indeed to the contrary it was Jesus' cross and as such it had a highly specific nature. Namely it is the kind of suffering that is to be expected when the power of non-resistant love challenges the powers that would rule this world by violence.[8] That it was such does not mean that other forms of our suffering are unimportant or humanly insignificant. Indeed the Church must be the kind of community in which we can care for one another in our sufferings. But we are able to be that kind of community only because Jesus in his cross has in fact redeemed humanity in a manner that does not require our "collaboration." Rather it requires our willingness to live trusting that the power of his cross is more profound than the powers of this world.

Thus exactly what we do not find in our work is "a small part of the cross of Christ" (27). On the contrary, what we find in our work is opportunity of service to one another reminding us of our need as a people for a redemption not accomplished through our work. John Paul II's attempt to give our endeavors such great theological status results not in a renewed sense of dignity of common work, but rather only underwrites our already overwhelming temptation to attribute too much significance to our individual efforts.

It is useful to ask ourselves why John Paul II considers it necessary to renew our sense of the dignity of common work. For his account has all the marks of the kind of things that those who no longer have to work feel they need to say about those who do. Perhaps then, the best definition of work is "that from which the rich are exempt." The rich thus must attribute meaning to work in an effort to morally legitimate their own parasitical status.

But there are also ecclesiological presuppositions at work here. His account of work lacks any sense of how work contributes to the growth of actual communities such as the Church. To be sure, he notes that work "first and foremost unites people" (20), but he neglects to mention that uniting occurs because we see how often our very mundane tasks contribute to the lives of others. That I have a plumber I can trust means more to me than some of the things we classify as really important. Exactly because we know we can count on one another as people, we do not need to attribute overriding significance to plumbing itself.

The Church is crucial for sustaining work not because it can provide a philosophy of work, but because it is a group of actual people who have learned to rely on one another, to depend on one another. We do not need to attribute ultimate significance to our work because we see how our work helps sustain the lives of other people. Moreover we know that work can estrange as easily as it can unify—we therefore require a community whose unity can see us through the conflicts that our interaction in work can so easily entail.

John Paul II's theological analysis of work describes the character of work as we actually experience it. In effect his account develops a systematically distorting analysis which fails to encounter the economic challenges of our day and in particular the contribution the church can and should make.

The Problem With *Laborem Exercens'* Economics of Work

On a more positive note it is extremely important that *Laborem Exercens* represents a welcome return to the economic issues that inspired and generated *Rerum Novarum, Quadragesimo Anno*, and *Mater et Magistra*. Moreover, John Paul II has rightly reemphasized some of the profound insights of those encyclicals. Particularly strong is his return to the theory of just wage and the common good as crucial indicators of the justice of an economic system. Thus he says:

> the justice of a socioeconomic system and, in each case, its just functioning, deserves in the final analysis to be evaluated by the way in which man's work is properly remunerated in the system. Here we return once more to the first principle of the whole

ethical and social order, namely the principle of the common use of goods. In every system, regardless of the fundamental relationships within it between capital and labor, wages, that is to say remuneration for work, are still a practical means whereby the vast majority of people can have access to those goods which are intended for common use: both the goods of nature and manufactured goods. Hence in every case a just wage is the concrete means of verifying the justice of the whole socioeconomic system and, in any case, of checking that it is functioning justly (19).

This strikes me as a sober and realistic position that is in many ways at odds with John Paul II's more romantic theology of work. For here work is rightly seen not as providing fulfillment or playing a role in God's continuing creation, but rather as the way we earn our living. Moreover the just wage has the virtue of being concrete and empirical. For a just wage precisely is that "remuneration which will suffice for establishing and properly maintaining a family and for providing security for its future" (19). Of course there will be arguments about what will constitute such a wage, and how best to accomplish it, but at least such a standard puts the argument where it should be.

The attractiveness of the just wage is that it does not pretend that in order to bring a moral perspective to economics we are required to provide an alternative theory to either capitalism or socialism. Rather it simply directs our attention to the important moral and social purposes our economic systems are meant to serve — namely, to support and sustain our ability to have and raise children. Moreover this criterion reminds us that all economic questions are also fundamentally moral questions insofar as they draw on our assumptions about what we are or should be as a society capable of welcoming and sustaining future generations.

Of course the standard of the just wage leaves many questions unanswered. For example, what kind of family must an economy be capable of supporting? Do the number of children make any difference for our consideration of what kind of remuneration the society must provide? Does it make any difference if the family is understood in intergenerational terms? What kind of child-rearing practices and educational opportunity must the economy make possible? Why, for example, does John Paul II assume mothers rather than both parents should be made free to nurture and educate children? Why should men be excluded by economic necessity from accountability for that most important role?

Such questions, except the last, are left unanswered in *Laborem Exercens*, and rightly so. For they are exactly the questions that the appeal to the just wage is meant to occasion as central for any society's setting of economic priorities. The just wage, so to speak, is not an economic theory, but rather a moral challenge to any theory or system in that it reminds us what we should be about. While it involves no utopian ideal of a harmonious or egalitarian economic system, it stands as a simple reminder that any system must at least deal with these matters.

Alas, John Paul II could not leave it at that but assumed that a theory beyond the just wage was needed. He thus attempts nothing less than to supply us with a new "meaning of human work" (2) that can provide a perspective for all economic questions from production to distribution. The Church, in its lofty position as universal teacher, must by extension supply mankind with an alternative global economic theory through which our problems will be ameliorated. We are told that "work is the key to the whole social question" (3), not in the sense of just wage; but that from an analysis of work rightly understood, a theory which avoids the weakness of both capitalism and socialism can be developed and implemented.

The basic premise of this theory is the "principle of the priority of labor over capital" (12). This is assumed by John Paul II but never analyzed or demonstrated as foundational. Rather we are told that the theory entails "labor is always a primary efficient cause, while capital, the whole collection of means of production, remains a mere instrument of instrumental cause" (12). This principle is the economic restatement of the primacy of man over things—i.e., work is to serve human purposes not vice versa.

On the basis of this theory John Paul II supports positions that are generally recognized as commendable. Thus he, in line with past social encyclicals, supports private property yet reminds us that ownership can be subordinated to the right of common use (14); he supports the right to employment, to unionize; the rights of farmers, the disabled, and the particular responsibility states have in the process of immigration. The problem, however, is that John Paul II did not need his elaborate theology and theory of work to arrive at and support these particular positions.

Even more problematically his theory distorts a realistic account of our economic alternatives. Because he utilizes a "personalistic" account of work he neglects exactly the primary issue at stake in any labor dispute—i.e., power. He fails to point out that the issue is not work itself, but why the holders of capital should be able to have power over others simply because they possess the resources to define the value of work.[9] What John Paul II either does not recognize or does not confront is that the very definition of terms of modern economic theory already entails and underwrites power relations that may well be unjust in terms of his own criteria of just wages. It is, of course, a good thing to condemn "rigid capitalism" (14), but that is not very interesting since that species exists now for the most part only in the ideology of the Republican party. The problem with John Paul II's analysis is that he simply fails to direct our attention to where the real conflicts are occuring within and between advanced capitalist economies and the developing nations.

It is, for example, simply misleading and distorting to tell us on the basis of a "correct understanding of work" that in principle capital cannot be opposed to labor (13). Nor is it the case that an economy almost by a will of its own is or can be coordinated to achieve the common good (10). And it is naive in the extreme to assume that the "mutual dependence of societies and states" is sufficient to sustain a call for them to collaborate to secure international full employment (18). The assumption of an organic and harmonious theory of society as in social encyclicals of the past fails to acknowledge the inherent power-relations of economic systems. Some possess power over others; they are not about to relinquish that power because it fails to sustain a system of fulfilling work for everyone.

As Christians, however, we need no alternative social and economic theory to capitalism or socialism to recognize that injustice exists. We need only the presence of the poor, the uncared-for widows and orphans, the disabled, the unemployed. All we need to know is that a worker cannot support his or her family. Based in that knowledge, we can challenge the greatest pretensions of all economic and social theories — whether capitalist, socialist, supply-side, Keynesian, or even Papal. For the pretext of all such theories is the claim they really know what is going on and as a result ask some to suffer for the good of the whole on the basis of theory. Such is the idealogy that the Pope must challenge, unfortunately missing from his *Laborem Exercens*. Instead of a prophetic challenge to the pretension of those who claim to be in control, who claim to know what is going on economically, we get only another theory.[10] Thus the church abdicates its most important role, which is simply to point out: "The Emperor has no clothes."

Are Social Encyclicals Still a Good Idea?

The problem with *Laborem Exercens* however, is not in many ways unique, but rather exhibits characteristics of the more recent encyclicals. In those the church, as represented by the magisterial office, is seen as a universal teacher of basic truths for all people. As a result, most of what they say is of such a general nature that it cannot be rescued from the charge of being platitudinous. The encyclicals seem to be written in a purposively ambiguous manner so that all sides are left to interpret them in a manner that does not challenge our essential self-interests.

For example John Paul II echoing recent encyclicals tells us that "Commitment to justice must be closely linked with commitment to peace in the modern world" (2). The problem with such claims is they in no way indicate the price that is required for anyone to hold them. For example, nowhere does John Paul II indicate that in the interest of peace we must seek to achieve justice in a manner that may be less effective than violence for eradicating immediate forms of injustice.[11]

Laborem Exercens is no exception in this respect; nowhere does John Paul II indicate what kind of costs might be required for the achievement of the just wage. The encyclical gives the impression that universal employment and just wage are compatible demands requiring only the cooperation of people of good will. In fact, good will is not enough, not only because we cannot assume its universal existence; even if good will existed on everyone's part it by no means follows that we know how to form an economy sufficiently productive to create the resources for just wages for everyone.

As a result the social encyclicals, and *Laborem Exercens*, appear to many to be less than morally serious documents.[12] They have next to no effect on people who are having to make the economic decisions that affect thousands of lives. Rather they primarily reinforce the notion that the Church, through the papal office, has some ideas about economics but these ideas are not very clear or useful. Although pleased with the impression that the Church has taken a courageous stand, in fact that stance has required little of Pope or members of the Church. Moreover exactly because the Church must try to address all people and situations, John Paul II must base his position on a general theological and economic theory that simply cannot stand up to rational analysis. As a result, the Church reiterates to the world little more than what has been known for some time.

Perhaps, then, the Papacy should cease celebrating the anniversary of *Rerum Novarum* by writing new encyclicals. For the encyclicals betray the Church's very most important social fact—namely its presence throughout the world in diverse social settings and economic contexts. The great moral strength of the Church is that it is of a people scattered amid the nations in a manner defying all geographical and political boundaries. Yet instead of drawing on that rich resource the Papacy articulates universal political and economic theories that cannot help but be lifeless abstractions. In contrast, what the Papal Office should be doing is providing the means for Christians in diverse lands to show that the unity formed through sharing a common eucharistic meal requires them to defy the economic injustices created by clan and nation.

For example, at the very least the church should remind its rich members that our souls are in danger because of our possessions. If the church, not the Church of Rome but the Church of the Holy Redeemer of Peru, Indiana, raised that question seriously we might well find that the church would have something interesting to say about work and the economic order. For then the membership would have paid the price that is required by genuine challenge to our assumptions about the naturalness of the economic inequities that surround us. What is required is not better economic theory or a more profound account of work, but a church more ready to be a people caring for each other rather than economic systems.

It may be objected that calls to be concerned about people rather than economic systems are romantic at best but more importantly a false alternative that comes close to being immoral. After all, economic systems are people. Of course that is right, but it is a point that fails to take seriously my challenge. Attention to actual economic relations might help us see that the church must draw on its best resource when dealing with such matters—namely the actual experience of Christian men and women who must find ways to negotiate the extraordinarily complex economic systems in which we find ourselves caught.

For example, it might be extremely wise for the church to raise once more the issue of usury as a significant moral issue for discussion in the church. No doubt the prohibition of usury was defended by some remarkably bad arguments, but the principles informing it are still relevant. Namely, is it appropriate for Christians who are pledged to care for one another to take advantage of others who are in economic distress?[13] Of course it is true that money is often lent for reasons other than economic distress, but that is exactly the kind of distinction that the required discussion might make in trying to deal morally with questions of the legitimacy of usury. Such an issue does not ask us to choose between capitalism, socialism, or some "middle way;" it reminds us that if we are to make any headway on the morality of certain transactions, we must begin by asking how Christians should conduct their economic relations with one another and thus within the world in which they find themselves. Only by so beginning can we know whether, if and how, Christians might participate in the surrounding financial milieu.

NOTES

1. All references to *Laborem Exercens* will give the paragraph number in the text of the paper. I am using the translation provided by the United States Catholic Conference: Publication No. 825, Office of Publishing Services.

2. I am indebted to Mr. Phil Foubert for this point.

3. Gerhard Von Rad, *Genesis: A Commentary*, translated by John H. Marks (Philadelphia: The Westminster Press, 1961), pp. 57-58.

4. Ibid., p. 58.

5. Ibid., p. 59.

6. James Gustafson, *Ethics from a Theocentric Perspective*, I (Chicago: University of Chicago Press, 1981). For my evaluation of Gustafson's critique of "anthropocentricism" see my "God the Measurer," *Journal of Religion*, (Forthcoming).

7. One has the feeling that if John Paul II had read Studs Terkel's *Working* (New York: Avon Books, 1972) before he had written, he might have produced a much more realistic work. In particular he might have been more impressed by the quiet heroism of many workers who need no grand explanations to sustain their work.

8. John Howard Yoder, *The Politics of Jesus* (Grand Rapids: Eerdmans, 1972), pp. 97,132.

9. For example C. B. Macpherson argues that "liberal-democratic theory must treat a man's power, in the developmental sense, as a quantity, and must measure it in terms of external impediments to the exercise of his human capacities, that is, impediments to the maximum attainable in principle at any given level of social productivity and knowledge. One impediment, namely, lack of access to the means of labour, has been shown to diminish a man's power in three respects. First, it sets up a continuous net transfer of the material value of the productive power of the non-owner to the owner of the means of

labour, the amount of which transfer, in each of the repeated transactions, is the excess of the value added by the work over the wage paid. Second, it diminishes each non-owner's productive power beyond that market-measured amount, by denying him the essentially human satisfaction of controlling the use of his own productive capacities: This value is lost, not transferred. Third, it diminishes his control over his extra-productive life. Of these three deficiencies in a man's power, the first is numerically measurable and is in fact measured by the market. The other two are not so measurable." *Democratic Theory: Essays in Retrieval* (Oxford: Calendon Press, 1973), pp. 69-70.

10. For a Protestant equivalent see Robert Benne, *The Ethic of Democratic Capitalism: A Moral Reassessment.* (Philadelphia: Fortress Press, 1981).

11. Though disagreeing with the specifics of some of the alternatives my criticism in this respect is very similar to Paul Ramsey's critique of some of the social statements of the World Council of Churches. See Ramsey's *Who Speaks for the Church* (Nashville, Abingdon Press, 1967).

12. P. T. Bauer even suggests that the Pope's recent encyclicals which insist on large-scale aid, land reform, debt cancellation, commodity agreements have so little to do with economic realities they are not just incompetent, but they are "immoral because they are incompetent." "An Economist Replies: Ecclesiastical Economics is Envy Exalted," *This World*, I (Winter-Spring, 1982), p. 69.

13. John Noonan, Jr., *The Scholastic Analysis of Usury* (Cambridge: Harvard University Press, 1957). Noonan rightly notes the importance of the shift from treating usury as a sin of uncharitableness or avarice to treating it as a sin of injustice. For when that shift occurs it is necessary to try to base the church's prohibition on "natural law" that in many ways distorts exactly the moral commitments that made the condemnation of usury intelligible as an ethic among and for Christians. I am grateful to Anne Harley Hauerwas for reminding me of the moral importance of usury in this context. I am also in her debt for the skillful editing of this essay.

CHAPTER 3

Human Work and the Story of Creation: Theology and Ethics in *Laborem Exercens*

by David Hollenbach, S.J.

THIS ESSAY WILL ADDRESS THE ENCYCLICAL LETTER *LABOREM EXERCENS* FROM the viewpoint of theological ethics. There is a certain irony in the assumption that a theologian might have anything useful to say about the significance of work. Can one think of a reality which is more of "this world" than human labor and toil? If one supposes that religious belief and the worship of God are pre-eminently activities of the Sabbath—the day of rest—then work would seem to be quite beyond the pale of the theologian's concern. The same irony is present in the idea that a religious leader like Pope John Paul II might be able to add anything useful to an appreciation and understanding of work. Indeed, in Hannah Arendt's interpretation of the Western history of ideas about work and politics, the Christian religion has contributed to a significant devaluation of these two chief poles of public life. According to Arendt, the

Christian ethic, "while it is incapable of founding a public realm of its own, is quite adequate to the main Christian principle of worldlessness and is admirably fit to carry a group of essentially worldless people through the world."[1]

Laborem Exercens forcefully challenges the presupposition that Christian faith is concerned with the sabbath to the exclusion of interest in the everyday or interested in the *vita contemplative* to the detriment of the *vita activa*. The Pope's claim to be able to make some contribution to our understanding of the meaning and value of work is based on two complementary aspects of the Christian doctrine of creation: God is the active creator and sustainer of all that is, and human beings are created and sustained by God in their very being and their every action. In the view of the encyclical the divine action of creation and the created human activity of work are not related to each other as sabbath to weekday or as sacred to profane. There is a dynamic interrelation between God's action as creator and the human activity of work. As the encyclical puts it:

> The word of God's revelation is profoundly marked by the fundamental truth that the human person, created in the image of God, shares by his work in the activity of the creator and that, within the limits of his own capabilities, the human person in a sense continues to develop that activity, and perfect it as he advances further and further in the discovery of the resources and values in the whole of creation.[2]

In other words, human work "is a participation in God's activity."[3]

This claim is a bold one, both from the point of view of Christian theology and from the perspective of our ordinary experience of what work is really like. Theologically it runs the risk of arrogantly inflating the significance of what we humans can do and who we humans really are. Karl Barth, the great theologian of the "otherness" of God, has warned us against the pretence that can be operative in such claims about human work. Though Barth would agree that a human being can in some sense participate in the activity of God, he insists that "this does not mean that he becomes a co-creator, co-saviour or co-regent in God's activity. It does not mean that he becomes a kind of co-God."[4] In addition to this possible arrogance, such claims for the significance of human work risk trivializing our understanding of the creative action of God. In cultures where work is alienated or increasingly meaningless for large numbers of people, the close linking of human work with the activity of God is no compliment to God. Further, such linkage could bestow a false aura of religious legitimacy on social patterns that should be challenged or simply overthrown by those who not only believe that God is creator but also that God is good.

Laborem Exercens is not unaware of these dangers. For example, it calls for a perspective on human work which shows "the maturity called for by the tensions of mind and heart"[5] which permeate work life in the present day. It asserts that its interpretation of the value of labor "will require a reordering and adjustment of the structures of the modern economy and of the distribution of work."[6] It challenges all patterns of work which alienate the worker from work when it affirms that "in the first place work is 'for persons' and not persons 'for work.' "[7] It also argues that capital or the means of production are *instruments* for the enhancement of human creativity and human fulfillment. They must never be allowed to become the determining forces in the economic process.[8] It directs these criticisms at both "rigid capitalism" and at the state capitalism of bureaucratic collectivism.[9] The encyclical challenges the present international distribution of labor as a threat to human dignity and says that "both within the individual political communities and in their relationships on the continental and world levels there is something wrong with the organization of work and employment, precisely at the most critical and socially most important points."[10]

These criticisms of present structures of work are advanced in the name of an understanding of the relation between God as creator and the human person as creature. Other papers prepared for this symposium will analyze the arguments on which they are based in greater detail. This essay, however, will focus on a limited part of the argument: the theological interpretation of the interconnection between human work and the creative and preserving action of God. It will be argued that the encyclical's approach to this theological question is useful but incomplete, and that this incompleteness leads to an oversimplification of the issues which arise in a Christian ethical approach to the problems of the domain of work.

The argument will have three phases. First, the encyclical's use of the Book of Genesis will be considered, for the theology of *Laborem Exercens* rests squarely on this biblical source. Second, some suggestions will be made about how a more complex understanding of the tensions and conflicts of the world of work is called for in a theology based on a more nuanced reading of the first book of the bible. Finally a few suggestions will be advanced about the ethical implications of these first two considerations. Thus this essay will not deal with many of the valuable points raised in the encyclical. It has the modest purpose of exploring the theology of *Laborem Exercens* and a few of the ethical consequences of this theology.

The Implications of Genesis 1-11 for a Theology of Work

Laborem Exercens bases its analysis of the significance and proper ordering of human labor on a number of intellectual sources. It relies on the past social teachings of the Church on related social-economic questions and claims fundamental continuity with this tradition.[11] True to the Roman Catholic natural law tradition with its emphasis on the significance of human experience and reason as sources for theology and ethics, *Laborem Exercens* affirms that philosophical and social scientific analyses play a legitimate and important role in shaping its conclusions. John Paul II, however, asserts that the Church's contribution to the discussion of work is formed "not only in the light of historical experience, not only with the aid of the many methods of scientific knowledge, but in the first place in the light of the revealed word of the living God."[12] As René Coste has noted, the Pope's aim is the presentation of a "truly theological anthropology of work."[13]

The keystone of the encyclical's theological discussion is its interpretation of the first chapters of the Book of Genesis. An indication of the importance of the Genesis accounts in the Pope's reflection is the fact that twenty-one of the document's ninety-one footnotes contain references to the first book of the bible. Indeed the encyclical is quite explicit about the relevance of Genesis to its understanding of work: "The church finds in the very first pages of the Book of Genesis the source of her conviction that work is a fundamental dimension of human existence on earth. An analysis of these texts makes us aware that they express — sometimes in an archaic way of manifesting thought — the fundamental truths about the human person in the context of the mystery of creation itself."[14] Thus, without excluding what can be learned about the structure and dynamics of work from all the human sciences, John Paul II relies on biblical sources to support his assertion that what the encyclical presents as "a conviction of the intellect is also a conviction of faith."[15] In other words, it is the Pope's appeal to the biblical sources and their interpretation in living Christian tradition that warrants his claim to a distinctive though not exclusive competence to speak on the meaning and values of human work.

There are several verses from Genesis to which the Pope repeatedly refers in developing the theme of human work as a participation in the creative activity of God. Most prominent among these are three verses in the so-called Priestly account of creation found in Genesis 1, i.e. verses 26-28.

> [26]Then God said, "Let us make *adam* in our image, after our likeness; and let them have dominion over the fish of the sea, and over the birds of the air, and over the cattle, and over all the earth, and over every creeping thing that creeps upon the earth." [27]So God created *adam* in his own image, in the image of God he created him; male and female he created them. [28]And God blessed them, and God said to them, "Be fruitful and multiply, and fill the earth and subdue it; and have dominion over the fish of the sea and over the birds of the air and over every living thing that moves upon the earth."

These verses provide a central part of the foundation of the encyclical's theology of work. John Paul II employs them to support the link he sees between human work and the creative activity of God.

In the Image of God

First, human beings in some way reflect and embody the nature of God. This is the meaning of the affirmation that human beings are created "in the image of God." Throughout the history of Christian thought the creation of humankind as *imago Dei* has been interpreted in a variety of ways. It has been taken to mean that, like God, human beings are persons rather than animals or things. That is to say, humans are capable of self-conscious awareness.[16] In a closely related interpretation, humans are seen as images of God through their possession of both reason and freedom, faculties which give them the capacity for both self-determination and moral responsibility.[17] Others have interpreted the divine image as the human capacity for interpersonal relationship, for friendship, for community life in society and for love.[18]

None of these readings of the meaning of the image of God in human persons is excluded by *Laborem Exercens*. Rather, John Paul II has focused on an interpretation which is more explicitly suggested by the biblical text itself. Human persons are like God through their commission to subdue the earth and have dominion over the rest of creation.

The significance of work is directly linked to the creation of humankind in the image of God through this interpretation of the *imago Dei*. In the words of the encyclical: "The human person is the image of God partly through the mandate received from the creator to subdue, to dominate, the earth. In carrying out this mandate, humankind, every human being, reflects the very action of the creator of the universe."[19] The encyclical thus understands all the creativity of civilization and the economy as an expression of the image of the Creator in the human creature. Whether work be agricultural or industrial, physical or intellectual, more traditional in form or in the technologically advanced spheres of electronics and scientific research, the encyclical affirms that all forms of creative activity by which nature is brought to the service of human ends are an expression of the image and likeness of the Creator in the human creature.

The biblical language which speaks of human "dominance" over nature and of the commission to "subdue the earth" has been criticized as a prime source of ecological irresponsibility in Western society and culture.[20] Recent biblical studies have shown, however, that the attitude toward nature expressed in Genesis 1:26-28 is one of stewardship rather than exploitation.[21] John Paul II has elsewhere expressed his sensitivity to the responsibility humans have for the preservation of the natural and biological worlds. In his first encyclical letter, *Redemptor Hominis*, he affirmed that this same biblical passage commissions the human race to be "master" and "guardian" rather than "exploiter" and "destroyer" of nature.[22]

It is unfortunate that this emphasis has not been reiterated here. This omission has occurred, it seems, because the encyclical's primary purpose is to emphasize what it calls the "subjective dimension" of work. The *imago Dei* motif is brought forward to emphasize that in work human beings must remain true agents and that both the means of production and the fruit of labor are at the service of those who work. A person's activities in work "must serve to realize his humanity, to fulfill the calling to be a person that is his by reason of his very humanity."[23] Thus the theological interpretation of human "dominance" over nature supports the encyclical's fundamental principle that work is not simply "merchandise" to be bought and sold. Rather, the account of creation set forth in Genesis 1 stands as a critique of any economic system in which persons are "treated on the same level as the whole complex of the material means of production."[24] The great strength of the encyclical lies in its willingness to direct this critique against both national economic systems and against transnational and international economic arrangements which violate this principle.

The major theological contribution of the encyclical, therefore, lies in the grounding it provides for a very positive evaluation of human work through the interpretation of the *imago Dei* as expressed in the subjectivity of workers. This is undoubtedly a most important theme in the Genesis narratives. Indeed there are additional episodes in these narratives which can further reinforce the positive evaluation of work and the critical principle of the subjectivity and dignity of workers which the Pope wants to emphasize. For example, Genesis 2:15 describes God placing the first human being in the Garden of Eden with the charge to "till and keep it." Thus work is part of human life in its created, paradisiacal state. It is created by God as "very good." It is not merely the result of human sin. The geneology contained in Genesis 4:17-22 portrays the origins of civilization, with the emergence of urban culture, animal husbandry, the arts and technology. These developments are regarded as signs of God's continuing blessing on the creativity of humankind. In Genesis 8:22 God promises to Noah that this blessing shall continue "as long as the earth remains," and Genesis 9 extends the promise of God's preservation and blessing in an "everlasting covenant" with "all flesh that is upon the earth."

The Question of Sin

Despite the legitimacy and value of the encyclical's powerful biblical argument for the dignity of both work and worker, the picture which it offers us seems to me to be an incomplete one. The absence of the qualifications on the meaning of human "dominance" over nature which are called for by a critical exegesis of the whole creation narrative raises a question about the overall use of Genesis in *Laborem Exercens*. The narratives of Genesis 1-11 are a rich and complex whole. They present a description of human existence and the human predicament by recounting a set of highly compressed narratives about cosmic and human origins. The full biblical theology of the relation between Creator and human creature must take the whole of the Genesis creation story into consideration and also situate it in the context of the rest of the Old and New Testaments.

The exposition of such a fully developed biblical theology of creation and work is both beyond my competence and beyond the scope of this essay. In responding to *Laborem Exercens* from the perspective of theological ethics a more limited point can be made. Elaboration of the theology of the participation of human work in the creative activity of God calls for greater attention to the aspects of the Genesis narrative which focus on the problematic and even sinful dimensions of human agency and human action. The Genesis account of human origins, taken as a whole, is less sanguine about the ease with which human civilization and human productivity can be brought into harmony with the creative and preservative blessing of God than *Laborem Exercens* appears to be.

The Genesis narratives are myths and certainly not to be confused with scientific or historical documents. The value and religious significance of these myths derive from their ability to form and express an appreciation of the ultimate shape of human existence as a whole. As Paul Ricoeur has put it, "the 'Adamic' myth is the anthropological myth *par excellence*."[25] The accounts of the origins of cosmos and humanity found in Genesis are narratives which recount events from primal time in order to describe the *present* condition of human existence. These mythic narratives are attentive not only to the potentialities inherent in a world which has been created as radically good. They also evoke the limits of human capacities and the hardships to which human beings are subject. They describe the origins not only of human creativity but also of human "deviation" or "going astray."[26] Moreover, as the biblical scholar Claus Westermann has shown, the context for the initial elaboration of the Genesis narratives was that of danger, the struggle for survival and the experience of the self as threatened.[27] The subsequent recounting of the creation myths "had the function of preserving the world and of giving security to life"[28] by situating danger, threat and sin in the larger context of a good God and a good creation. A fully adequate interpretation of the depiction of human agency and human work as they are portrayed in Genesis must take this into account.

Laborem Exercens takes note of the fact that the Genesis accounts include evocations of the limits, burdens and threats to human creativity. The encyclical points out that, because of the disobedience of Adam and Eve to the command of God, human work is often full of toil: "In the sweat of your face you shall eat your bread" (Gen 3:19). Work is sometimes sterile and unproductive: "Thorns and thistles it shall bring forth to you" (Gen 3:18).[29] These references to the ambiguities of the situation of human agency and labor, however, are considerably less developed in the encyclical than they are in the creation account in the first eleven chapters of Genesis.

These are five major events in the total narrative of origins which mythically portray the emergence of sin and the destructive capacity of human agency: the disobedience of Adam and Eve and their consequent expulsion from the Garden of Eden (Gen 3), Cain's murder of his brother Abel (Gen 4:2-16), the marriage of the "sons of God" with the "daughters of men" and the limitation on the span of human life because of this infraction (Gen 6:1-4), God's destruction of the earth by flood as a result of pervasive wickedness in human hearts (Gen 6:5-7:24), and scattering of the peoples of the earth and the confusion of their languages as a result of the people's attempt to build a city "and a tower with its top in the heavens" (Gen 11:1-9).

It is not our purpose here to present a detailed interpretation of these passages. Two brief observations will serve to show their importance for an understanding of the relation between human work and the creative activity of God. First, an underlying motif in the narratives is the distortion of the capacities of human freedom and agency which follows from a failure to recognize the limited nature of these capacities. This is most evident in the serpent's temptation of Adam and Eve by holding out the possibility that they might become "like God" (Gen 3:5). It is present in the overstepping of the boundary between the divine and the human expressed in the myth of the marriage of the "sons of God" with the "daughters of men." It reappears in the story of the tower of Babel, where the desire of the people to "make a name" for themselves (Gen 11:4) leads them to try to climb the heavens through the tools of their own technology.[30] The motif of the creation of human persons "in the image of God" is thus held in tension with the powerful warning that human superiority over nature is the occasion of a perpetual temptation to try to become "like God" through knowledge, sexuality, technology or other human capacities. Though created in God's image, human beings are creatures, not God or even demigods. If they deny their creatureliness they obscure the *imago Dei* as well.

Second, the Genesis myths concerning the origin of sin directly link the distortion of the relation of creature to God with the distortion of the relations within the human community as well. Among the consequences of the effort of the first couple to become "like God" is a distortion of relation of mutuality and equality which characterizes their status as created by God into a relation of domination and subordination (Gen 3:16).[31] The story of Cain and Abel should be understood as a further elaboration of this distortion of human relationships which follows upon the failure of humans to accept their creatureliness. The words which God addresses to Adam after he has eaten the forbidden fruit, "Adam, where are you?" are directly paralleled by the words God addresses to Cain after the murder of Abel, "Where is Abel, your brother?" The alienation from God which follows upon the effort to transcend the status of creature is paralleled by the alienation from fellow humans which follows on the effort to escape the responsibility of being our "brother's keeper." And finally, the tower of Babel story not only portrays an act of rebellion against humanity's earthbound nature but also gives an account of how human history has become a battleground of conflict and misunderstanding because of this rebellion.

On the basis of his exegesis of all these passages from Genesis, Westermann has concluded that the breakdown in the participation of human activity in the creative action of God and the breakdown in the life of human society are inseparable from each other.

> In the biblical account of the origins sin is not the narrow, individualistic notion that it has become in church tradition. It is viewed in a broader perspective. It is seen as that other limit, that inadequacy or overstepping of limits which determines the whole of human existence. Sin shows itself in many forms in all areas of human life and not merely in a personal confrontation of man and God. It is to be reckoned within all aspects of the human community, where man is at work as well as in the world of politics.[32]

The first eleven chapters of the book of Genesis thus evidently contain an interpretation of human capacity and agency which is in marked tension with the theology which sees human work and dominance over nature as manifestations of the image of God in human beings. The theology underlying *Laborem Exercens'* valuation of work is indeed warranted by the Genesis narrative of origins. *Laborem Exercens*, however, does not present us with the *whole* of the biblical perspective on the potentialities and limits of human creativity in work. The problem of presenting a complete and unified interpretation of the biblical perspective on *any* question of fundamental human importance is notoriously difficult. The biblical sources are internally pluralistic and cannot be simply harmonized into a tightly integrated theological framework.[33] The fact that there is a certain selectivity in the way *Laborem Exercens* reads the Book of Genesis, therefore, should not be surprising. Nevertheless, a balanced theology of work calls for greater attention to the aspects of the biblical story which are de-emphasized in the encyclical. In what follows a few suggestions will be made about how such balance might be sought.

The Theology of Work on a More Complete Biblical Basis

Historical-critical analysis of the narratives of origins has concluded that there are two main sources upon which the redactor of Genesis has relied in constructing the text as we have it in the canonical bible. The theology of *Laborem Exercens* relies heavily, one might almost say exclusively, on passages which can be traced to the so-called Priestly or P source of the sixth-fifth century B.C. By contrast, the narratives of Adam and Eve's disobedience, of Cain and Abel, of the marriage of the "sons of God" and the "daughters of men," and of the tower of Babel can all be traced back to the older tenth-ninth century B.C. author known as the "Yahwist."

This earlier Yahwistic theology is considerably more attuned to the ambiguities of human creativity and work than is the Priestly author. Gerhard von Rad has called the Yahwist "the great psychologist" among the biblical writers. Like his Christian successors Augustine, Pascal, and Reinhold Niebuhr, the Yahwist's theology includes deep reflection on the "riddles and conflicts" of human behavior and the "mistakes and muddles" present in the human heart.[34] The Priestly author, on the other hand, is more the architect than the psychologist. His is concerned with establishing a well-integrated social system with temple cult, theocratic governance and religious law as the soul of this system. In the words of Bernhard Anderson:

the Priestly writer does not portray sympathetically the human side of the historical drama: the people's conflicts, frustrations, anxieties, doubts. He lacks the "human interest" that we find in the Yahwist's story of Paradise Lost or in the narrative of Abraham's supreme test of faith; for his concern is with the laws and institutions that were given to the people in the climatic period of Sinai.[35]

Westermann, among others, has pointed out that the Priestly tradition originated in the context of that phase of Jewish religion which had as its primary focus the rebuilding of the temple in Jerusalem and the reestablishment of Jewish society after the Babylonian exile.[36] The positive valuation of human creativity in the Priestly source is directly linked with the religious developments taking place in response to the author's social-historical context. The Priestly tradition elaborates a theology of human creativity which is considerably more expansive than one which would affirm that the building of temples is the prime focus of human work. Nevertheless the connection between an almost entirely positive valuation of the fruits of human culture and the religious aims of the Priestly author is not accidental. The Priestly theology is a theology for a religiously centered and organically integrated society.

One should not be surprised to discover a similar conjunction of religious and social-cultural interests in a contemporary document like *Laborem Exercens*. Pope John Paul's preference for the Priestly strand in the Book of Genesis can be explained at least in part by the analogies which exist between the social-historical context of the Priestly author and the context which has shaped the Pope's thought. Both have experienced severe restriction on the religious and national aspirations of their people—the Priestly author through exile in Babylon and the Pope through the restrictions imposed on the Polish people by a succession of foreign powers. Both are convinced that the preservation of nationhood and the preservation of religious identity are closely interconnected. Thus both defend a close connection between cultural creativity, historical tradition and religious fidelity. The highly positive estimation of the value of human creativity as an expression of the image of God in human existence serves to link religion and culture closely together in both the Priestly theology and the theology of *Laborem Exercens*. Their theologies of work are developed as components of this understanding of the organic link between religion and culture.

John Paul II has made this larger cultural concern most evident in a recent address at the headquarters of UNESCO. In this address he stated that the justification for his presence in a forum such as UNESCO was "*the organic and constitutive link* which exists between *religion* in general and Christianity in particular, on the one hand, and *culture* on the other hand. This relationship extends to the multiple realities which must be defined as concrete expressions of culture in the different periods of history and all over the world."[37] The social paradigm for the Pope's reflections is that of a society in which Christianity and social, economic and cultural life are closely interwoven. This model of social-religious-cultural integration governs the Pope's analysis of work. It also serves as the basis of *Laborem Exercens'* repeated appeals for solidarity among workers and for collaboration and cooperation among all components of the economy. John Paul's theology, in other words, gives primacy to organic unity and integration among the diverse elements of social, economic and religious life. An organically unified social life is seen as an expression of both the fullness of what it means to be human and the depths of what it means to be Christian. It is in this sense that one can say that the theology of *Laborem Exercens* is a Priestly theology.

The Yahwistic account of human and cosmic origins is much less optimistic about the ability of the human race to achieve this kind of harmonious integration than is either the Priestly author or *Laborem Exercens*. The story of the tower of Babel, which von Rad has called "the keystone to the Yahwistic primeval history," presents us with a picture of the very antithesis of human community bound together by bonds of solidarity and cultural integration.[38] The potential of work, technology, culture and even religion to become sources of conflict and destruction is a leitmotif of the Yahwist narratives. Because all these achievements of human creativity can and in fact sometimes do lead to rebellion against God and murder of fellow humans, the Yahwist continually reminds humankind of its limits: "You are dust, and to dust you shall return" (Gen 3:19). A balanced theology of work must take this perspective into account.

Where, then, does this leave us in the effort to understand the participation of human work and creativity in the creative action of God? One possibility would be to say that we are left free by the biblical sources to choose between the Priestly or Yahwist emphases according to the needs of our own cultural or economic situation. Such an approach is to some extent inevitable, for a complete unification of these diverse emphases in a single theology is not finally possible. If the biblical witness, however, is to serve as a challenge to the cultural milieu and not simply as a legitimation of it then this kind of selectivity cannot be a fully adequate response to the pluralism of biblical theologies. An alternative approach would be to try to find some sort of compromise between the alternatives contained in the two biblical sources examined here. This could take the form of a search for a least common denominator or for a theological midpoint between them. The danger of this solution is the elimination of theological tension which it entails. The biblical view of the relation between human and divine creativity is not some neutral perspective halfway between Priestly optimism and Yahwist pessimism. It includes both of these emphases.

The Tension between Goodness and Perversity

The beginnings of a solution to this problem can be uncovered if we consider the fact that the two traditions we have been discussing have in fact been woven together by the editors who produced the Book of Genesis in the final form which it takes in the bible. It is this document, in the context of the whole bible, which is normative for a Christian theology of work and human creativity. The Genesis account as a whole presents us with the biblical picture of the origins and potential of human work. Thus it is possible to read Genesis as an account of two *aspects* of human creativity rather than as a simple juxtaposition of two different accounts of human creativity.

The most probing recent discussion of the relationship between the two aspects of the mythic narrative is that of Paul Ricoeur. Ricoeur has shown that the Yahwist myth of the "Fall" and expulsion from the garden, together with its consequences of murder and cultural conflicts, is a narrative way of evoking an experience of a fundamental "rift" in human existence. This "rift" is the deep tension between the ontological goodness of the God-created human being and the actual perversity which is written on the pages of human history. It is the experience expressed in the classic words of Rousseau: "Man is born free, and everywhere he is in chains."[39] In the Yahwist strand of the Genesis narrative the goodness of created humanity is evoked by the portrayal of a state *before* the advent of murder and historical conflict. Evil is not a necessary consequence of created human nature but rather the result of the free human attempt to transcend the limits of creaturely good-ness. Evil and sin are real and powerful realities, but they are the con-tingent results of human freedom rather than the necessary outcome of human nature. Thus the Yahwist's account of the conflicts which emerge in the free exercise of human creativity is set against the back-ground of the affirmation that "sin is not our original reality, does not constitute our first ontological status; sin does not define what it is to be a man."[40] The Yahwist account, in other words, makes its assertions about the capacities of human creativity in the negative mode: the human quest for knowledge leads to loss of innocence—but it need not be so; the productivity of technology leads to strife and cultural conflict—but it need not be so; the religious quest to be like God and to ascend the heavens leads to rivalry and murder—but it need not be so. These same assertions about the goodness of human capacity and creativity are made by the Priestly tradition in directly affirmative and positive terms. The Priestly author focuses in the first place on the on-tological status of human capacities—they are very good—rather than on their actual exercise in history and in civilization. The Priestly tradi-tion has taken the Yahwist's affirmation of the contingency of sin and evil and transformed it into a positive theological assertion of the on-tological goodness of human capacities and human nature. As Ricoeur has put it, the Yahwist's "it need not be so" is "the radical intuition which the future editor of the second creation-story (Gen. 1) will sanc-tion by the word of the Lord God: 'Let us make man in our image, after our likeness.' "[41]

These two traditions, therefore, are reflecting on human existence and human capacities for creativity from two different points of view. The Priestly tradition is principally concerned with the created being or essence of humanity. To apply a category drawn from another time, the Priestly theology is rooted in an ontological and metaphysical in-terest. The Yahwist, on the other hand, is preoccupied by the historical and social expressions of these capacities in all their ambiguity. His theology is rooted in the categories of historical, social, cultural and religious critique. An adequate theology of work cannot disregard either of these perspectives. Pure ontological reflection on the created goodness of the human person risks irrelevance to actual historical con-flict and oppression if it ignores the Yahwist's sensitivity to such realities. Purely historical reflection on the outcomes of the exercise of human creativity in society risks leading one to the conclusion of Qoheleth: "Vanity of vanities! All is vanity. What does a man gain by all the toil at which he toils under the sun?" (Ecclesiastes 1:2-3) An adequate theology of work and human creativity needs *both* a deep sensitivity to the capacity of human beings to be co-creators with God *and* a ruthlessly realistic assessment of the conflicts and oppressions which human freedom can and does create. Without the first the theology has no basis for hope and thus cannot be Christian. Without the second the theology will not be capable of generating an ethic that is usable in human history—the time between Paradise and the coming of the kingdom of God.

Conclusion: An Ethical Implication

The implications of this analysis for ethical reflection on human work are multiple. By way of conclusion a single brief comment on the ethical approach of *Laborem Exercens* will be offered here. The encyclical presents a strong case for an ethic which seeks to promote cooperation, collaboration, solidarity and harmony between all persons involved in the work process.[42] The same concerns are evident in the Pope's discussion of international and transnational economic processes.[43] These ethical emphases are rooted in the encyclical's theology of both the genuine creativity of human work and its emphasis on the capacitites of human beings for genuinely communal cooperation. The creation of human beings in the image of God is the ultimate foundation for such an ethical standpoint. This ethic is also capable of providing real support for some important new developments presently underway in national and international economic discussions. This aspect of the encyclical deserves support and gratitude.

It can be asked, however, if *Laborem Exercens'* ethic is adequate for use in situations where collaboration, solidarity and cooperation are unlikely or impossible. From the foregoing analysis it is evident that John Paul II has de-emphasized the conflictual elements of the Genesis account of human existence and human work. In another series of reflections on the Book of Genesis he has made clear his conviction that the Priestly tradition represents a theological advance over the Yahwist. In the Pope's words the Priestly source "is much more mature both as regards the image of God, and as regards the formulation of the essential truths about man. . . . Man is defined there, first of all, in dimensions of being and existence ('*Esse*'). He is defined in a way that is more metaphysical than physical."[44] John Paul II, in other words, gives

primacy to a style of theology which is more metaphysical and ontological over theological approaches which are more historical and
social.[45] This approach is quite capable of denouncing all situations
which do not conform to the structure of human personhood as this
structure is discerned through ontological analysis. Its danger, however, is that it will lack the categories which are necessary to guide action in non-ideal circumstances.

To paraphrase Ricoeur, the gap which exists between the ideal
possibilities of created human nature and the realities of history is
paralleled by a gap between a description of personhood set forward in
ontological terms and an ethic which can guide action in the midst of
conflict.[46] *Laborem Exercens'* contribution lies in its description of and
theological support for the possibilities of human creativity. It is less
developed in its approach to the practical ethical questions which arise
in the actual struggle to realize these possibilities. This limitation is
rooted in the document's theology.

An elaboration of the implications of this observation is beyond our
scope here. Suffice it to say that both the traditional ideologies of liberal
capitalism and Marxist socialism, each in different ways, are more attentive to the realities of conflict and struggle in the world of work than
is *Laborem Exercens*. The encyclical is certainly aware of the need for
worker struggle and it reaffirms such techniques of struggle as labor
unions, the strike, and the right to a just wage. What remains unclear
is how these legitimate rights are to be exercised in practice according
to the encyclical's ethic of collaboration and solidarity. More detailed
analysis of the practical possibilities and actual impediments to such
collaboration is needed if the gap between ontology and ethics is to be
bridged. A theology which is based on a more complete reading of
Genesis than that found in *Laborem Exercens* would help make it clear
that such detailed analysis is essential in a religious vision of work as
co-creation.

NOTES

1. Hannah Arendt, *The Human Condition* (Garden City, N.Y.: Doubleday
Anchor Books, 1959), p. 49.
2. *Laborem Exercens*, Para. 25. All citations are to the text published by
the United States Catholic Conference: Publication No. 825, Office of Publishing Services.

3. Para. 25.

4. Karl Barth, *Church Dogmatics* III/4, trans. A. T. MacKay et al. (Edinburgh: T. and T. Clarke, 1961), p. 482.

5. Para. 25.

6. Para. 1.

7. Para. 6.

8. Para. 12.

9. Para. 14.

10. Para. 18.

11. Para. 1. For an analysis of the claim to unbroken continuity in the modern Catholic social tradition see Richard McCormick, "Notes on Moral Theology 1981," *Theological Studies* 43 (1982), pp. 97-102, and John Coleman "Development of Church Social Teaching," *Origins* 11 (1981), pp. 33-41.

12. Para. 4.

13. René Coste, "Le travail et l'homme. L'encyclique 'Laborem exercens,' " *Esprit et vie*, January 21, 1982, p. 37.

14. Para. 4.

15. Para. 4.

16. See Harold L. Creager, "The Divine Image," in Howard N. Bream, et al., *A Light unto My Path: Old Testament Studies in Honor of Jacob M. Myers*, Gettysburg Theological Studies IV (Philadelphia: Temple University Press, 1974), pp. 103-118.

17. See Vatican Council II, *Gaudium et Spes*, Pastoral Constitution on the Church in the Modern World, no. 17, in Joseph Gremillion ed., *The Gospel of Peace and Justice* (Maryknoll, N.Y.: Orbis Books, 1976), p. 256.

18. The prime modern representative of this interpretation is Karl Barth. See *Church Dogmatics* III, 1, pp. 193 ff. and III, 2, p. 324. This notion is also found in the teaching of the Second Vatican Council. See *Gaudium et Spes*, no. 12. A forceful argument that Barth has misread Genesis in developing this interpretation has been developed by Phylis Bird in " 'Male and Female He Created Them.' Gen 1:27b in the Context of the Priestly Account of Creation," unpublished manuscript.

19. Para. 4.

20. See, for example, Lynn White Jr., "The Historical Roots of Our Ecologic Crisis," *Science* 155 (1967), pp. 1203-07.

21. See James Barr, "Man and Nature: The Ecological Controversy and the Old Testament," *Bulletin of the John Rylands Library* 55 (1972-73), pp. 9-32; and Bernhard W. Anderson, "Human Dominion Over Nature," in Miriam Ward, ed., *Biblical Studies in Contemporary Thought* (Somerville, MA: Greeno, Hadden and Co., 1975), pp. 27-45.

22. *Redemptor Hominis*, no. 15.

23. Para. 6.

24. Para. 7.

25. Paul Ricoeur, *The Symbolism of Evil*, trans. Emerson Buchanan (Boston: Beacon Press, 1967), p. 232.

26. Ibid., p. 233.

27. Claus Westermann, *Creation*, trans. John J. Scullion (Philadelphia: Fortress Press, 1974), pp. 12-13.

28. Ibid., p. 11.

29. Para. 9.

30. The most evident instance of the limits of *Laborem Exercens'* use of Genesis occurs in its single reference to the tower of Babel story. In a list of various professions which are referred to in the Old Testament *Laborem Exercens* includes the work of "the builder" (Para. 26). The footnote cites Gen 11:3, a text which describes the preparations for the construction of the tower: "And they said to one another 'Come, let us make bricks, and burn them thoroughly.' And they had brick for stone and bitumen for mortar." One could not easily find a less appropriate text to support the encyclical's basic perspective, for the Genesis myth attributes all the conflicts of world history to this construction project.

31. See Phyllis Trible, *God and the Rhetoric of Sexuality* (Philadelphia: Fortress Press, 1978), pp. 126-128.

32. Westermann, *Creation*, p. 19.

33. For a thorough and perceptive reflection on this problem see David H. Kelsey, *The Uses of Scripture in Recent Theology* (Philadelphia: Fortress Press, 1975).

34. Gerhard von Rad, *Genesis. A Commentary* Revised edition, trans. John H. Marks, (Philadelphia: Westminster, 1972), p. 25.

35. Bernard W. Anderson, *Understanding the Old Testament*, third edition (Englewood Cliffs, N.J.: Prentice-Hall, 1975), p. 434.

36. See Westermann, *Creation*, p. 51.

37. John Paul II, "Address to UNESCO," June 2, 1980 in *The Person, the Nation and the State, Texts of John Paul II (October 1978–January, 1980)*, William Murphy, ed. (Vatican City: Pontifical Commission "Justitia et Pax," 1980), p. 48.

38. von Rad, *Genesis*, p. 152.

39. Jean-Jacques Rousseau, *The Social Contract*, in Sir Ernest Barker, ed., *Social Contract. Essays by Locke, Hume, and Rousseau* (New York: Oxford University Press, 1967), p. 167.

40. Ricoeur, *The Symbolism of Evil*, p. 251.

41. Ibid., p. 251.

42. Para. 8.

43. Para. 17 and 18.

44. Pope John Paul II, *Original Unity of Man and Woman. Catechesis on the Book of Genesis* (Boston: St. Paul Editions, 1981), p. 24.

45. For an analysis of the limits of ontological thinking as a vehicle for the expression of Christian faith see Johann Baptist Metz, *Faith in History and Society: Toward a Practical Fundamental Theology*, trans. David Smith (New York: Seabury, 1980).

46. See Paul Ricoeur, *Fallible Man: Philosophy of the Will*, trans. Charles Kelbley (Chicago: Henry Regnery, 1967), p. 217.

PART TWO

Conceptual Foundations: Creativity, Freedom and Justice

Both the original industrialization that gave rise to what is called the worker question and the subsequent industrial and post-industrial changes show in an eloquent manner that, even in the age of ever more mechanized "work," the proper subject of work continues to be man.

Laborem Exercens, Para. 5

Only in freedom can man direct himself toward goodness.

Gaudium et Spes, Para. 17

It is necessary to situate the problems created by the modern economy in the wider context of a new civilization. These prob-

79

lems include human conditions of production, fairness in the exchange of goods and the division of wealth, the significance of the increased needs of consumption and the sharing of responsibility.

Octogesima Adveniens, Para. 7

Once more the fundamental principles must be repeated: the hierarchy of values and the profound meaning of work itself require that capital should be at the service of labor and not labor at the service of capital.

Laborem Exercens, Para. 23

In Robert A. Caro's first volume on the life of Lyndon Johnson, *The Path to Power*, there is a chapter devoted to Johnson's mentor in Washington, Sam Rayburn, the famous Speaker of the House of Representatives. Caro writes of Rayburn's youth in the eighteen-eighties and nineties on a Texas cotton farm:

> Except for four months each year in a one-room, one-teacher school house, Sam Rayburn spent his boyhood in the cotton rows . . . If, Sunday, chores were light, they were supposed to be replaced not by play but by piety. "Many a time when I was a child and lived way out in the country," Sam Rayburn later recalled, "I'd sit on the fence and wish to God that somebody would ride by on a horse or drive by in a buggy—just anybody to relieve my loneliness." Terrible as were the toil and the poverty, the loneliness was worse. Poverty, he was to say, only "tries men's souls"; it is loneliness that "breaks the heart. Loneliness consumes people."

Unknown to the Rayburns, there was help in sight for the loneliness, if not the poverty, experienced by so many farm families like the Rayburns. Up in Michigan, outside of Detroit, lived a never-do-well farmer turned mechanic. In 1889, this man announced to his young wife that he was going to build a horseless carriage, that the farm and the city would one day be brought closer together, and that our cities would be crowded with these vehicles. Four years later Mr. and Mrs. Henry Ford successfully tested in their kitchen Ford's first internal combustion engine. Ten years later, in 1903, Ford sold his first car when he was forty years old. By 1923, Ford was famous for his Model T—a vehicle designed and priced for farmers like the Rayburns. Ford was a pioneer not only for his product but for the assembly-line factory, for integrated production and distribution, and for the radically high wages he paid his workers for only an eight-hour day. He was an industrial genius, and he had many of the qualities described by the philosopher, Bernard Murchland, in his essay on the essential marks of creativity: restlessness, eccentricity, receptivity, discipline, commitment, and originality — to name only a few. Murchland quotes Plato's idea "that the greatest benefits come to us through that creative madness which is the gift of the gods." To Murchland, Henry Ford with his creativity, "first born of our human gifts," represents something akin to the mark of divinity within us.

Joseph Pichler, the author of the next essay, is a business executive and ethicist. Drawing on the two disciplines of philosophy and economics, he focuses on the possibilities of freedom and creativity in our capitalist society. Pichler rejects any trade-off between religion and what for him are the high ideals of capitalism: " A full implementation of capitalist preconditions (liberty, property, and voluntarism) would assure a high degree of distributive justice to all partners in co-creation."

In his essay on the continuity and change in the social teachings of the church, Bryan Hehir accepts John Paul II's declaration at the beginning of *Laborem Exercens* that his reflections are intended "to be in organic connection" with Catholic social teaching extending from Pope Leo XIII, who published *Rerum Novarum* in 1891, to Pope Pius XI, Pope Pius XII, John XXIII, and Paul VI. For Hehir, Pope John Paul II brings to the papal office and to his writings a unique, personal style: ". . . a fascinating personality with an activist conception . . . a proven intellectual, wedded to a belief in the power of the word, he is also an actor with a sensitive appreciation of the power of gestures — political and personal."

In the final essay of Part Two, Denis Goulet, the developmental economist, writes of the duty of the church to confront powerful institutions, like capitalism and the corporations, to "sanctify, or at least tame, them." But how should the church approach this responsibility? Goulet suggests two dangers: first, there is a possibility that the church will be co-opted by business power and propaganda, much like, he argues, military chaplains and plantation preachers. On the other hand, Goulet sees an opposite temptation: ". . .that of rejecting corporate legitimacy in some naive spirit of unhistorical moralism. Genuine ethical strategies transcend moralism, accepting relativities of time and place, limited virtue, unavoidable evils and the value of intermediate ends." Goulet seems to adopt a form of Christian realism which argues that we have to accept less-than-perfection in order to make progress. But even with this caveat, Denis Goulet looks hopefully over the myriad of economic systems and experiments to find innovative social and economic policies which can inspire needed reform.

CHAPTER 4

Creativity and the Social Order

by Bernard Murchland

Industrial society will open the way to a new civilization only by restoring to the worker the dignity of a creator. —Albert Camus

IN GENESIS GOD IS ENCOUNTERED AS A CREATOR. THAT MAN AND WOMAN ARE created in His image means that creativity is the first born of our human gifts, a genuine mark of divinity within us. This has been a common perception among philosophers from Plato to modern times. In the *Phaedrus* Plato argued that the greatest benefits come to us through that creative madness which is the gift of the gods. Many prophets and priests and poets, he pointed out, conferred splendid benefits on Greece when under the divine spell but did little or nothing when they were in their "right minds." In modern times philosophers like Nietzsche, Bergson, Imgarten, Croce, Collingwood, Maritain and Whitehead have affirmed the primacy of creativity. Whitehead, for example, asserts that creativity is the ultimate brute fact of existence, the most basic general character of nature. If, says Whitehead, all the characteristics of nature were abstracted, one by one, there would result a final residual element from which no further abstraction could be accomplished. This final element is creativity.

Our theme is, then, an important one. I shall try to shed some light by doing three things. I want first of all to present a phenomenological sketch of creativity. Secondly, I will discuss John Paul II's encyclical in light of this sketch. Finally, I will make some closing remarks about creativity and the social order.

The Phenomenon of Creativity

I have determined that there are ten essential marks of creativity. I present this taxonomy, if it might be called that, as relatively complete and reliable despite some overlap and imprecision. It has been worked out over a number of years, is deeply indebted to various philosophical and psychological theories and has been often tested against the experience of creative people. Of course, it is far from perfect and I welcome comments and criticism. It is a fact that creativity is still largely mysterious terrain; we don't know very much about it. Two cautionary remarks. I don't present these characteristics in any particular order of importance although some of them are clearly more important than others. Secondly, I believe creativity to be isomorphic. While I take most of my examples from the work and comments of creative artists I do not claim they are more creative than anyone else but merely privileged (and highly visible) instances of a pervasively human trait. Creativity can be found in all walks of life, among very different kinds of people and is to be found to some degree in everyone.

1. *Restlessness*. Because man is not ontologically grounded he must complete himself through creative effort. Augustine expressed this condition in a famous line: Our hearts are restless until they rest in Thee. Kierkegaard located the source of creativity in the tension between the finite and infinite poles of our being. Sartre makes the point graphically when he says that we have a hole in our being; we are driven by lacks and wants. All creative effort is motivated by unsatisfied needs, unrealized potential. As Carl Rogers put it: The mainspring of creativity is man's tendency to actualize himself, to become his potentialities. All human life manifests the urge to expand, to extend, to develop, to mature. Creative people are searchers and adventurers. They are dissatisfied with any given state of affairs including their own creative accomplishments. Thomas Mann spoke for the breed when he asked: "To me too has not unrest been ordained? Have I not been endowed with

a heart that knows not repose? The story teller's star, is it not the moon, lord of the road, the wanderer who moves in his station one after another, freeing himself from each?"

2. *Eccentricity.* Creative types are characteristically colorful, odd, different. As the saying has it, you don't have to be crazy to be creative but it helps. Frank Barron used such objective tests as the Minnesota Multiphasic Personality Inventory and the California Psychological Inventory to determine that creative groups have more psychopathology than do "more representative members of the same profession." The average creative writer, he reported, is in the upper 15 per cent of the general population on all measures of psychopathology. The distant source of this condition is the *mania* theory found in Plato's dialogues and coming down to us through the alchemic and Romantic traditions. Eccentricity can be merely amusing as when Woody Allen wears sneakers with a tuxedo; bizarre as when Hamlet teases Polonius with different interpretations of a cloud; neurotic as when Van Gogh cut off his ear and sent it to his brother by first class mail; or deep as when Henry Thoreau went into the woods because, he said, "I wished to live deliberately, to front only the essential facts of life, and see if I could learn what it had to teach, and not, when I came to die, discover that I had not lived. I wanted to live deep and suck out all the marrow of life." Thoreau sought his own vantage point in the flux of things. Thus we must not identify eccentricity with the merely bizarre or neurotic. Rather we must take the word to mean, in its literal sense, off-center; to mean an individual's ability, as Emerson said, to establish an original relationship with the universe. Creative people see reality freshly and uniquely; they have their own angle of vision; they march to an inner music; they rejoice in the insight that comes from particularity. Whence Gerald Manley Hopkins praised God "for all things counter, original, spare, strange."

3. *Receptivity.* We cannot will creativity; the Muse cannot be forced to come before her time. The testimony of artists bears ample proof to the involuntary, pre-conscious source of their insights. That is why they spend a lot of time in what appears to be doing nothing at all: daydreaming, walking by the sea, watching the fire, prodding and probing in a passive effort to contact the intuitive springs of the creative process. Rollo May speaks to this point in his *The Courage to Create.* The creative person, he writes, "stands in a state of openness, heightened sensitivity, incubating the creative idea, with a sharpened readiness to

grasp the creative impulse when it is born." William James said he learned to skate in the summer and to swim in the winter. Saul Bellow reports on the same quality in himself. "A writer is on track when the door of his native and deeper intuitions is open. I've always felt a writer is something of a medium and when something is really working he has a certain clairvoyant power." The creative person is significantly the involuntary instrument of something deeply felt. The picture paints the painter. The poem writes the poet. The book reads the reader.

No one has written better about the reflexive character of creativity than Stanley Burnshaw. His *The Seamless Web*[1] is a gold mine of evidence about how experience is ingested by creative poeple. Creativity, Burnshaw proclaims in a bold biological metaphor, is a metabolic experience. "A creative artist inhales the surrounding world and exhales it. Whatever is taken in is given back in altered condition and transformed into matter, action, feeling, thought. Creative artists exhale words, sounds, shapes capable of acting upon others with the force of an object alive in their surrounding worlds." And: "The poet knows for sure he is being used. A poem begins as dictation with the poet listening to something that speaks to him; he listens and sees the words. They command his attention. They break through and into his awareness; they will not be ignored."

4. *Discipline.* Burnshaw makes clear that the creative process is not only passive and reflective. The other side of this process is expression. Otherwise we would know even less about creativity than we do. Creativity seeks a medium. That is why the creative person does not merely walk by the sea but at the appropriate moments must work very hard. By discipline I mean first of all mastery of a technique. A writer will learn how to use words; a politician will become adept at matching laws to community needs; an athlete will learn how to hit the ball. What we often notice first about creative people is precisely this mastery of technique. We refer to this variously as style, craftsmanship, expertise, mastery, professionalism. Hopkins, watching a falcon riding the winds, exclaimed: "the mastery of it, the sheer mastery of it!" Many of us fail to be as creative as we could be because we give up too easily; we take the line of least resistance; cut corners; let George do it. In a word, we don't master the tools of our respective trades. Flannery O'Connor tells us in her memoirs that she went to her study every day from 9-12. And, in a delicious comment on the creative process, she notes that she didn't always get much done but "if an idea comes along

between 9-12 I'll be there to greet it." What Martha Graham said about dancers applies, *mutatis mutandis*, to all creative effort: "It takes ten years to produce a dancer. That's not intermittent training; that's daily training. You go step by step. In ten years, if you are going to be a dancer at all, you will have mastered the instrument. You will know the wonders of the human body, how the ears rest next to your head, the way the hairline grows, the little bones in your wrists, the magic of your feet, the miracles of muscular control." The poet William Stafford exhorts us "to row that easy way, the rage without met by the wings within that guide you anywhere the wind blows." The disciplined person gives direction to the winds of creativity that blow up from the unconscious depths.

5. *Suffering.* At one level, we can understand suffering in its etymological sense of patience. Creative persons have to be patient because so much creativity takes place in the pre-conscious areas of chaos and non-direction. They must so often create their meanings in the dark; in some cases it takes a lifetime before they can express what is churning within them. At another level, we can understand suffering as a tolerance for frustration and ambiguity and the failure that is inevitable in any creative work. All creative people must learn to cope with loneliness, misunderstandings, the sense of hopelessness that arises when they perceive the discrepancy between the ideal and the real, between what they have dreamed and what they have realized. Shadows are the constant companions of creativity.

At the deepest level, however, we must understand suffering in its rich, spiritual meaning as a journey into the dark night of the soul, into the belly of the whale. Because we are doubled creatures, with a constant civil war waging within us, we must undergo the purgative fires of suffering. Creativity is born of our struggles with non-being. Paul Tillich has said that the measure of creativity is the amount of negativity we can absorb. Archibald MacLeish makes the point well when he writes: "We poets struggle with non-being and force it to yield being. We knock upon silence for an answering music." Creative people feel the pain of insufficiency acutely; each effort they make is a raid on chaos, a defiance of human limits, a gesture towards infinity. Often their suffering is symbolized by some physical defect. Toulouse-Lautrec said that had his legs been six inches longer he would never have been an artist. His creativity was both generated by and a compensation for his self-consciousness in this regard. Sickness often goes hand in hand with creativity. Nietzsche was once asked why the Jewish people are so creative. "Because they know how to suffer," Nietzsche answered. And I know of no one else who has written so deeply and so beautifully about the suffering that attends creativity as Nietzsche himself.

6. *Originality*. The best general definition of creativity we can offer is the bringing of something new into existence. Artists continually shape and reshape their materials in an effort to do something that has not been done before. The creative mind, according to Jacob Bronowski, "is a mind that looks for unexpected likenesses." All nature is akin, said Heraclitus. The trick is to uncover the similarities. A tree is only a tree until it is painted by Cezanne; it then becomes an original statement about reality. Aristotle considered the ability to create metaphors the premier sign of genius. This is because metaphor is precisely where disparate strands of meaning come together at a unified point of illumination. In the light of metaphor, as in a flash of intuition, new worlds come into being, connecting our experience to larger patterns of meaning.

I understand originality here much as Kierkegaard understood subjectivity. "The mode of apprehension of the truth is precisely the truth," he said. We could argue about the epistemology of that definition; but it accurately states an essential aspect of creativity. The subjective thinker is the original thinker. Such a person has the following traits: inwardness, a capacity for hard choices, a sense of ultimacy, fearlessness before the absurd, a passion for the infinite, the ability to live life forward, great powers of appropriation—that, is, the power to make the truth one's own, to stamp reality with the impress of one's own personality. We are not talking here about mere individualism; and we go beyond what is connoted by the idea of eccentricity. Here we speak of one's strong desire to be more and different, the unique way in which each "existing individual" encounters reality. When Kierkegaard goes to see the middle of a play or reads the third part of a book he is being eccentric; when he redefines Christianity he is being original. He gives evidence of a core within against which all experience is evaluated.

7. *Commitment*. Originality implies a degree of ultimacy. Creative people are, in Nietzsche's image, "pregnant with their creations. They know and hear nothing except about the pregnancies and deliveries of the spirit. This is what gives birth to that terrible artist's egoism that has the look of bronze and knows itself justified to all eternity in its work." Thus highly creative people will go to any extreme to ac-

complish their tasks: they will work interminably, sacrifice material needs, neglect family and friends, and even suffer death itself to realize their goals. Hemingway wrote Charles Scribner in 1940: "I have to write to be happy whether I get paid for it or not. But it is a hell of a disease to be born with." The word that perhaps best conveys this compulsive, do or die character of creativity is passion. I hate this age, complained Kierkegaard, because it lacks passion. Socrates, whom he regarded as the very embodiment of the subjective thinker, felt this compulsion. Just before he died he told his friend Crito that his philosophy rang in his ears like the passionate music of the worshippers of Cybele. He could hear no other music but the music of his arguments; he felt no other conviction than the conviction of his philosophy. His life itself was a small thing to give in that cause.

8. *Enthusiasm.* Enthusiasm includes everything included under commitment. But it adds one further determination: creativity is life affirming. Hitler and Stalin were committed; but they did not affirm life. Art teaches nothing but the significance of life, Henry Miller said. It is true, as Freud argued, that life is a struggle between Thanatos and Eros, between the forces of death and the desire for life; it is also true that Thanatos in the short run carries the day. But creativity is in the service of life and affirms immortality. Towards the end of *The Brothers Karamazov* Alyosha is asked: "It is true what religion says that we shall see one another again?" He answers: "Certainly, we shall see one another again. We shall joyfully tell one another everything that has happened." This is the attitude of enthusiasm. Not to desire immortality is to let the absurd reign.

Enthusiasm literally means to be filled with the gods, filled with a portion of the Divine substance (the milk of Paradise, Coleridge called it) out of which all life springs. In Hindu religion Brahma is the protector of artists because they are creators. And creation is called "lila" or the enjoyment of God. To affirm life, to enjoy God, to create—all synonomous expressions. Thoreau in *Walden* advises his readers to "love your life." However mean your life is, he wrote, "meet it and live it; do not shun it and call it hard names. It is not so bad as you are." Let Picasso have the last word: "The essential in this time of moral misery is to create enthusiasm." We look to creative people to love life, to praise life, to teach us something about life in its multiple forms and infolded mysteries.

9. *Freedom.* Creativity is the strongest argument against determinism. It flows from freedom and, as Camus said, increases "the sum of

encyclical also draws a close parallel between work and value formation. Work concerns not only personal values but social values as well. From the first page we are told that work contributes to "the cultural and moral level of society." Man works to earn his daily bread but bread is defined in fecund value terms as "the bread of science and progress, civilization and culture."[7] The Pope, then, speaks of work not in any narrow sense but from "the viewpoint of its human value and of the moral order to which it belongs."[8]

This is a noble appreciation of work. Although the Holy Father acknowledges that work can be mechanical and less than human, he effectively rejects the "alienation of labor" thesis which found its classic formulation in the writings of Karl Marx. By alienation Marx meant the state of being unconnected and lacking in inner substance. The worker is alienated when he experiences himself as an object, a thing, rather than a subject or person. He is alienated when he is cut off from the product of his labor. What he creates stands over against him as an alien object in which he no longer recognizes his image and over which he exercizes no control. In alienated labor the vital link between man and his work is torn, leading to an eventual loss of individuality and to dehumanization. Thus the worker is defeated by his work. He finds in it misery instead of well-being, isolation instead of community, and experiences himself as a means rather than as an end. In sum, the worker is alienated when, through his work, he fails to realize his potential or to fulfill his basic needs.

Marx's alienation thesis can be conveniently summarized in the following points. (1) The worker has no control over what he produces and is to that extent enslaved by the blind forces of the market instead of controlling them; (2) his labor is characterized not by community or fellowship with his co-workers but by competition, exploitation, envy, mistrust, and various forms of conflict; (3) instead of becoming more human in his labor, the worker becomes more machine-like, sometimes a mere appendage of the machine and, like it, an object; (4) because he cannot adequately fulfill himself in his work, the worker becomes an occasion of human impoverishment. His existence fails to realize its potential and remains, as Marx put it, "poor, one-sided, animal-like."[9]

Marx's influence has been profound. He has inspired a whole contemporary literature on the subject. Studs Terkel's *Working* may be taken as representative of the genre. Intellectuals are prone to find evidence of alienation everywhere in the work world. But I fear much of what they say is moonshine. One notices that they themselves do very little of the kind of work they profess to analyze. I think the poet Gary Snyder is closer to the reality of things when he says that Americans are never so happy as when they are working. Be that as it may, the view of work put forth in *Laborem Exercens* refutes, almost point for point, the Marxist analysis and offers a more wholistic, much more sophisticated position. I found it refreshing.

I was, however, made uneasy by the close conjunction one finds in the encyclical between work and "mastering nature." The word "dominion" (or some cognate) is used over 30 times in the first part alone. That terminology has an odious ring to it in these days and I think the Pope badly skewed the notion of creativity by too directly associating it with the dominion theme. In a sense, everything he takes away from the Marxists in his analysis of work he gives back by tying it to a somewhat simplistic interpretation of the biblical injunction "to increase and multiply and subdue the earth." Lynn White, in an influential article, has traced the present ecological crisis to a perverted interpretation of that same injunction. Many thinkers, often inspired by Marx, carry this analysis further to indict technological society as such.

Herbert Marcuse may be considered typical. In his widely read *One Dimensional Man*,[10] Marcuse contends that technological society is one of total domination, that is, technological society is totalitarian. This is so, he claims, because the technological imperative has expanded to every aspect of society. It has become a political universe and a psychological universe, abolishing the distinction between public and private, individual and community, and turning to its own ends such traditional institutions of freedom as representative government, the press and even free enterprise itself. Totalitarian technology maintains its hegemony by depriving all opposition of its critical function, that is its capacity to think negatively against the system, and by imposing false needs through advertising, market control, the media, and so forth. Two of the paradoxes of technological society Marcuse makes much of are: liberty itself has become an instrument of domination and dark irrationalities parade as reason.

The mechanism by which the individual becomes absorbed into the technological universe is called introjection by Marcuse to signify a process by which we transform the outer to the inner. But, says Marcuse, this supposes an inner fulcrum, a subjective core, to activate the process of introjection. But this is precisely what is lacking. Therefore he opts for the term alienation which in its extreme form means not solely that we are cut off from values in society but are deprived of

inner powers of selection and choice. To be one-dimensional, therefore, is to think and feel and live according to the univocal norms imposed by technology. The result is a naivety and simple-mindedness
that does not easily accomodate the complexity of human reality but
does render society amenable to technological dictates.

Now I don't think Marcuse is right about all of this. But his position
is representative enough and cogent enough to be taken seriously and
I think the Pope was poorly advised to use emphatically a language that
could make him liable to the criticism of the technological determinists.

Two other marks of creativity are happily accentuated in *Laborem
Exercens*. Bearing in mind the reservations just expressed, we can com-
mend the Pope for connecting work with the professions in general and
technology in particular. The litany of the professions in Paragraph 26
makes this point as does, more philosophically, the objective definition
of work as technology. Whatever may be said of technology it is a fact
that, for better or for worse, science-technology (the hyphenation indicates what I take to be a pragmatic identity between the two) is the
cutting edge of creativity today. To be creative implies some technological mastery. The encyclical takes note of technological developments in agriculture, in industry and in electronics. These manifest a
high degree of creativity, have changed the nature of society, and
altered man's relationship to both culture and himself. These developments have not done away with the problem of work but, the Pope says,
rather mildly, "provide grounds for reproposing in new ways the question of human work."[11] It is good not to encounter the whining, negative
attitude toward technology that is common in religion documents! The
technology question must be faced, and must be faced in creative terms
rather than the carping negativism of the determinists. These words
deserve further study: ". . . technology is undoubtedly man's ally. It
facilitates his work, perfects, accelerates and augments it. It leads to an
increase in the quantity of things produced by work and in many cases
improves their quality."[12] It is not an exaggeration to claim that the
greatest social challenge facing us today is to devise ways of keeping
technology on a creative track. This is especially true when we contem-
plate the destructive powers of modern technology. It will take all the
creative energies we can muster to make it to the end of the century
without blowing the planet to bits. The Pope offers encouragement and
guidance in this task.

I want also to note that the encyclical is "enthusiastic" in the sense
of life-affirming. The theological ground of enthusiasm is the paschal

mystery. And it is here that John Paul II seeks to justify the ultimate significance of human work. In this mystery, bathed as it is in the light of the Resurrection, "we always find a glimmer of *new* life, of the *new* good as if it were an announcement of the *new* heavens and the *new* earth."[13] To praise God is to praise life; to evoke the divine power that is imminent in the world and sustains it is to appeal to the power that enables us to affirm life; to see work as a principal expression of the Divine mystery is to learn deeply about the nature of human freedom. I was puzzled by the fact that the one mark of creativity least in evidence in *Laborem Exercens* is freedom. It is mentioned, although rarely, but at no point stressed or devleoped. One might wonder why this is so.

A Creative Society

In brief, we can say that a creative society will be one in which creative work is possible. More broadly, we may say a creative society is one which provides for the constructive release of human energies, which enhances the ways in which people fictionalize their lives. It combines the maximum amount of freedom compatible with a disciplined existence. We should, therefore, expect a creative society to be ordered, liberal and value-directed. Now, beyond such generalities, can we specify what political and social arrangements might best promote a creative society? If we were to live as *Laborem Exercens* directs us to, what kind of society would be living in? On this point the encyclical is less helpful. The Pope, no doubt wisely, declines to enter into ideological dispute.

He rejects the extremes of capitalism and socialism; he finds the language of class conflict unpalatable. Labor and capital are not polar concepts but rather "inseparably linked."[14] Economism is to be rejected because it reductively sets the one in opposition to the other. At times the Pope is partial to such socialistic measures as collectivizing the means of production—or some of them at any rate. But he then skates on the other side of the river and strongly condemns collectivism—or at least the extremes of collectivism. The right to private property is upheld but it is not "absolute and untouchable." Capitalism is good; but "rigid" or "primitive" capitalism is bad. And so on. It is hard to get a clear reading here. Perhaps this is the most "creative" posture the Pope could take. One of his concerns, after all, is finding "new meanings" of work for our time and consequently new social institutions. This part of the encyclical is in the nature of a probe, an invitation to further discussion. What is safeguarded throughout is the principle of subjectivity: the primacy of the worker ("the real efficient subject") over the means of production. It would no doubt be profitable for a gathering such as this to discuss the political and economic implications of what is here suggested.

For myself it reduces to a pragmatic question: when I look about me I see that everywhere democratic capitalism has provided greater freedoms, more justice and a higher standard of living than all alternatives. And I see everywhere that socialism has tended to produce stagnant economies and repressive political regimes. Where today does one find democratic socialism? At the same time I am aware that democratic capitalism is undergoing a severe crisis. One of the best analysts of the pathology of capitalism is Daniel Bell.[15] When I read Bell I have to ask myself where we are headed and by what means shall we get there. It seems unlikely and excessively dramatic to expect capitalism to be succeeded by, say, socialism. Nor can one imagine anything like pure socialism coming into being. But we have to entertain the possibility that some new amalgam of the two will transpire.

Drawing on Bell, but not wholly so, let me note five critical paradoxes of contemporary democratic capitalism. The first is that greater prosperity leads to greater government intervention in the private sector. Prosperity gives rise to complexities and ideals (e.g. the end of poverty) that give the government plausible reasons for stepping in. Secondly, the moral basis of capitalism is eroding. Capitalism grew out of a philosophy that had quite definite convictions about human nature. Without its natural moral support no economic system can survive, let alone prosper. Bell discusses this paradox under the rubric of hedonism. A third paradox concerns the nature of learning. At a time when general learning (call it liberal education in the old-fashioned sense of the word) is critically necessary, the educational establishment is turning more and more to specialized and career-oriented education. In a time of moral crisis, value neutrality is defended as one of academia's highest goals, indeed almost a civic virtue. Never, to paraphrase Churchill, have so many schools done so little for so many. The average college graduate today is appallingly ignorant, not only of his own tradition and common cultural referents but of contemporary society as well. A friend of mine no longer attends graduation ceremonies; they remind him too visibly of failure. Another paradox, that may have devastating consequences, is the fact that the burden of defending freedom may spell the end of freedom. The United States, virtually alone in the free world, is shouldering this burden which causes stresses and strains in both foreign and domestic affairs, gives excessive powers to the military and such agencies as the IRS and CIA, and disposes the populace to favor demagoguery in its political leaders. Haunting each of us is the question: How are we going to pay for all of this?

Let me call the final paradox a category confusion between the material and ideal aspects of democratic capitalism. I have always been much impressed by Santayana's saying to the effect that everything material has an ideal fulfillment and everything ideal has a material base. I like it because it establishes a dialectical (as opposed to a dualistic) relationship between two poles of what is in reality a continuum. Too often in capitalism ideal values are regarded as merely epiphenomenal, as when a corporate executive (otherwise ignorant) buys an expensive painting for his office. Similarly, proponents of values often either condemn the material out of hand, as a long line of humanists have condemned capitalism, or they seek to impose their values from above in an artificial and inevitably unsuccessful way. John Dewey, in his *Individualism Old and New*, wrote: "The American problem is that of making the material an active instrument in the creation of the life of ideas and art." He was arguing against those who complain that America is too materialistic, rightly seeing that it is the least material of nations. The dilemma we face may be put this way: ideal values must not only be congruent with their material base but they must *grow out of* that base. Dewey puts it well: "To return to a dualism consisting of a massive substratum of the material upon which are erected spiritually ornamented facades is flatly impossible, except upon the penalty of spiritual disenfranchisement . . . "

I think John Paul II might like Dewey's words. Yet I wonder if he himself has avoided the confusion. He sustains an almost Sartrian *en soi-pour soi* distinction between things and persons, between the means of production as object and the worker as subject. Does this imply "a massive substratum of the material?" Is there not lurking here somewhere an unwieldly dualism? It is not clear where the *tertium quid* is, the common denominator between the two realms. By stressing the subjectivity of the worker it is easy to risk reifying the objectivity of the work. The encyclical condemns this error in dialectical materialism. But how, in Christian terms, do we get around it? It may well be obvious, as we read in Paragraph 13, that "materialism is incapable of

7. Para. 1.

8. Para. 24.

9. For a more sympathetic view of Marx's thesis, see John W. Houck, "Early Historical Traces of the Contemporary Debate about Work Alienation" in *A Matter of Dignity: Inquiries into the Humanization of Work*, ed. W.J. Heisler and John W. Houck (Notre Dame, Ind.: University of Notre Dame Press, 1977), pp. 49-63.

10. Herbert Marcuse, *One Dimensional Man* (Boston: Beacon Press, 1964).

11. Para. 5.

12. Ibid.

13. Para. 27, emphasis added.

14. Para. 13.

15. See Daniel Bell, *The Cultural Contradictions of Capitalism* (New York: Basic Books, 1976), and *The Coming of Post-Industrial Society* (New York: Basic Books, 1973).

16. Langdon Winner, *Autonomous Technology* (Cambridge, Mass.: M I T Press, 1977).

17. Hans Jonas, *Philosophical Essays: From Ancient Creed to Technological Man* (Englewood Cliffs, N.J.: Prentice-Hall, 1974).

CHAPTER 5

Business Competence
And Religious Values –
A Trade Off?

by Joseph A. Pichler

A NATION'S ECONOMIC STRUCTURE EXPRESSES SOCIETAL VALUES, INFLUENCES the ethical development of citizens, and shapes the expression of personal codes. The structure is a significant part of the macro-moral context within which individuals encounter and respond to micro-moral issues.[1] Therefore, considerations of ethical values in economic behavior should be founded on an analysis of that context.

Some economic systems are inherently evil because they are based upon slavery, warfare, or other immoral conditions. Others are conceptually moral, but capable of producing evil if they are not fully implemented. The distinction is important for public policy. If a system is inherently evil, it must be rejected in favor of a morally acceptable alternative. If, on the other hand, immorality is caused by a failure to fulfill some precondition of an acceptable conceptual model, then it may be possible to resolve the problem by achieving a more complete implementation.

Capitalism has been criticized for being a conceptual system that is grounded in purely materialistic values. Its competitive dynamic has been identified as a force that inevitably crushes micro-moral standards, produces worker alienation, despoils the environment, and yields an unjust distribution of wealth. Empirical evidence of exploitation, poverty, and waste have been cited in economies that are nominally based upon capitalism.

Citizens of capitalist nations must give careful thought to these criticisms. Executives have a particular responsibility in this regard because their decisions give life and content to the competitive dynamic. Their competence affects the system's efficiency and their values help to shape its direction.

The first section of this essay addresses macro-moral issues. It presents the value judgments upon which capitalism is based, lists the system's structural preconditons, and analyzes competition's economic and moral implications. The second treats the role of public policy. The conclusions of the first two sections are then applied to a review of *Laborem Exercens*. The final segment poses certain micro-moral considerations for executives who must function daily within an imperfect capitalist economy.

Values, Preconditions, and Implications

Three value judgments form the philosophical ground for classical capitalism:

> *Liberty Principle*. Individuals should be free to pursue their self-interest without restraint provided that they do not restrict the freedom of others to do the same.

> *Property Principle*. Liberty is based, in part, upon the individual's ability to acquire, use, and dispose of property.

> *Voluntarism Principle*. Property is to be acquired and exchanged only by voluntary agreement.[2]

The Liberty Principle is a fundamental statement in favor of self-determination and is the basis for the Property and Voluntarism Principles. Limitations on the acquisition or use of property are, necessarily, limitations upon certain dimensions of self-determination.[3] Slavery, discrimination, fraud, and other forms of coercion are forbidden because they are inconsistent with both the Liberty and the Voluntarism Principles. Ideally, this norm would be self-enforced by ethical standards. However, liberty requires that due process measures be taken, when necessary, to protect persons or property and to enforce voluntary contracts.

The unit of analysis is the individual as an integral being. No single role or dimension is identified as being necessarily more important than any other. The definition of self-interest allows the broadest scope to motivation and endows individuals with the right to select goals and choose the roles to be emphasized. Those who wish to define their lives in terms of work and acquisition may do so. Others are free to be aesthetes or ascetics. The only limitation upon life-plans and instrumental actions is the requirement that they not inhibit the rights of others to pursue their own goals. It is this constraint which differentiates liberty from license.

The principles assume that individuals are rational, i.e., that they are able to make choices among goals and select instrumental acts that will achieve them.

Complex social structures, such as corporations, may be created by voluntary transactions provided they do not possess a leverage that limits the rights of outsiders (or members) to seek their self-interest. The earliest economists recognized that specialization and cooperation may multiply the productive capabilities of individuals.[4] Under certain circumstances, this gain is best achieved within the structure of a formal organization.[5]

Finally, the principles do not guarantee that individuals will achieve their self-interest nor do they preclude situations in which only one party can achieve a mutually desired goal. The principles *do* guarantee individuals the right to implement their chosen strategies without interference from others.

Capitalism is a system which implements the Liberty, Property, and Voluntarism Principles in economic activity. The system is defined by five structural preconditions:[6]

1. Individuals, singly and in combination, are permitted to acquire, operate upon, exchange, or otherwise dispose of property.

2. Voluntary agreements to exchange labor, resources, and goods are enforceable at law.[7]

3. No legal restrictions are placed upon relative prices, the generation and flow of information, or the mobility of labor, resources, and goods.

4. No economic entity is large enough, relative to the size of its industry, to control the prices of goods or resources. Individuals and organizations may not control prices by agreement.

5. There is a recognized medium of exchange.

The first four preconditions are derivable from the Liberty, Property, and Voluntarism Principles. Taken together, they allow individuals to pursue economic interests through voluntary exchange. They also constrain behavior that would limit the freedom of others to do the same. The fifth condition is necessary for exchanges to generate relative prices.

To the extent that these preconditions can be implemented, prices and profits are determined by consumer choice operating through the competitive dynamic. Individuals seek out and purchase an array of goods that provides the highest expected satisfaction per dollar expenditure. Relative prices fluctuate as preferences change. When a good becomes popular, its price is bid up and the supplier earns an above average return. This provides an incentive for the original supplier to expand output and for new firms to enter the industry. The expanding industry draws labor and resources either from an unemployed status or from other industries who offer less satisifactory prices, wages, or working conditions. As the supply of the product increases, inventories eventually build and suppliers find it desirable to reduce prices in order to generate additional sales. The exceptional profit begins to decline with reductions in price. This process may be accelerated if the high profits attract less expensive substitute goods into the market and/or the cost of attracting additional resources and labor increases. The dynamic moves toward an equilibrium price at which the expected profit in the industry just equals the highest return that can be earned elsewhere. A reverse process occurs when a good becomes unpopular: prices and profits decline, firms reduce capacity and leave the industry, and other industries bid away labor and resources.

There is no central planning system to allocate resources and labor among industries. Rather, the allocations emerge from the revealed preferences of consumers and the responses of firms and employees. The process is entirely voluntary; resources are drawn rather than sent to alternative uses.

The market will not produce the desired quantities and types of goods if legislative or monopolistic restrictions are placed upon information flows, price levels, or the mobility of labor and resources. Restrictions on market processes also generally entail encroachments on liberty in areas of life beyond economic activity.[8]

Personal income is determined by one's physical and human resources and the degree to which these are allocated in accordance with relative prices and wages. Those who inherit valuable physical or human resources have an advantage over the less well endowed. However, the beginning "stake" will be eroded if it is not allocated in accordance with consumer desires. Conversely, skillful allocation can multiply a modest endowment. If an individual defines self-interest in terms of high wages and profits, capitalism bends that drive toward the service of consumer desires.

The system rewards producers who utilize resources most efficiently in serving consumer needs. Profits equal the difference between the revenues from the sale of a product and the cost of the resources used to produce them. It can be shown that, for any state of technology, costs are solely a function of consumer demand.[9] Losses are incurred by those who produce unwanted goods or use wasteful technologies. Thus, capitalism contains powerful incentives to conserve resources.

The third precondition releases the competitive dynamic that drives the system. Self-determination cannot be achieved if individuals are prevented from searching out the resources, goods, and employments that are most satisfying. Thus, media freedom is essential. Capitalism reinforces this freedom by rewarding those who provide information that is interesting or useful. This precondition also has significant moral implications. Individuals are free to engage in ethical discourse intended to shape the behavior of others, provided that coercion is avoided. If community norms and practices are repugnant, persons may move elsewhere without having to explain the reasons or seek official permission.

It is unfortunate that economics texts generally emphasize the efficiency aspects of capitalism and neglect its second order, value implications. This may explain the erroneous belief that capitalism's value orientation is purely material and that the competitive dynamic inevitably drives out morality. In fact, the reverse is true:

> The preservation of competition enables consumers, investors, and employees to apply their personal ethical systems to market activities by dealing only with the economic units whose behavior

they find appropriate. When many suppliers are available, consumers need not buy from firms that discriminate, pollute the environment, exploit employees, or engage in immoral activities. Competition assures diversity and diversity assures the ability to select among firms on the basis of ethical principles as well as product price and quality.[10]

In summary, capitalism does not impose a moral code, but provides individuals both the opportunity and the responsibility to express ethical norms in economic behavior. The economy will respond with equal efficiency whether purchases are directed toward Bibles, bubble gum, or brothels.

The system is open-ended with respect to the economy's direction, the identification of resources, and the implementation of new technologies. It provides incentives for individuals to construct new strategies for serving present and future consumer needs more efficiently. This has important implications for societal risk. Capitalism permits a far greater range of strategies to be implemented simultaneously than is possible under a centrally coordinated system. Individuals are free to make varying assessments of future conditions, to develop a response, and to profit if they are correct. As in the case of any investment process, diversification reduces risk when there is no proven heuristic for projecting the future. Centralized planning, on the other hand, necessarily excludes or limits some alternatives.

The structure of capitalism permits individuals to seek self-interest, but it also generates forces that set limits upon behavior. Most of these develop from interactions with others who are exercising their liberty. If the preconditions could be perfectly implemented, exploitation of workers, resource holders, and consumers would be impossible. If one employer attempted to drive down wages, rivals could earn a profit by offering somewhat higher pay. The profit opportunity would exist as long as any wage remained below the competitive level and the bidding would continue until the wage was returned to equilibrium. A parallel response would occur if a firm attempted to raise prices above the market level. Rivals would have a profit incentive to expand production and new entrants would be drawn to the industry as long as an above-average profit could be earned. These reactions would drive prices back to the equilibrium levels.[11] In summary, competition protects workers and consumers by triggering forces that constrain even the most avaricious entrepreneur.

As stated earlier, the highest incomes are earned by those who are able to satisfy consumer desires most effectively. Thus, income differentials are justified on efficiency grounds because they provide the incentive to maximize output from the nation's resources. Can differentials be justified morally? Yes, up to a point. In his brilliant work, *A Theory of Justice*, John Rawls argues that differentials are acceptable if they are necessary to motivate individuals to engage in economic activities that also benefit the least advantaged members of society.[12] For example, high incomes would be justifiably paid to induce incentive to develop alternate fuels that would reduce heating costs for everyone. One cannot prove that the income distribution generated by capitalism or by any other conceptual economic system meets this condition.[13] At best, we can conclude that differentials are not necessarily immoral and that there may be circumstances under which mandatory transfers of income from high to low earners need not result in an appreciable loss of productivity.

A few final words about self-interest. It is naive to believe that rejection of capitalism in favor of another system will destroy the drive to achieve self-interest. More likely, this desire will re-emerge in an altered and perhaps more virulent form—especially in systems which permit a favored group to control the economic activity of others. By diffusing power through voluntary market forces capitalism reduces the opportunity for economic self-interest to become economic predation.

The Role of Public Policy

A major economic function of government is to implement the structural preconditions that define capitalism. American public policy has achieved this goal to a substantial degree. The Constitution and its Amendments of 1781 expressly protect life, liberty, and property; guarantee a free press; establish a judicial system; forbid legislative impairment of contractual obligations; prohibit states from interfering with mobility of persons and products; and establish a uniform medium of exchange.[14] Shortly after the Civil War, when powerful "trusts" began to develop, Congress passed the Sherman Act outlawing all monopolies and collusive arrangements. Except for wartime and recent flirtations with formal controls, the nation has not interfered with wage and price fluctuations. Our laws do include notable departures from the capitalist ideal, especially regulatory protection for certain industries and occupations, but the underlying framework remains intact.

Public policy is also responsible for implementing macro-economic policies to achieve prosperity and full employment. In a capitalist system, monetary and tax policy are preferable to public expenditure policy as a means of obtaining these goals. The preference is based upon considerations of liberty. When cash balances, disposable incomes, and interest rates change, individuals and firms may freely adjust their purchasing and investment patterns in accordance with self-defined interests. Changes in public expenditures, on the other hand, reallocate resources between the public and the private sectors. When government spending increases, resources are drawn from the private sector and utilized in accordance with politically determined purposes rather than consumer preferences as reflected in the price system. Although some level of public expenditure is necessary to maintain government and to provide goods that the market system cannot efficiently produce, alterations in public expenditure levels to achieve macro-economic goals represent a greater infringement upon liberty than do adjustments in the money supply and tax rates.

A third role of public policy is to deal with three problems that cannot be effectively solved by the market. These are inherent deficiencies that would exist even if capitalist preconditions could be perfectly implemented. The first concerns those few industries with such enormous economies of scale that a monopoly firm inevitably emerges from free competitive processes. Public utilities are the classic examples. A multifirm equilibrium cannot be reached because the long run marginal cost declines through the output that saturates the market. The firm that expands most rapidly can continue lowering the price until it has driven all rivals from the market. If several firms enter the market, resources are wasted until one grows to optimum size and achieves a monopoly. At that point, the firm could raise the price above the competitive levels. Thus, the market solution is inefficient and exploitive.

Public policy can resolve the "natural monopoly" problem by limiting the number of firms that can enter the industry and regulating the prices and/or profits they may earn. Ideally, the regulatory body sets the price at a level that allows the firms to earn the competitive rate of return and to attract just enough capital to meet consumer demand.

The other two technical cases involve problems of economic externalities or "neighborhood" effects. Certain resources, by their nature, must be held in common and cannot be the subject of voluntary transactions among individuals. Examples include air, rivers, and the ozone layer. In the absence of transactions prices a firm can use such resources without charge even though use imposes a true economic cost on others. Thus, the market will not efficiently allocate such resources. For example, a firm that dumps toxic waste into a river bears little cost for using this resource, but generates an external cost that is borne by pesons downstream.

Public policy measures must replace the market allocation system in order for such resources to be allocated efficiently. This can be achieved by imposing a use tax at a rate that will either indemnify neighbors for the loss of the resource or induce the firm to initiate technological changes that will hold usage to acceptable levels. For example, an appropriate tax imposed on effluents released into the air will make it efficient for firms to install electrostatic scrubbers. The cost of the equipment will be borne by consumers in the form of an appropriately higher product price. This result is consistent with both the philosophical basis of capitalism and the market solution for resources that can be privately held.[15]

Goods and services may create positive externalities if they provide substantial benefits to persons other than the primary consumer who pays the price. For example, the entire nation benefits when citizens invest in their own education. These external gains include an enriched level of culture, more efficient technology, and a more discerning electorate. In some cases, external benefits are so widespread that they cannot be appropriately priced through private transactions. This is the case for such public services as police and fire departments. The market may not provide sufficient quantities of such goods and services. Therefore, it is necessary for public policy to replace the price system by taxing secondary beneficiaries in order to support an appropriate level of expenditure. This public policy solution does not necessarily require that the services be *provided* by the government.[16]

Few economists disagree about the need for public policy to replace or augment the market in solving the natural monopoly and externality problems. There is far less consensus on the correct approach to four other areas: information on hazardous products, income distribution, civil rights, and labor unions. All merit discussion because they involve significant moral issues.

It was noted earlier that capitalism assumed rationality. This implies that children and the mentally handicapped must be sheltered from market forces either by family or some other appropriate agent. A corollary is that rational individuals must have reasonable access to information that will enable them to make choices in accordance with their self-interest. The structural precondition forbidding censorship generates forces to achieve this condition. Individuals may pursue as much information as they believe necessary to make choices. That pursuit creates a market that offers a profit incentive for others to provide information through advertising, news stories, consumer unions, certification by private test laboratories, etc. To these must be added the greatest sources of product knowledge—informal communication with fellow consumers.

Such information channels are generally adequate even for products that can cause injury. Producers have strong incentives to provide adequate warnings and instructions for use because the publicity from injury would ruin their reputation and inhibit future sales. In most developed countries, injured persons may seek indemnification through the judicial system. An award is appropriate if the producer had knowledge of the danger and failed to disclose it or if the firm was unaware of the problem because it had failed to engage in adequate pretesting.[17]

Indemnification may not be an adequate remedy for products that pose unusually severe hazards to health and welfare. Pharmaceuticals and high energy industrial devices are examples of such products. Public policy may address this area by requiring appropriate testing and disclosure of results regarding potential injury *before* the product is released. This policy represents only a minimal interference in the market.[18] However, it is inappropriate for government to ban hazardous products if there is a channel for imparting full product knowledge to the consumer. Individuals should remain free to make a reasoned choice in favor of using the product if the potential consequences will not impose significant externalities upon others. For example, cancer patients should certainly have access to marijuana as a means of reducing chemotherapy's side effects if they have full knowledge of the known consequences. It is even less appropriate for government to ban products which have been "proven" to be ineffective and which have no notable injurious effects. Thus, an individual should be free to try laetrile despite a preponderance of evidence that it is ineffective.

In a capitalist system, income is a function of productivity. Personal income depends upon an individual's resources and the extent to which these are allocated to their most profitable uses. This is a "just" result in a distributive sense, but it does not address the needs of those who possess inadequate resources or have no employment opportunities. One can imagine a society in which ethical and religious norms are so firmly established that productive individuals will voluntarily support those in need. Public policy can encourage this generosity by granting tax deductions or other incentives for voluntary income transfers. Some might believe that voluntary transfers alone will solve the problem. Unfortunately, the proposition can be tested only by a social experiment that might result in great misery. Thus, I believe it is appropriate for public policy to establish income transfer programs supported by mandatory taxes. Determination of the appropriate level of support and the conditions for receipt go beyond the scope of this paper. However, three general principles can be suggested. First, the tax rate should not be so high as to reduce the incentive for capable persons to be productive. Second, the level of transfer payment should ensure a minimum living standard provided the total product of society is sufficient and that the necessary tax rate does not violate the first principle. Third, the conditions of receipt should be based solely on need and should screen out those who are unproductive by choice rather than unavoidable circumstance.

If capitalist preconditions could be fully implemented and individuals responded according to the profit incentive, there would be no need for a civil rights protection. Employment opportunities and income would be based strictly on productivity rather than race, creed, color, or sex, etc. There is ample evidence that such conditions do not always prevail in economies based upon capitalism. Our own nation's history is an example. Certain discriminatory preferences were so strong and widespread in our culture that they overcame profit incentives. When such conditions exist, it is appropriate for public policy to intervene in private transactions by requiring that employment choices be based strictly on productivity considerations. The Civil Rights Act as interpreted in *Griggs vs Duke Power* achieved this end by setting a policy that constrained employment choices only to the extent that they reflected personal preferences unrelated to job performance. It is also appropriate to require that firms found guilty of discrimination make restitution to the injured parties.[19]

Civil rights is a subclass of more general issues associated with labor. Labor is unique for several reasons. The resource is inseparable from the resource owner. This "integrity" has value that extends far beyond the realm of economics. The entire person is affected by the danger, noise, tedium, achievements, and exhilaration of employment. This is far different from other resources that may be employed without notable effect upon the resource owner other than the gain or loss of an economic return. Labor is both a factor of production and a beneficiary of economic activity.

These observations are sufficient for arguing that public policy should be constructed with particular care to limit the human cost of allocating labor. Much of this goal could be achieved by the following policies that would perfect the labor market and utilize the competitive dynamic to prevent exploitation. First, employer collusion in setting wages and working conditions should be forbidden. Monopsony is every bit as exploitive as monopoly. Second, a public labor market information system should be available without charge in order that individuals may maximize their self-determination in employment. Third, unemployment compensation should be available to support workers for a reasonable period of job search. Fourth, low-interest mobility loans can ease the burden for families who must move a long distance to secure employment. These policies are particularly desirable during the early stages of economic development and in depressed areas where the infrastructure is not adequate to provide a smoothly functioning labor market.[20]

In most nations, labor is not content to rely solely upon public policy to prevent exploitation. The drive for self-determination is almost universally manifested through the formation of unions. In the American case, labor unions are economic combinations whose major function is to negotiate wages and employment conditions. The antitrust laws forbid such cartels in all other resources, but the Clayton Act of 1914 expressly exempts unions from coverage:

> . . . the labor of a human being is not a commodity or article of commerce. Nothing contained in the antitrust laws shall be construed to forbid the existence and operation of labor . . . organizations . . . ; nor shall such organizations, or the members thereof, be held or construed to be illegal combinations or conspiracies in restraintive trade, under the antitrust laws.

The Wagner Act (National Labor Relations Act of 1935) went beyond the Clayton exemption by giving workers a legally *protected* right of self-organization and collective bargaining. In passing the Wagner Act, Congress explicitly recognized the right of association among employees, the industrial strife that resulted from a denial of this right, and the bargaining advantage that employers enjoyed because the labor market was imperfect.

The formation of labor unions is inconsistent with the structural preconditions of capitalism. Yet, in a more fundamental sense, unions implement the Liberty Principle. Freedom of speech and association cannot be granted to the laborer as citizen and denied to the laborer as worker without also denying integrity of the individual. This does not mean that labor unions should be permitted to operate without restraint. Workers at other firms and the unemployed should be free to improve their condition by accepting employment on economic terms that have been rejected by strikers. That right cannot be denied without violating the Liberty Principle. These third party rights form a market constraint upon unionized workers that is far preferable to direct government regulation of collective bargaining. American public policy chose this market constraint in the *Mackay* decision which established the right of employers to permanently replace workers who strike for purely economic reasons. Permanent replacement is not permitted if the strike results from an employer unfair labor practice.

This section has dealt with public policy response to four significant moral issues. I judge these to be appropriate even though they represented limited departures from strict capitalist preconditions. Does this mean that policy is ultimately an *ad hoc* process and that the principles of capitalism can be honored only in the breech? I think not. Four propositions might be posed to guide public policy on significant moral issues within the context of capitalism:

1. Can the issues be addressed by perfecting one or more structural preconditions of capitalism? If so, that solution is to be preferred. If not, proceed to question 2.
2. Does the problem result from one of the technical imperfections inherent in capitalism? If so, implement the recommended solution. If not, proceed to question 3.
3. Is there a non-market solution that will respect the Liberty Principle? If so, implement it. If not, proceed to question 4.
4. Are the moral values in question more important than the loss of liberty that will inevitably result from a non-market solution? If so, implement the solution and establish a "sunset" date for review. If not, choose liberty.

Capitalism and *Laborem Exercens*

Conceptual capitalism and *Laborem Exercens* are in fundamental agreement on the primacy of self-determination as the goal of economic activity. The capitalist view is based upon a philosophical commitment to liberty. The encyclical's position is grounded in the theological premise that man is the subject of work:

> Man has to subdue the earth and dominate it, because as the "image of God" he is a person, that is to say, a subjective being capable of acting in a planned and rational way, capable of deciding about himself and with a tendency to self-realization.[21]

They also agree that the relationship between labor and capital is cooperative rather than antagonistic, that production is a joint product, that public policy plays a key role in establishing an economic framework, and that there should be a national commitment to full employment. The modified capitalist view expressed in the last section of this paper corresponds even more closely to the encyclical on the subjects of free trade unions and the need for transfer payments to support those who are involuntarily unemployed.[22]

There are significant areas, however, in which *Laborem Exercens* is either contrary to capitalism or states propositions in such oracular terms that there is potential conflict. These problems of interpretation largely result from the encyclical's failure to pose a unified system against which to evaluate alternative structures. There are disturbing signs that the lack of conceptual rigor may be caused by a disregard for or mistrust of economics as a field of study. First, the encyclical does not include economics in the listing of "sciences devoted to man."[23] Second, the use of the term "economism" to describe the treatment of labor as merchandise casts economic theory in an ambiguous light.[24] On the one hand, the term might be directed to systems which hold that labor has no value beyond its economic worth and that material goods are superior to mankind. If so, the condemnation is appropriate but very restricted in scope. On the other hand, the warning against the dangers of "treating work as a special kind of 'merchandise' or as an impersonal 'force' needed for production . . ." can be read as a more general criticism of economic theory which treats labor and other resources as conceptual constructs in order to trace their allocation toward the competitive dynamic. Such abstraction is appropriate for analytic reasons and does not denigrate labor to purely a material value. Third, *Laborem Exercens* adopts an unfortunate usage of the term "capitalism" in referring to the treatment of man as the instrument rather than the subject of work.[25] This is confusing and pejorative. Although the document recognizes that capitalism has a definite historical meaning, it purposely adopts the term to describe any system ". . . whatever the program or name under which it occurs . . ." that makes man an instrument of production. The same paragraph identifies the materialistic view of work as ". . . the error of early capitalism. . . ." Readers will be excused if they read or misread this play on words as a rejection of conceptual capitalism.

The absence of economic rigor and the failure to make a distinction between conceptual systems and empirical results cause particular problems when *Laborem Exercens* attempts to critique the capitalist dynamic and to prescribe corrective public policy. The encyclical identifies the conflict between capital and labor as resulting from the actions of entrepreneurs who attempt to maximize profit and minimize wages.[26] A later paragraph amplifies this view:

> The attainment of the worker's rights cannot however be doomed (sic) to be merely a result of economic systems which on a larger or smaller scale are guided chiefly by the criterion of maximum profit.[27]

It is not clear whether the encyclical is condemning conceptual capitalism or the exploitation that may result when the system is not fully implemented. If the preconditions are fulfilled, the competitive dynamic constrains the actions of firms that might attempt to drive down the price of any resource, including labor, and the profit-maximizing motive is channeled to serve consumer needs in the most efficient manner. Should the drive for maximum profits be condemned in such cases? Would profit maximizations be an acceptable motive in a capitalist system where moral agents, such as the church, educated consumers to define self-interest in terms of high ethical standards? These questions are left unanswered because of the encyclical's failure to distinguish between conceptual systems and empirical results.

The failure is even more apparent when the document proposes specific public policy recommendations. It describes the "disproportionate distribution of wealth" and expresses an unqualified opinion that wealth should be leveled out in both developed and underdeveloped countries.[28] The issue of appropriate income distribution is a highly complex area which defies simple conclusions. Rather than stating an unqualified policy proposal, the encyclical should have attempted to shape minds and hearts in a manner that would encourage voluntary redistribution and/or enable economic growth to occur with narrower differentials. This would have required the document to adopt the tone of teacher rather than critic.

The immigration issue is a final example of the manner in which the absence of a conceptual system cripples *Laborem Exercens*. Paragraph 23 refers to immigration as a "material evil " that causes some level of moral harm. It argues that the immigrant's new country has less right to the individual's contribution than did the country of origin. There is no conceptual basis offered in support of this conclusion. Its relationship to the proposition that "Man has the right to leave his native country for various motives . . . in order to seek better conditions of life in another country"[29] is by no means clear. Is it really a material evil for workers to leave a poverty-stricken country to improve their lives? Is it evil even if emigration also improves income for those who remain behind in their native country?

Laborem Exercens identifies liberty as essential to self-realization.[30] However, the encyclical generally limits the discussion of liberty to persons in their role as workers rather than persons as integrities who are free to select and emphasize roles in accordance with their self-determined interest. Such partial analysis raises certain analytic difficulties in dealing with the function and structure of economic activity. Specifically, it leads to the conclusion that ". . . the sources of the dignity of work are to be sought primarily in the subjective dimension, not in the objective one."[31] In emphasizing the sanctity of work as a *process*, the encyclical understates the sanctity of its *purpose* which is to provide consumers with material goods to help them achieve self-determination. Novak has made the point very succinctly: "To serve human needs, desires, and rational interests is also in its fashion, to serve human liberty, conscience, and God."[32]

The encyclical's discussion of the relationship between capitalism and labor is difficult to interpret. Paragraph 12 asserts the principle of labor's priority over capital, but Paragraph 13 opens with an unequivocal statement that capital cannot be separated from labor.[33] There appears to be an error of logic or an inconsistency of definition. How can a construct or substance have priority over something from which it cannot be separated? There are more fundamental difficulties. What is the meaning of the term priority? In the absence of a clear definition, the term could apply to relative income shares, the locus of decision authority regarding the nature of products, a preference for labor-intensive rather than capital-intensive technologies, or several other economic relationships. The principle also may be read to favor the priority of labor over persons who provide capital. These ambiguities are serious in the light of the encyclical's statement that a labor system can be morally legitimate if it overcomes the opposition between labor and capital by recognizing labor's "substantial priority."[34] If moral legitimacy is secured by "labor's priority," then the meaning of this term should be clearly stated in order to guide policy.

Several of the problems already discussed come to a focal point in the passages of *Laborem Exercens* dealing with private ownership. Paragraph 14 opens with an historical review of the Church's position in favor of private ownership, but cautions that this right is subordinate to the right of common use. The means of production must not be possessed in opposition to labor ". . . because the only legitimate title to their possession . . . is that they should serve labor . . . and thereby achieve the principle of common use."[35] Again, there are definitional problems. Does the encyclical intend to state that labor has a priority over capital or a priority over capitalists? Specifically, is the term labor being used with reference to all persons versus the material means of production or with reference to one subset of persons versus another? If the former, then it would be better to discuss the common use principle in terms of persons as consumers, i.e., the common users.

Laborem Exercens then argues that, under certain (unspecified) conditions, socialization may be appropriate to ensure common use. It rejects the dogma of an exclusive right to private ownership and demands that this right should undergo a constructive revision both in theory and in practice.[36] The encyclical goes on to suggest possibilities ranging from profit sharing to co-determination to joint ownership. After a warning that elimination of all private ownership would not achieve the desired reforms, the document suggests that labor and capital might pursue the common good through intermediate bodies that are autonomous from government. The section closes by condemning the dehumanizing effects of excessive bureaucratic centralization and stating that, in order to be acceptable, any form of socialization must protect the personal values that were the basis for St. Thomas' preference for private ownership.

There is no argument with the encyclical's warning against the immorality that can result from either extreme of absolute private ownership or by absolute socialization. Nor is there any difficulty with profit sharing or labor ownership of stock provided that they result from voluntary transactions. Such benefits are common in American industry, including the non-unionized sector. Co-determination has recently been introduced voluntarily in a number of industries through membership by union officers on boards of directors. Perhaps this voluntary evolution is what *Laborem Exercens* has in mind when it proposes intermediate bodies. If so, the encyclical does not suggest any radical change in the industrial relations system that is practiced in the United States. It should again be stressed that these relationships have developed voluntarily and that they may not be desirable or desired in all relationships. If the encyclical intends to propose that such relationships should be imposed by public policy, then serious objections must be raised.

Micro-moral Considerations

If the preceding analysis of conceptual capitalism is accepted, then three conclusions may be stated regarding the macro-moral context of executive behavior. First, capitalism is not an intrinsically evil system. When the structural preconditions can be adequately implemented, incentives are established to produce goods in an efficient manner by means of voluntary transactions. The term "efficient" means that the goods are desired by consumers and that minimum resources are used to produce them. The moral quality of the goods depends upon the manner in which consumers define self-interest and the degree to which resource suppliers (including labor) respond to economic incentives. Second, there are three allocation problems that cannot be efficiently solved through market processes. All have well-accepted public policy solutions that may be implemented as limited exceptions to the capitalist framework. Third, opinions are divided regarding the system's ability to resolve several other economic problems that have moral significance. Some believe that these can be solved only by public policy that involves some interference with the market mechanism. Others believe that no interference is necessary and that the solutions lie in a more perfect implementation of capitalist preconditions.

These conclusions form a necessary, but not sufficient, basis for arguing that executives may function in a capitalist system without trading off moral values. Achievement of this goal requires certain understandings and actions. It may also require a willingness to define self-interest in terms that are broader than profit maximization.

The chances of achieving morality are markedly greater if the executive has a thorough understanding of capitalism's structure, competitive dynamic, and philosophical base. By now it should be clear that the preconditions are crucial to establishing the incentive system and constraining behavior to preserve liberty. Executives who embrace capitalism may preserve their integrity only if they support public policy that implements the structure and resolves the three inherent deficiencies. The ideal mentality for considering such policy is the "Veil of Ignorance" condition as described by Rawls.[37] The condition requires, among other things, that individuals reason as though they had no knowledge of their social and economic position. Some executives might find it necessary to sacrifice profit opportunities in order to adopt this stance if their firms are benefiting from an abrogation of one or more preconditions. This would include, for example, firms that receive government subsidies and those who are protected from competition by regulation.

Particular attention must be devoted to the moral issues on which there is debate as to capitalism's efficacy. The initial step is to *recognize* that there are moral implications to such matters as income distribution, civil rights, and collective bargaining. This should be followed by careful weighing of the implications of market versus non-market solutions. The four propositions posed at the conclusion of the section on public policy may assist in this process.

No conceptual economic system can be perfectly implemented. In the case of capitalism, the resulting interstices may provide the executive with a certain amount of discretionary power which permits a temporary avoidance of competitive constraints. For example, employers in "one industry" towns may possess a certain degree of monopsony power until the market returns to equilibrium. These discretionary situations call for careful moral reasoning, particularly when they involve the very special resource of labor. Decisions involving safety, layoffs, promotions, and shutdowns exert a vital influence on employees and their families. The alternatives must be carefully weighed in terms of the human cost and benefits.

In another context, I have argued that respect for liberty and justice are especially valuable guides to action involving micro-moral issues. Considerations of liberty require that every effort be made to establish conditions under which trading partners can exercise their right of informed free choice. In circumstances of differential power, liberty forbids coercion and also ". . . establishes a positive obligation to provide others with the information they need to make rational choices and to evaluate the consequences of their decisions."[38] This obligation extends to consumers, employees, suppliers, and shareholder. Differential knowledge is a frequent source of differential power and the obligation to provide the other party with reasonable information for making an informed choice. Respect for liberty is essential in dealing with persons who are not capable of rational choice because of age, infirmity or psychological condition. Exploitation under these circumstances is an absolute violation of capitalism's foundation.

Justice requires that:

> . . . (we) give equal treatment to individuals who are equal. Stated somewhat differently, the principle *requires* that we be able to justify every case of unequal treatment by showing the differential treatment is based upon morally accepted distinctions among individuals.[39]

A full implementation of capitalist preconditions would assure a high degree of distributive justice to all partners in co-creation. When this cannot be achieved, executives must make every effort to use their authority in a manner that will, at minimum, approximate the capitalist result. This self-imposed norm could help solve a broad spectrum of problems ranging from race discrimination to price discrimination.

Situations involving discretionary power provide opportunities as well as responsibilities. When competitive forces do not pose an immediate threat, the firm has more time to consider alternative technologies, product characteristics, employment practices, etc. This permits a search for morally preferable options. It also gives broader scope for expressing esthetic and social values.

Executives have a moral obligation to develop their technical knowledge as well as their competence in moral reasoning. Poor decisions made with the best of intentions may create as much human suffering as purposive immorality. Decision makers at all levels must consider the grave consequences that may accompany an uninformed decision: unemployment, industrial accidents, consumer injury, etc.

A system based upon private ownership implies special obligations towards shareholders and creditors. Executives have a fiduciary responsibility to these capital suppliers. Many are enumerated in the complex security laws and the Foreign Corrupt Practices Act. However, there is a responsibility beyond the law to protect assets and use them strictly in accordance with corporate purposes. The Liberty Principle requires that those purposes be clearly elucidated and that managers provide stakeholders with accurate information regarding the state of the firm.

Business decisions are usually made within the context of an organization structure and a web of formal relationships that distribute power and determine communication flows. Executives are frequently called upon to make decisions at organizational levels and geographic distances that are several times removed from actual events. John Lachs has preceptively argued that this can create a moral vacuum brought about by the "psychic distance" between the executive who makes the decision and the subordinate who implements it.[40] Executives should give careful consideration to designing organizations in a manner that will narrow or remove this moral gap. Particular attention must be directed to achieving accurate information flows that will retain significant nuances of events that must be judged at a great geographic or organizational distance. Lachs also argues persuasively that executives should train themselves to understand the nature and relationships of all operations so that each manager ". . . begins to think of the corporation as *his*."[41]

Finally, executives should bring joy to their organizations by whatever means is appropriate to their personalities. This must not be reduced to a human relations formula or a cynical desire to increase productivity. It is a fundamental obligation that involves celebration of achievement, enthusiasm for others, and grace in times of hardship.

NOTES

1. See Richard T. De George, "Moral Issues in Business," in *Ethics, Free Enterprise and Public Policy*, ed. Richard T. De George and Joseph A. Pichler (Oxford University Press, 1978), p. 8.

2. A more complete formulation of the three principles may be found in Joseph A. Pichler, "Is Profit Without Honor? The Case for Capitalism," *National Forum*, Summer, 1978. Much of this section is derived from that article.

3. The Property Principle can also be derived from Locke's argument that "operations on" resources create "a property" in them which is the basis of ownership and the reward for turning resources into usable commoditites.

4. Adam Smith, *The Wealth of Nations*, ed. Edwin Cannan (Chicago: University of Chicago Press, 1976), pp. 7-16.

5. Kenneth Arrow, for example, has argued that, under certain circumstances, formal organizations have a comparative advantage over the marketplace in screening and coding certain types of information. See Kenneth J. Arrow, *The*

Limits of Organization (New York: W.W. Norton & Company, Inc., 1974), pp. 52-59.

6. A slightly different formulation of the preconditions may be found in Pichler, "Capitalism in America: Moral Issues and Public Policy," in *Ethics, Free Enterprise and Public Policy*, p. 20.

7. Physical resources are defined as tangible objects that can be converted to goods in a production process. "Labor" is a resource that includes technologies as well as personal attributes that have economic value. "Goods" are objects and services acquired for consumption rather than for the production. A substance may attain or lose resource value with technology. For example, natural gas did not become a resource until the late 19th Century when it replaced whale oil. See Walter B. Wriston, "The Whale Oil, Chicken and Energy Syndrome," (Address to the Economic Club of Detroit, February 25, 1974).

8. For a discussion of the effects of price control on the nation's energy supply, see: Joseph A. Pichler, "Capitalism: Efficiency and Morality," (Address to Institute of Entrepreneurship, Benedictine College, Atchison, Kansas, Fall, 1981).

9. Pichler, "Capitalism in America: Moral Issues and Public Policy," in *Ethics, Free Enterprise and Public Policy*, p. 22.

10. Ibid., p. 27.

11. The return to equilibrium requires differing amounts of time in various industries.

12. They may also be justified if the high incomes do not worsen the condition of the poor. See John Rawls, *A Theory of Justice* (Cambridge, Mass: Belknap Press of Harvard University Press, 1971), pp. 276-7.

13. Lloyd J. Reynolds, *Economics*, 4th ed. (Richard D. Irwin, Inc., 1973), pp. 575-579.

14. For an extended discussion of the Constitution as a basis of the capitalist system see: Charles A. Beard and Mary R. Beard, *A Basic History of the United States* (New York: Doubleday, Doran & Company, 1944); Pichler, "Capitalism in America: Moral Issues and Public Policy," in *Ethics, Free Enterprise and Public Policy*, pp. 23-26.

15. The externality problem becomes more complex for underdeveloped countries. A nation may find it in the common interest to sacrifice its environmental purity in order to attract industry and employment through lower production costs. Such a policy would seem to be appropriate if there is 100% consensus in the country and if the resulting pollution does not affect neighboring countries. The situation is not easily resolved if there is a division of opinion within the nation because those who oppose the policy will have a portion of their common resources consumed without indemnification.

16. Milton Friedman, *Capitalism and Freedom*, (The University of Chicago Press, 1962), p. 75f.

17. Joseph A. Pichler and Richard T. De George, "Ethics: Principles and Disclosures," *World*, Peat, Marwick, Mitchell & Co., Spring, 1979, pp. 28-32.

18. For further discussion of this matter see: Milton Friedman and Rose Friedman, *Free To Choose* (Harcourt Brace Jovanovich, 1979), pp. 203-210.

19. Subsequent public policy went beyond the *Griggs Decision* to impose quota systems that inevitably injured individuals who had not participated in discriminatory practices. See: William T. Blackstone, "Is Preferential Treatment for Racial Minorities and Women Just or Unjust," in *Ethics, Free Enterprise, and Public Policy*.

20. Public support of these activities may be justified by the externality argument.

21. John Paul II, *Laborem Exercens*, Para. 6. All citations to *Laborem Exercens* are to the text published by United States Catholic Conference, Office of Publishing Services: Publication No. 825.

22. Para. 19 and 20.

23. Para. 4.

24. Para. 7,11,12,13.

25. Para. 7.

26. Para. 11.

27. Para. 17.

28. Para. 2.

29. Para. 23.

30. Para. 6.

31. Ibid.

32. Michael Novak, "Can a Christian Work for a Corporation?" in *The Judeo-Christian Vision and the Modern Corporation*, ed. Oliver F. Williams, C.S.C. and John W. Houck (Notre Dame, Ind.: University of Notre Dame Press, 1982), p. 187.

33. Paragraph 12: "the principle of the priority of labor over capital." Paragraph 13: "that capital cannot be separated from labor."

34. Para. 13.

35. Para. 14.

36. Ibid.

37. John Rawls, *A Theory of Justice*, p. 136.

38. Pichler and De George "Ethics: Principles and Disclosures," in *World*, p. 30.

39. Ibid.

40. John Lachs, "I Only Work Here: Mediation and Irresponsibility," in *Ethics, Free Enterprise, and Public Policy*, p. 211.

41. Ibid., Italics in the original.

CHAPTER 6

John Paul II: Continuity and Change in the Social Teaching of the Church

by J. Bryan Hehir

MY PURPOSE IS TO ANALYZE DIMENSIONS OF CONTINUITY AND CHANGE IN JOHN Paul II's contribution to Catholic social teaching. The analysis will consist first, of a sketch of the social teaching he inherited; second, of an examination of general issues of substance and style which shape the Pope's impact on the received tradition; and third, of a discussion of specific issues where lines of continuity and change can be identified.

Catholic Social Teaching: Leo XIII-Paul VI

John Paul II declares at the outset of *Laborem Exercens* that his reflections are intended "to be in organic connection" with the twentieth-century tradition of Catholic social teaching. The phrase "social teaching" has beome a technical term in Catholic theology, referring to the body of papal, conciliar and synodal teaching which extends from Pope Leo XIII, who died in 1903, to John Paul II.[1] In order to give the phrase its proper specificity it is necessary to distinguish Catholic social teaching from the social implications of Catholic faith. There has always been a social dimension of Christian faith; the detailed history of the social consequences of Christianity is found in Ernst Troeltsch's *Social Teaching of the Christian Church*. Christianity, with Catholicism in a specific way, has been a social institution of significant proportion.

The phrase social teaching, however, refers to the twentieth century effort to provide a systematic, normative theory relating the social vision of the faith to the concrete conditions of the twentieth-century. John Paul II refers to and draws upon this normative doctrine even as he reshapes and extends it in *Laborem Exercens*. To assess his contribution it is necessary to have a sense of the historical development and analytical categories of the social teaching. In Part One of the latest encyclical he notes the fact of development in the social teaching, distinguishing the "labor question" from the global perspective which one finds in the post-World War II period. It is possible to be more specific and distinguish three stages of growth in the social teaching between 1891 and 1978. Each period is marked by a "sign of the times" to which the social teaching responds.

For the first period, the question is the Industrial Revolution; the relevant texts span the period from Leo XIII's *Rerum Novarum* (1891) to Pius XII's *Pentecost Address* (1941). In these documents the unit of analysis is the nation and the theme is economic justice in nations undergoing industrialization. The topics addressed included: 1) the role of the state in the economy; 2) the right of laborers to organize; 3) the conditions of work in factories; and 4) proposals for diversifying ownership of productive property. The ideas and issues of this first stage of the social teaching persist to the present and find new expression in the work of John Paul II, but the outbreak of World War II and the post-war developments, politically, economically and socially produced a new set of issues which required change and development in the social teaching.

The question of the second period is the interdependence of the post-war world. The reality of interdependence as it is found in the social teaching has multiple causes: the emergence of over 100 new states in thirty years; the increasing interpenetration of economies among the industrialized nations (Western Europe, the United States and Japan), and the impact of these societies on the developing world; the fact of material interdependence highlighted by trade, financial and raw materials exchange between the North and South; the recognition of transnational problems (population, energy, environment), and the rise of transnational actors (private or governmental). The social teaching notes the increasing material interdependence of all the international system and focuses on the challenge of shaping moral interdependence which will yield both institutions and ideas equal to the challenge of a new age. In this second period the unit of analysis in papal teaching is no longer the nation but the international system. The topics addressed include:

> 1) the need for a political authority beyond the nation-state, one capable of addressing the needs of the "international common good;" 2) the protection and promotion of human rights in a world of nation-states; 3) a critique of prevailing patterns and institutions of international economic exchange because of their impact on developing countries; 4) an emphasis (since John XXIII) on agricultural development, the need for land reform, the imperative of a food security system which addresses the problem of hunger and malnutrition; 5) a critique of superpower policies which subordinate the needs and self-determination of small states to larger geopolitical designs.

The third stage of development is found in Paul VI's 1971 apostolic letter, *Octagesima Adveniens*, which addresses the "new social questions" of post-industrial society. This document is perhaps the most creative yet least known of the social teachings. It recapitulates the two previous periods and also opens new issues for discussion. The "new social questions" which Paul VI identifies are issues arising in the societies which first underwent the Industrial Revolution and now are highly urbanized, pluralistic and secular, penetrated by mass communication and continually changed by revolutionary technologies. In this complex setting Paul VI probes issues like the role of women, the task of education, and the existing but inadequate modes of political and social organization seeking to direct these societies. While the stress in the letter is on these issues, the international themes are revisited, including a series of questions on Christian-Marxist dialogue and the political vocation of Christians. The role of utopian vision in Christian social thought and the place of the local church in the social ministry are mentioned but left for further study and discussion.

While this historical explanation of the social teaching allows us to trace major themes, it does not provide a complete framework to assess the contribution of John Paul II. A different method of analysis, focusing on the structural categories of the social teaching provides a second means of understanding the legacy inherited by John Paul II. Structurally, it is possible to distinguish two major themes which have shaped the papal and conciliar social teaching in the last two centuries. The two themes coalesced and were stated with a new tenor and orientation at Vatican II. The two pervasive questions of the nineteenth and twentieth centuries have been the "church-state" controversy and the "church-society" issues. In an authoritative commentary on the social thought of Vatican II, John Courtney Murray writes:

> The first point here is the new conception of the problematic. Its terms are not now, as they were for Leo XIII, the Catholic Church and human society in Europe. The terms are wider— religion in its full ecumenical sense and human society throughout the wide world. The second point is that, again in continuity with Leo XIII, the Council situated the narrow issue of Church and state within the context of its own widened problematic. Thus it effected a further transformation of the state of the narrower question. And in consequence it opened the way to a development of doctrine on the matter.[2]

John Paul II indicates in *Redemptor Homines, Laborem Exercens* and his *Address at the United Nations* that he will be a key contributor to the development of doctrine. He inherits the church-state/church-society questions as they have been formulated by Vatican II. Behind the conciliar texts are two broad arguments, which comprise the social teaching. The church-state argument is rooted in the nineteenth-century Catholic response to the democratic revolutions. This argument extends from Gregory XVI, through Pius IX and Leo XIII to Pius XII and John XXIII.[3] The dynamic of the argument illustrates a slow but progressive assimilation by the church of key tenets regarding "the democratic freedoms" and the "human rights" language which supports them. Leo XIII is a pivotal figure in opening Catholicism to dialogue with the constitutional state, but he was not able himself, conceptually or historically, to formulate an affirmative response. This task was left to Pius XII, who significantly enhanced the human rights content of the social teaching, and John XXIII whose *Pacem in Terris* joins themes of the natural law and natural rights traditions in his statement of a Catholic case for a society based on justice, love, truth and freedom. This line of development culminates in the church-state teaching of *Dignitatis Humanae* at Vatican II. The issues in the church-state argument have been political and juridical in character; they have been principally concerned with how the institution of the church relates to the institution of the state and how both are called to the service of the human person. This argument has been principally a western phenomenon, with its roots in Europe, its terms drawn from the clash of the organic natural law ethic and the contractual liberal philosophy, and its dynamic one in which the church has significantly been a learner, a useful critic but eventually an advocate of the position which seeks to limit state power by the instrument of law for the purpose of protecting the freedom and dignity of the person.

The church-society argument has had different themes and a wider scope than the church-state question. It is the church-society discussion which runs through the social encyclicals. The themes are not political but socio-economic; the emphasis is less institutional and more on the presence of the church as a teacher, a community and a leaven in the society. The key figures in this argument have been Leo XIII, Pius XI, John XXIII and Paul VI. The conciliar text which states the church-society issue and which constitutes a major development in the argument is *Gaudium et Spes*.

This distinction between the "political" tradition and the "socio-economic" tradition is identifiable in the social teaching but it is not an absolute dichotomy. The relationship between the church-state and church-society themes is a structured relationship. The first is the inner core of the second; the limited, institutional definition of how the church relates to the political process of a country often sets the general tone for the wider activity of the church in society. This does not mean that the church takes its direction for social ministry from the state, but that different forms of the state provide different challenges for the church. To function in a secular democracy is one question; to face an authoritarian military junta is a very different task; and to relate to a theocratic regime presents other questions.

Post-Vatican commentators have noted the shift in Catholic teaching which today gives the church-society question primacy of place, seeing the church-state issues as subordinate to the larger issue of the church's total witness in society. *Laborem Exercens* fits into the church-society argument; it draws upon earlier stages of this tradition (e.g. *Rerum Novarum*), it expands Catholic teaching on key issues (e.g. workers' rights) and it generally does not address structural political questions in detail. John Paul II, however, has addressed the church-state side of the argument in other writings, particularly on the issue of religious liberty. In his political writings he shows a keen sense of the importance of the state, of a theory of the state and of the need for a church-state theology.

In the following two sections, I will comment on the influence of John Paul II on both dimensions of the social teaching, showing how he relates the two and what his contribution is to each.

John Paul II: Substance, Style and Social Teaching

Prior to examining specific issues in the social thought of John Paul II, this section will concentrate on general characteristics of his teaching. Specifically, the proposition being argued here is that John Paul II's impact on Catholic social teaching is a mix of what he says, how he says it and what he does. The proposition implies, therefore, that he shapes the social tradition as both a teacher and an actor, as a moralist and a statesman. In examing these three modes of influence, I shall relate each to an issue affecting the development of Catholic social teaching today.

The first issue which opens the way for a contribution by the present Pope is the post-conciliar state of Catholic social teaching. In 1966 Fr. Murray described the state of the question:

> The simple conclusion here is that the two conciliar documents, *Dignitatis Humanae* and *Gaudium et Spes*, have made a joint contribution toward the renewal of traditional doctrine with regard to the ancient issue of church and state. . . . The relevant principles have been stated with a new purity, which was made possible by the new perspectives in which the whole issue was viewed. . . . This doctrinal work was inspired by the maxim of Leo XIII, "Vetera novis augere et perficere". A work of systematization remains to be done under the same inspiration.[4]

Principal among the systematic tasks to be achieved is a work of *integration* of the social teaching with other constitutive dimensions of the faith. The need for integration is precisely the product of the multiple developments which have marked the social teaching from Pius XII through Paul VI. The conceptual advances made in this period have decisively shaped the tradition. The developments have been in moral argument (e.g. the precision given to human rights claims in *Pacem In Terris*) and in ecclesiological understanding (e.g. the significant advances in *Gaudium et Spes* and *Justitia In Mundo*). The developments have been diverse and rapid; a work of integration is required if this understanding of the significance of the social dimension of the faith is to be made available to the whole Church.

From the beginning of his pontificate John Paul II has cast his social teaching in a systematic framework which can be used to relate the social teaching to the core of Catholic faith. The framework is most clearly evident in the *Puebla Address* and in *Redemptor Hominis*, but aspects of it appear throughout the papal writings including *Laborem Exercens*. The framework is rooted, as much of John Paul II's theology is, in *Gaudium et Spes*, but he pushes the conciliar teaching forward.

The framework has four interrelated categories: anthropology, christology, ecclesiology and social ethics. There is an inner logic among the categories, each one building on the previous one. At the heart of John Paul's social thought is a statement of (theological) anthropology: the "complete truth about the human being constitutes the foundation of the Church's social teaching and the basis also of true liberation. In the light of this truth, man is not a being subjected to economic or political processes; these processes are instead directed to man and are subjected to him."[5] The person has long been the center of Catholic social thought and John Paul II's stress on the theme places him squarely in the line of Pius XII's *Christmas Addresses*, John XXIII's *Pacem In Terris* and the conciliar texts *Dignitatis Humanae* and *Gaudium et Spes*. But John Paul is not simply repeating previous teaching; he uses both his developed philosophical skills and his experience of struggle with an authoritarian regime (precisely over the question of whether the church or the state would own the person's allegience) to sharpen and deepen Catholic teaching on the dignity of the person. In his extraordinary intellectual biography of John Paul II, Professor George H. Williams observes: "In the perspective of generations of Christian scholarship it will come to be noted that the evolving papal stress on the dignity of man received its most notable and swift expansion in the prepapal and papal pronouncements of Pope John Paul II."[6]

An example of how the Pope puts his distinctive stamp on the theme of human dignity is his personalist treatment of work in *Laborem Exercens*. Catholic teaching has never been satisfied with an explanation of the meaning of work in purely instrumental terms; the human investment in work always was the reason behind the social encyclical's insistence on a just wage. But *Laborem Exercens*, drawing upon both biblical and philosophical themes, invests the process of work with new meaning and purpose: "Work is a good thing for man—a good thing for his humanity—because through work man not only transforms nature, adapting it to his own needs, but he also achieves fulfillment as a human being and indeed in a sense becomes 'more a human being.' "[7]

The Pope's tendency to relate biblical and philosophical themes is a topic addressed below, but it must be cited here as a characteristic of his framework for social teaching, particularly in the way he moves from anthropology to christology. Here again he shows himself to be, in the words of Father Henri de Lubac, "a man of *Gaudium et Spes*."[8] One of the striking characteristics of the conciliar pastoral constitution is its christological stress. Each of the first four chapters closes with a resounding christological summation of the theme being analyzed.[9] In this respect the treatment of the human person in its chapter one is notably different from that of *Pacem In Terris* only two years earlier. John XXIII's defense of the person was elegantly cast in the philosophical terms of natural law; *Gaudium et Spes* roots human dignity in theological soil. John Paul II is decisively on the side of the conciliar text because he believes that only in the person of Christ is the true potential of human dignity perceived. Williams summarizes the case: "In a word, he has been saying that Christ is not only a revelation *of God* and his salvific will for all mankind through the church but also a revelation *of man*, of what man was intended to be at creation and is by reason of the Incarnation of the Son of God and by reason of the Crucifixion, Resurrection and Ascension of the God-Man Jesus Christ."[10]

The logic of the Pope's argument moves from anthropology and christology to ecclesiology. Here again, the contribution of John Paul II may be primarily to relate in explicit terms dimensions of the social teaching which have been developing in parallel fashion but require systematic integration. The social teaching as found in the social encyclicals always had a strong grounding in human dignity but a noticeably weak ecclesiology. *Pacem In Terris* is eloquent about human dignity and human rights and is prophetic about specific social issues, but it is silent about ecclesiology. This gap leaves the social ministry in a precarious position, devoid of legitimation in terms of a definition of the church's essential ministry. The decisive contribution of *Gaudium et Spes* was to provide the social ministry with a sound ecclesiological basis; this development has been solidified in the 1971 and 1974 synodal documents, *Justitia In Mundo* and *Evangelii Nuntiandi*. John Paul II uniquely enhances this theme both by his use of the conciliar text and by his personal reflections on the linkage of ecclesiology and anthropology. Relying on paragraph 76 in *Gaudium et Spes* (i.e. the church is called to be "a sign and a safeguard of the transcendence of the human person."), John Paul II makes the striking affirmation that "man is the primary route that the church must travel in fulfilling her mission: He is the primary and fundamental way for the church, the way traced out by Christ himself, the way that leads invariably through the mystery of the incarnation and the redemption.[11]"

The consequence of John Paul's teaching on anthropology and ecclesiology is that it ties together in creative fashion the social tradition's emphasis on the person and a definition of the church's pastoral ministry which places the person — with all his/her needs — at the center of the church's work. The defense of human dignity and the protection of human rights are not simply significant humanistic and moral truths, they are today for the Catholic Church an ecclesiological imperative. From this imperative flows the need for a social ethic — the fourth element in John Paul's framework; the function of a social ethic is to specify the challenges confronting the church in defense of human dignity.

The second contribution of John Paul II to the social teaching requires less specific commentary but it should be noted. It is not *what* he is saying but *how* he speaks on social issues. There has been in Catholic social ethics a growing discussion of *how* the church should cast its social message.[12] The terms of the debate are set by *Pacem In Terris* and *Gaudium et Spes*. As noted above, John XXIII's encyclical epitomized the "classical" Catholic social ethic, a strong philosophical statement, rooted in a religious vision but expressed in terms accessible to all people of goodwill. The conciliar text is dramatically different (only two years later) with its pervasive theological themes of christology and ecclesiology and its extensive use of biblical imagery. There are assets in each of these traditions, the philosophical and the theological, and the post-conciliar debate in social ethics has sought to adjudicate the cost/benefit relationship for each style. The issues at stake, of course, are much larger than terminology; *how* the church speaks to a social question is due in part to its conception of who the audience is, how the church conceives its social function and what style of analysis is judged to be most adequate in assessing complex social issues.

These questions cannot be adjudicated here; the more modest point is to define the question and to locate John Paul's teaching in light of it. A noted authority on the Pope's writings has said: "The core of John Paul the Second is undoubtedly philosophical. In his pastoral writings, addresses and sermons, as well as in his pronouncements concerning the Church's politics, the premises of his thought refer, in the last analysis, directly to properly philosophical views."[13] In light of this commentary it is surprising to examine the Pope's social thought, since it is decidedly on the *Gaudium et Spes* side of the debate in social ethics. Both of the Pope's encyclicals, *Redempton Hominis* and *Dives in Misericordia* are strongly biblical-theological documents and his general framework, discussed above, continually leads him from philosophy to theology. There are exceptions such as his *U.N. Address*, which faithfully reflected the argument of *Pacem In Terris*. Undoubtedly the Pope's own commitment to philosophical reflection will assure a strong philosophical grounding to the social teaching, but his style thus far enhances the strain in contemporary Catholic thought which stresses a biblical and theological explicitness in the Church's social message. The ultimate direction of the larger debate will be affected by many voices, but the Pope's orientation thus far is significant if not determinative.

The third general impact of John Paul II on Catholic social teaching is related to his actions as Pope. The office of the papacy is always a unique forum in world affairs; now a fascinating personality with an activist conception of his ministry fills the office. Commentators as different in their perspective as George Will and Tad Szulc both agree that John Paul II is the most significant single figure on the world stage.[14] It is too simple to adopt a rubric that we should watch what the Pope does rather than what he says, but it would be an inadequate interpretation which ignored the nature and consequences of his major initiatives. Assessing the relationship of word and deed in John Paul requires an essay in itself; a proven intellectual, wedded to a belief in the power of the word, he is also an actor with a sensitive appreciation of the power of gestures—political and personal. The analysis here will be limited to a comment on his style of leadership and then a set of examples intended to highlight the consequences of his actions.

There is always a risk in using secular political analogies to probe ecclesial questions, but I will run the risk and argue that papal style today is significantly Gaullist. A strong leader with a well-honed conceptual design; a decisive style which is prone to act and let others react; a tendency to appeal directly to his constituency (i.e. the church or, at times, world public opinion) over the heads of organized elites; a remarkable self-possession and a capacity to move mass opinion by word and deed; all are found in John Paul II. The long-term impact of this style of leadership, on both church and state, cannot be assessed as yet, but many of the Pope's most celebrated actions have influenced the social ministry. Two forms of action are of interest.

First, John Paul's willingness to be specific about controverted, complex questions. Most of the social teaching, including his own, is understandably cast in general terms, leaving specific application to others in church and society. Several of John Paul's public positions complement his general teaching. Examples include his support for the SALT II treaties expressed not only in one of his weekly addresses in Rome but also in his reference to them while in Washington just as the Senate was about to consider the treaties; his support for the Camp David agreements, a particularly difficult choice given the Holy See's position on the Middle East; and his decision to send members of the Pontifical Academy of Science to heads of state in the United States, the Soviet Union, France, and Great Britain to warn about the escalating nuclear arms race. All of these actions, while nuanced and carefully shaped, were understood in very concrete terms.

Second, while on pilgrimage to various countries the Pope has been willing to match cautionary statements about the Church's political involvement with specific comments about social injustice. The two pre-eminent cases have been his statement in Oaxaca, Mexico, about the justification, under specified circumstances, to resort to expropriation of property; and his direct comment to President Marcos of the Philippines that claims about state security are not justifications for "subjugating to the state the human being and his or her dignity and rights."[15]

These general characteristics of John Paul's social style set the background for examining specific issues. Issues come and go, and are always limited and often local in their significance, but the horizon of the Pope's words and deeds serves to give larger meaning to his specific teaching on concrete cases and questions.

Continuity and Change: Issues and Examples

The issues selected for examination are drawn from the categories used in Part One of this paper: church-state; church-society and one specific international question.

The Church and Politics: The classical church-state issue is how the church as an institution relates to the political order. It is a perennial question which has produced a wide spectrum of responses from the Roman Empire through twentieth-century democracy.[16] Surprisingly the issue has not received much sustained attention in the church-society literature. John Coleman's masterful review of the encyclical tradition notes the reticence to speak directly about the church and politics.[17]

John Paul II has not been reluctant to address the question and his statements have stressed the non-political nature of the church's ministry. The texts abound from his Puebla Address in 1979 through his remarks to the Jesuit Provincials in Rome in 1982.[18] The strength and frequency of these cautionary statements have inevitably raised the question whether the Pope's cautious church-state views are designed to restrict the church's witness on the church-society issues of justice, peace and human rights.

To assess the content and consequences of John Paul's church-state teaching it is necessary to place it in the context of the framework established by Vatican II. One way to interpret the conciliar theology is to say the church has become less political but correspondingly more active in its social witness. The church is less political in that it seeks no special status or privileged position in the political order. The thrust of the Council's document *Dignitatis Humanae* was to say that the one demand the church makes of the political process is the freedom to fulfill its ministry.[19] The church seeks *freedom from* interference; it does not *ask for* special status. In this sense the church is less tied to any existing government. John Paul's statements reinforce this sense of distance from the state.

Freedom, however, is not an end in itself, but a pre-condition for the church to fulfill its social witness. The controlling text for interpreting this witness is *Gaudium et Spes*, paragraphs 40-42; one cannot make sense of John Paul's social teaching apart from these passages.[20] In a terse compact fashion they set forth the parameters of the church's social witness:

1) the church has no specifically political mandate or ministry;
2) the church is a religious community whose ultimate goal is to contribute to the building of the Kingdom of God;
3) the Kingdom, however, grows in history – mysteriously but actually;
4) hence, as the church pursues its religious objective it has four consequences: protecting the dignity of the person, promoting

human rights, fostering the unity of the human family and informing human activity with meaning.

These four consequences are not narrowly defined political goals, but
they cannot be pursued apart from the political process. The church
contributes to the realization of these four objectives in its own distinctive mode of action, but the consequences of a religious ministry
directed toward these ends will be felt in the political process. Both
John Paul's social teaching and his personal witness stress the importance of these goals—human dignity, justice, rights and peace—for the
church's life today. In the same speeches in which he cautions priests
not to play specifically political roles, he also urges them to include the
protection and promotion of human rights in their ministry.[21]

In summary, the conciliar legacy of a less political but more socially
engaged church is sustained in John Paul's social teaching. To be
precise, he does oppose specific forms of church engagement in the
political process—notably the participation of institutionally representative figures in elective office; but there is no basis for using these
specific limits to say that John Paul II is eroding or constraining the
church's social witness.

A final point which is relevant to this balance of the political and the
social is the Pope's strong sense of the distinction of roles and functions
in the church. For the social ministry this has meant a strong stress on
the vocation of the laity in the socio-political arena. This is hardly a
new theme, but it has received renewed attention from a Pope cautious
about church-state matters but activist in his sense of the social
relevance of Christian faith. Two points are significant about this stress
on the lay vocation.

First, anyone acquainted with the church's social ministry, theoretically or practically, recognizes the need for this emphasis. Particularly
in the United States we have been less than successful in the post-
conciliar period in providing the laity proper scope in the social ministry.
Second, the shift which did occur at Vatican II was not designed to
lessen the lay role, but it did describe the priestly and religious life in
a manner allowing for more direct involvement in the social ministry.
It is questionable, therefore, whether the model of distinct roles used
in the time of Pius XI and Pius XII can today be reinstituted. That
model proposed a "first-order" direct role for the laity in the socio-
political realm and a "second-order" role of education for the church
professionals. The present visible, active role which the bishops play

on social questions goes beyond a "second-order" function, and this makes it less likely that the old distinction will hold.

These broad comments on the church and politics have to be concretized in different cultures and political systems, some of which require very flexible interpretation of these principles. The central point is to see that John Paul's teaching stands in continuity with the conciliar framework; he may seek to restrain certain specific forms of political engagement, but he has not directed his teaching to a withdrawal of the church from the social witness advocated in post-conciliar Catholicism.

Human Rights: The principal way in which John Paul II addresses the social questions is through human rights categories. His use of this theme continues a pattern rooted in Pius XII and expanded by John XXIII and Paul VI. In itself this is a noteworthy theme in the social teaching, since papal thought in the nineteenth and early twentieth centuries was cautious about human rights language. The reason was well-known; it is a standard commentary to distinguish the eighteenth century natural rights tradition from the older natural law philosophy. The contribution of Pius XII and particularly John XXIII has been to incorporate aspects of the natural rights tradition within the natural law framework.

John Paul's use of human rights is notable in two ways. First, his frequent appeals for human rights on his pilgrimages not only allows him to speak to a variety of specific issues, but it also reinforces the human rights ministry of the local church. This was visibly the case in his address to sugarworkers in the Philippines and to laborers in Brazil.[22] It was uniquely the case, of course, in his visit to Poland.

Second, John Paul II not only applies the human rights teaching of his predecessors, he is also developing his own distinctive interpretation of human rights. His *Address to the United Nations* gave the broadest interpretation yet accorded to human rights in Catholic social teaching. He developed an interpretation of the international system based on human rights, going so far as to link the roots of war with human rights violations. Some would question whether the category of human rights can bear the weight the Pope places on it, but he may push our understanding beyond convenient interpretations of the theme.

His conceptual contribution to the human rights argument also moves in the direction of seeking a unified interpretation of different kinds of rights. The U.N. distinctions of political-civil and social-cultural-economic rights reflect a broader divergence rooted in distinct philosophical and political systems. The Pope's U.N. address sought to cut across this divide on the basis that both material and spititual values are essential to human dignity and must be provided for in any political system.

The human rights theme raises a final question on which John Paul's views are less well known. The 1971 synod of bishops raised the question of the role of social justice and human rights categories within the Church. This proposal to use the concepts traditionally applied to society in an assessment of ecclesial life and structures is still in its rudimentary stages in Catholic social teaching. There is an intellectual question here of determining how to make the transition from secular structures to analogous but not necessarily identical structures within the church. As yet John Paul has not addressed himself explicitly to this theme in spite of its connection with the broader human rights ministry with which he is so solidly identified.

War and Peace: Among the international issues in Catholic social teaching none has been more carefully assessed than the war and peace question. The extensive analysis of the morality of war from the biblical period through Pius XII faces a qualitatively new challenge in the nuclear age. Like his predecessors, John Paul II has felt compelled to confront the nuclear question, but in his own way.

In his analysis of the nuclear arms race, the Pope has cast his argument in terms of the relationship of technology, ethics and politics. The theme is a central one in his thought, one he uses to address medical-moral questions as well as international relations. In his first encyclical, the *Redeemer of Man* (*Redemptor Hominis*), and in his recent address at Hiroshima he used the prism of technology and ethics to analyze the meaning of the arms race. John Paul II's analysis involves two steps. First, the nuclear arms race is depicted as the most visible example of a larger question: how modern technology can move beyond both moral and political guidance thus submitting the human person to an impersonal power. The technological dynamic of the arms race fits this pattern—new improvements in weaponry are always one step ahead of the most recent attempts to control them.

Second, this technological dynamic means that the challenge for the human community is to reestablish the primacy of ethics and politics over technology. In his address to scientists and intellectuals at Hiroshima, John Paul II stated his basic theme:

> In the past, it was possible to destroy a village, a town, a region, even a country. Now it is the whole planet that has come under

threat. This fact should finally compel everyone to face a basic moral consideration: From now on, it is only through a conscious choice and through a deliberate policy that humanity can survive.[23]

The realm of moral choice on this issue lies ultimately, although not exclusively, in the political process. Scientists, journalists, educators and religious leaders prepare the atmosphere of choice, even shape the categories for choosing, but effective action on the arms race requires decisive political action. At the United Nations and at the White House in 1979, John Paul II acknowledged this and called for political measures to control and reverse the spiral of the arms race.

Four of the last five popes (with the exception of John Paul I) have made distinctive contributions to the social teaching. This paper points to the factors which guarantee that John Paul II will forcefully shape this tradition. He is a man of the tradition but knows that a living tradition must grow and develop. Development will be the product of many forces not simply papal teaching, but John Paul's voice will be a catalyst to other efforts.

NOTES

1. For a summary of the teaching, see Joseph Gremillion, *The Gospel of Peace and Justice: Catholic Social Teaching Since John XXIII* (N.Y.: Orbis Books, 1976); John Coleman, "Development of Church Social Teaching," *ORIGINS*, 11 (June 4, 1981) p. 34ff.

2. J. C. Murray, "Church and State at Vatican II," *Theological Studies* 27 (1966) p. 585.

3. J. C. Murray, "The Problem of Religious Freedom," *Theological Studies* 25 (1966) p. 503-575.

4. Murray, "Church and State," p. 606.

5. John Paul II, Puebla Address, *ORIGINS*, 8 (Feb. 8, 1979) p. 535.

6. George H. Williams, *The Mind of John Paul II: Origins of His Thought and Action* (N.Y.: Seabury Press 1981) p. 264.

7. John Paul II, On Human Work, *ORIGINS*, 11 (Sept. 24, 1981) Para. 9.

8. I am indebted to one of Fr. Henri de Lubac's students for this reference.

9. Vatican II, *Gaudium et Spes*, cf. Para. 22, 32, 39, 45.

10. Williams, p. 265.

11. John Paul II, *Redemptor Hominis*, Para. 14.

12. Cf. D. Hollenbach, et al, "John C. Murray's Unfinished Agenda," *Theolgical Studies* 40 (1979) p. 700-715.

13. A-T. Tymieniecka, "The Origins of the Philosophy of John Paul II," *Proceedings of the American Catholic Philosophical Association*, 53 (1979) p. 16.

14. T. Szulc, "Politics and the Polish Pope," *New Republic* (Oct. 28, 1978) p. 19ff.

15. John Paul II, "The Pope's Address to President Ferdinand Marcos," *ORIGINS*, 10 (Feb. 26, 1981) p. 591.

16. Cf. Murray, "The Problem of Religious Freedom."

17. Coleman, "Development of Catholic Social Teaching," p. 39.

18. Cf. Puebla Address; Pope to the Brazilian Bishops; Address to Filipino Men Religious, *ORIGINS*, 1979-1982.

19. Cf. Murray, "Church and State at Vatican II," p. 587.

20. Ibid., p. 582.

21. Address to Filipino Men Religious, *ORIGINS*, 10 (Feb. 26, 1981).

22. Address to Rural Peasants at Oaxaca, *ORIGINS*, 8 (Feb. 8, 1979).

23. Address at Hiroshima, *ORIGINS*, 9 (Oct. 11, 1979) p. 266.

CHAPTER 7

Economic Systems, Middle Way Theories, And Third World Realities

FOR TWENTY CENTURIES THE CATHOLIC CHURCH HAS WRESTLED WITH THE powerful institutions of society in an attempt to sanctify, or at least tame, them. In a book written thirty-five years ago Raissa Maritain traces the slow evolution of humanity's critical understanding of the moral requirements of God's revealed word.[1] It took Christian churches centuries to see the Gospel as radically incompatible with slavery, and to grasp that colonialism violates the political dignity of peoples. Nevertheless, wherever the Church finds leverage to do so, it intervenes in social arenas to mitigate evils. As it did in the Middle Ages when it persuaded warring parties to observe truces of God, the Church labors in all arenas of human activity not to annihilate, but to harness biological and social forces to constructive purposes. Its effort is perhaps most evident in the domain of sexuality. Sex, created by God, is obviously a good thing. But because sex is easily abused, the Church unremittingly promotes social norms for channelling sex towards permanent commitment and non-exploitative behavior.

Today the Church faces a major challenge: how to impose ethical discipline on transnational corporations, whose impact on vulnerable Third World societies produces an array of good and bad effects.[2] Like other large and powerful institutions, corporations have an inherent tendency to impose their own dynamics and rules upon society at large. Although churches cannot control corporations directly, they seek, through political and moral pressures, to bend corporate power to larger human purposes. The specific mission of the Church is to promote the forward march of human beings, individually and collectively, through the relativities of time and space toward their ultimate destiny, definitive union with God as a community of redeemed. Corporate behavior must ultimately be judged by that standard.

The present symposium on "Human Work and Co-Creation" must be seen in two broad contexts: (a) the historical process in which religious agencies try to achieve the moral domestication of dynamic social institutions, and (b) the answer churches must give to their constituents who press them to judge corporations in matters of social justice and human rights. The Gospel neither approves nor condemns corporations. Rather, it summons Christians to view the corporation like any other powerful or wealthy institution, namely, as a mere human creation which must be stripped of idolatrous pretentions. Christians cannot uncritically endorse corporate goals or claims to legitimacy any more than they can those of the state. Necessarily, therefore, dialogue between corporate officials and Christians will entail conflicts of values and interests, if only because corporations and churches pursue opposing goals and invoke distinct criteria of success.[3] It is the task of serious interlocutors in both institutions, particularly of those whose partial loyalties extend to both, to render these tensions creative, not destructive.

Ancient normative issues are at stake for, as Alfred Marshall puts it, "The economist, like everyone else, must concern himself with the ultimate aims of man."[4] Clarence Walton writes in a similar vein:

> There is a spiritual thirst for justice, freedom and fraternity. One knows it. In this moral maelstrom executives will either find refuge or give refuge. But their power precludes ethical evasiveness; they will be involved in the one great decision every society must take from time to time: *how to live in society and community?*[5]

Or, in the words of two recent authors, "Ethics is everybody's business."[6]

Protagonists in debates are prone to exaggerate. Not surprisingly, some corporate ideologues foolishly talk as if their mandate to earn profit were unconditional and immune to criticism.[7] They forget that corporations are mere creatures of kings and states: their "personality" is not absolute, but rests on a legal fiction validated by government.[8] Therefore, the legitimacy of corporations is constantly subject to re-negotiation with society at large. Churches, as legitimate actors in society, have a right to plead their case for ethical constraints on cor-porations. Yet religious authorities do well to practice restraint and avoid two opposing stances. The first of these is invoking theology as a weapon to legitimize corporate ideology. Christians have the duty to challenge all idolatries of power and influence.[9] Interestingly, the strongest pleas for placing checks upon corporations issue not from critics but from loyal partisans. Testifying before the Joint Economic Committee of Congress on January 28, 1982, Admiral Hyman Rick-over lamented that moral irresponsibility was fast becoming the general rule in large corporations. After reaffirming his loyalty to capitalism, Rickover declared that:

> If our free-enterprise, capitalistic system is to survive, it is in-cumbant upon corporate executives to exercise greater self-restraint and to accept moral responsibility for their actions, many of which appear to be having a negative influence on our economy and our society.[10]

Rickover blames executives who, "aided by shrewd, high-priced law-yers . . . seek to evade moral and legal liability for the companies they own and control by insulating themselves from the details." He argues that:

> If a corporation is to be accorded protection as a natural person under the Fourteenth Amendment, then all the obligations incum-bent on "natural persons" ought also to be binding on corpora-tions. And, since a corporation acts through its officials, they should be held personally liable for illegal corporate acts.[11]

Rickover rejects the "increasingly popular notion: namely, that the so-called forces of the marketplace are enough to motivate large corpora-tions to act responsibly and exercise self-restraint."[12] Finally, he stakes out a middle position in these terms:

The notion that we have a self-regulating, free-market economy that will itself prompt a high standard of ethical business conduct is not realistic in today's complex society. Those who advocate exclusive reliance on the market do disservice to capitalism, since the result is often increased government intervention, the very antithesis of their goal. On the other hand, the destruction of capitalism and the establishment of complete state control are inimical to economic and political freedom.

The survival of our capitalist system therefore depends on finding a proper middle ground between these two extremes.[13]

My point is obvious: Christians must not be beguiled into granting uncritical legitimacy to corporations. If the sociology of interests teaches us anything, it is that corporate propaganda will try to claim too much legitimacy and invoke religious values to buttress their own legitimacy, just as kings and politicans have always done. It is a Christian duty to subject corporate claims to a radically skeptical scrutiny.

An opposite temptation also faces Christians: that of rejecting corporate legitimacy in some naive spirit of unhistorical moralism. Genuine ethical strategies transcend moralism, accepting relativities of time and place, limited virtue, unavoidable evils and the value of intermediate ends. Simone de Beauvoir is right: our age cannot live without an ethic or ambiguity.[14] Ethics must become a "means of the means" if it is to serve as a value guidepost to effective policy action.[15] Any realistic Christian ethic of corporate power must therefore accept constraints and compromises. It helps greatly if Christian ethicists lucidly acknowledge the high risk they run of being coopted by a particular set of vested interests. The history of military chaplains and plantation preachers records this risk eloquently. Good intentions are of little help here, since Christians must often become the enemies of their own institutional vested interests if they are to avoid supplying good conscience to beneficiaries of exploitative structures, while providing pastoral consolation to the victims of those very structures. Clearly, any "theology of corporations" is worthless unless it directly confronts and disarms the temptation of serving as a mere rationalization system for the vested interests of corporations.

All intellectuals face analogous difficulties because historical precedents do not satisfactorily define the role of intellectuals. In the past intellectuals have served as counselors to princes, as apolitical specialists simply carrying out their specialized tasks, as ideologues of a cause, or finally, as free-lancers trying to remain pure and above the fray.[16] The problem with being a counselor is that princes prefer good news to truth and display an alarming proclivity to behead intellectuals who value integrity more than political expediency. Apolitical experts, in turn, are not rooted in historical constraints and easily become unwitting accomplices to an evil *status quo*. As for ideologues of causes, they are often forced to engage in mendacious ethical contortions in futile attempts to reconcile truth with propaganda demands of their party or movement, which is usually more interested in loyalty and "scoring political points" than in fidelity to truth. No less than their fellow human beings are intellectuals tempted to trim their sails to prevailing winds and reward systems. The fourth group, free-floating intellectuals, are responsible to no living community of struggle or of need. They think they can live ahistorically, unattached to time, place, and concreteness. They never "assume" the burden of their own historical relativity. They delude themselves, for as Peguy says: "Those who have clean hands have no hands."

These four intellectual role models instruct Christians who seek integrity and ethical behavior in corporations. Christian thinkers are so easily induced to sell out as moral counselors to corporations because the blandishments offered them are always packaged to appear so reasonable, non-threatening, urbane, and ultimately, necessary. Predictably, many flee responsiblity by washing their hands of complex moral issues, branding them as purely "secular" matters lying beyond the pale of religious elucidation. Alternatively, they may seek refuge by living morally in only one of the four ethical arenas engaging the responsibility of corporate personnel. These arenas include: (1) personal and professional behavior within boundaries of prevailing ethical ground rules and organizational roles; (2) corporate policy decision-making procedures, touching on complex issues of societal justice; (3) ethical arenas dealing with the overall systemic good and bad effects of corporate activity in the world; and (4) competing images and standards of success operative in business circles, on the one hand, and in the Christian religion, on the other.[17]

A new challenge now comes to Christians from John Paul II's encyclical *On Human Work*: They are enjoined to create a middle-way between two opposing ideologies of human labor—capitalism and Marxist collectivism. Middle- or "third way" economic experiments have a past history, however, which is now briefly reviewed.

Middle Ways: A View from History

On Human Work, like earlier papal encyclicals, denounces "the various trends of materialistic and economistic thought."[18] Because capitalism and socialism alike are criticized by popes, Catholic social thinkers have long yearned for "middle ways" which, so they hope, avoid the worst abuses of each system. They reject Marxist collectivism because it treats human persons as mere producers and capitalism because, notwithstanding noble rhetoric about individual liberties and political rights, it reduces workers to being mere "factors of production" ruled by impersonal economic laws. John Paul II reaffirms the traditional principle that:

> the basis for determining the value of human work is not primarily the kind of work being done, but the fact that the one who is doing it is a person. The sources of the dignity of work are to be sought primarily in the subjective dimension, not in the objective one.[19]

Papal condemnations of communism *in principle* on grounds that it is an inherently atheistic and materialistic system have been rendered obsolete, however, by philosophical breakthroughs achieved in Marxist-Christian dialogues. Serious communist philosophers now concede that "religious alienation" is dissociable from economic and social alienation.[20] Christians, in turn, especially in Latin America, experience no difficulty in calling themselves Marxists without falling into contradiction.[21] In 1963 Pope John XXIII distinguished between error and those who err in good faith.[22] In the encyclical John Paul II differentiates genuine from unsatisfactory socialization.[23] Christian socialists draw encouragement from papal overtures such as these.

The popes never condemn capitalism *on principle*, but denounce its abuses *in practice*, thus leaving unanswered the question whether capitalism's practical abuses are separable from its organizing principle of economic activity, competitive profit-seeking.[24] Critical interrogation by many Christians into the Gospel's application to economic ideologies has led them to conclude that middle-way models could ally capitalism's dynamic efficiency to socialism's compassionate regard for society's weak members. The enduring Christian dream is to find an economic system which is both efficient and just, and to inspire managers to be both hard-headed and gentle-hearted.[25]

The late Emmanuel Mounier articulated a communitarian personalist philosophy to steer a middle course between capitalism's atomistic competitiveness and communism's depersonalizing collectivism. Mounier wants not collectivities but communities or free associations of persons choosing to ratify their destinies as social beings. According to Mounier, true personhood requires community because, in its absence, persons cannot fully realize themselves. Therefore, economic and political life must be designed to foster this dual, interrelated growth. Liberal economics cannot be allowed to impose impersonal "laws" which subordinate persons to the process of production. Similarly, the Marxist "laws" of history are rejected because they condemn societies to be the playthings of ineluctable class struggle. The personalist believes that relations of production no less than the means of production can be organized in humane fashion.

Mounier died in 1950, but already in 1941 another French Christian movement had been founded. This was "Economy and Humanism," whose basic premise states that all societal arrangements—economic, political, and institutional—are subordinated to achieving the comprehensive good of the human person.[26] Like Mounier, "Economy and Humanism" condemned all reductionism and defined the societal task as the construction of a political economy which promotes a humanistic order and fosters civilizations of solidarity.

Manifestly, middle-way theories are nothing new in Christian circles and John Paul II's letter *On Human Work* brings no fresh elements to theoretical reflection on third ways. The Pope's letter is to be read as a fervent re-affirmation of the principle that no economic system or ideology is moral if it dehumanizes those who work in it. Problems arise because no successful strategy for making middle-way policies work has ever been devised.

In short, operational experiments are the key. Accordingly, it is instructive to review a few efforts launched under the banner of middle-way theories.

A. Yugoslavia. Yugoslavia under Tito had good reasons for not tying its economic destiny too closely to the Soviet Union. With economic dependence came intolerable levels of political and ideological subordination. And the centralized Soviet pattern of economic decision-making was largely inapplicable to Yugoslavia's regionally diverse groups: Serbians, Croatians, Montenegrins. More autonomy had to be left to decentralized economic units if conflicting political loyalties were to be retained by Yugoslavia's central authorities. In its search for a practical incentive system to make decentralization work, Yugoslavia resorted to worker-management within industry.

This essay is not the proper venue to describe or evaluate Yugoslavia's experiments in worker-managment.[27] Its purposes are adequately served by noting that middle-way strategies, like those they supplant, produce only relatively satisfying results. The very relativity of these results is a salutary reminder that "middle ways" are not panaceas.

Yugoslavia is not the only country, however, to have experimented with alternative approaches to socialism; several African nations have sought to frame indigenous models of "African" socialism.

B. African Socialism. Underlying the quest of African nations for their own brand of socialism is a two-fold aspiration. The *political* objective is to assert relative independence of the two super-powers, each epitomizing a dominant ideological system. The *cultural* goal is to tread a road to development which respects their past history and cultural heritage. Such ambitions can vary modally, however. Thus Julius Nyerere preaches "ujamma" or "familyhood" for Tanzania, whereas Leopold Senghor discourses on "negritude" as the basis of a distinctive identity and a unique "socialist" model for Senegal. Both leaders reject Marxism's one-dimensional emphasis on production and capitalism's atomistic competitiveness. Senghor does not want Africans to be mere consumers of civilization, because he believes they have their own contribution to make to the universal civilization in gestation. And Nyerere adds that, for him, "socialism" means subordinating individual goals to the needs of society, particularly those of its weakest members.[28]

Amilcar Cabral, theorist and military leader of Guinea-Bissau's independence struggle, likewise sought a development model suited to his country's specific conditions. Although he borrowed elements of social organization, ideology, and political practice from East and West, he urged Guinea-Bissau to create its own model in accord with past traditions and new conditions.[29]

These three African leaders all reject the central values held by the West's two main ideologies, capitalism and centralized socialism. Both systems undermine the traditional basis for solidarity, a value which accounts for the survival of African cultural identity through centuries of slavery and colonialism. If class conflict is taken as the law of life in society, solidarity becomes meaningless. Solidarity is likewise rendered meaningless if each person in society seeks only individual gains from collective efforts to produce and govern. This is why indigenous African socialists stand on a middle ground between individualism and impersonal collectivism.

In Africa as in Yugoslavia, however, practical results have been only relatively successful. Middle-ways are not panaceas and, on balance, their economic, political, and cultural performance record is not significantly better than that of societies following standard capitalist or socialist prescriptions. One must not suppose, however, that only socialism breeds hybrid systems: capitalism likewise generates alternative forms.

C. Neo-capitalism. Capitalism and socialism are generic labels which subsume, under their respective banners, various specific forms of social organization. Japanese capitalism displays its uniqueness, for example, through tenured lifetime work contracts, the practice of farming out work to artisanal family units, and fidelity to traditional seniority systems in promoting managers. Here we have a hybrid form of capitalism standing midway between U.S.-style reward systems and traditional Japanese work hierarchies. Indeed much of what in Asian countries is called "capitalism" constitutes a mixed system in which standard capitalist patterns merge with pre-capitalist institutional forms and values. This is most visibly the case in the continent's "successful" capitalist economies—Korea, Taiwan, Singapore, and Hong Kong.

Syncretistic patterns assumed by capitalism in another Asian country, Saudi Arabia, are especially interesting. Saudi rulers faced the challenge of preserving a feudal political order while harnessing the dynamic entrepreneurship of American capitalism to economic activities. That political order still rests on a strong and generalized adherence to Islamic beliefs and morality. Consequently, value tensions between capitalistic profit-seeking and Islamic norms for justice had to be harmonized through the creation of novel institutions and practices. The most intriguing of these is the Islamic bank, explicitly designed to circumvent the Koran's strict ban on usury, the charging of interest on monies loaned. Under modern financial conditions money is not some inert treasure to be preserved, but a dynamic asset for creating new wealth. Saudi Arabia's Islamic banks solve their moral dilemma by accepting deposits and making loans without charging interest to lenders and borrowers, although they do levy a service charge. A "shared risk" system allows banks to receive a percentage of profits realized by borrowers once their own investments bear fruit. In turn, Islamic banks distribute a "share" of their monetary receipts to their own depositors. Cynics may charge that funds circulating among borrowers, banks, and lenders are no different from "interest" or what the Koran would call "usury." Nevertheless, Saudis go to great lengths and expense to institute separate accounting, management and loan negotiation mechanisms to assure that "interest" is not paid. Saudis have devised an effective "middle way" between standard capitalist practices and traditional Islamic lending norms, which did not make use of mediating institutions such as banks.[30]

In many other Third World countries, "mixed" approaches to planning and economic management likewise characterize daily practice. To illustrate, capitalists hold that the recruitment and promotion of personnel should be based on merit, which is assessed by a combination of certified credentials and performance tests. In countless Third World countries, however, the nomination of people to posts is dictated by nepotism; traditional allegiances to family, kin, or ethnic community outweigh considerations of merit. Defenders of this practice point out that, notwithstanding rhetoric about the merit principle, matters may not work so differently in countries like the United States, where "old boy" networks of school alumni or social club members may play the functionally equivalent role exercised by nepotism elsewhere. The net effect in both cases is to circumvent the strict merit system.

D. Chile. No "third way" experiment is more illuminating than that conducted by Chile under Presidents Eduardo Frei and Salvador Allende between 1964 and 1973. Frei, leader of Chile's Christian Democrat Party, admired Konrad Adenauer and Alcide de Gasperi as creative practitioners of a "third way," more socially compassionate than capitalism yet free of Marxist totalitarianism. European and Latin American Christian Democracies alike drew their ideological nourishment from the social encyclicals, a specialized *corpus* of papal writings which defends several normative principles. These are:

(1) private ownership of productive assets is a natural right;
(2) this right is not absolute but relative, and its specific institutional modalities vary with circumstances and are always subordinated to the "common good" of society;
(3) this "common good" places an obligation on the state to assure sustenance to all its citizens at a level consonant with their spiritual dignity as persons. In a word, social justice is distributive as well as commutative;
(4) the salary system is not intrinsically exploitive;

(5) class conflict is not the inherent law of social history but a pernicious error which prevents labor and capital from joining efforts to pursue the common good;

(6) the so-called "laws of economics" must be subject to the demands of the spiritual vocation of all human beings; and

(7) the value of persons must not be judged solely, or primarily, on the basis of their contribution to economic production.

Christian Democratic parties translated this humanistic vision into a political platform which was simultaneously anti-communist and reformist. On the one hand, the platform censured communism as intrinsically evil because it is atheistic and totalitarian. On the other, it condemned capitalism, not in principle but in its concrete practice, because it valued competitive success more highly than providing essential goods to all members of society. Because history offered numerous examples of countries which were both capitalistic and democratic, Christian Democrats assumed that political welfare decisions could attenuate evils attendant upon capitalism. This politics could accomplish by distributing economic, political, and organizational powers over multiple institutions, each serving as a check upon the other.

Thanks to the towering stature and political shrewdness of Adenauer and de Gasperi, aided by post-war conditions and the visible presence of a communist enemy, European Christian Democrats achieved great prestige in the two decades following World War II. Latin American Christian Democrats gladly rode the coattails of that prestige. Indeed, in the late 1950's and early 1960's, they had not yet been disillusioned by revelations of widespread corruption, anti-reformist conservatism, and cynical perpetuation in power which, in later years, tarnished the guilded image of German and Italian Christian Democracy. Adenauer and de Gasperi were tough but noble and incorrupt politicians. Unfortunately, however, their party later became a seedbed of mediocre and cynical office-holders. More importantly, objective social conditions in Latin American countries differed radically from those found in Europe.

Unlike Germany and Italy, Latin American countries were peopled by vast majorities of poor; their economies were still in transition away from the production of primary commodities for export to manufacturing; their labor unions were relatively powerless at the bargaining table; their political institutions were not pluralistic or democratic; and their press had no tradition of free and critical public education. Latin American Christian Democrats saw government's role to be promoting structural reform, not merely balancing competing interest within a framework presumed to be equitable in its foundations. Chile's first generation of Christian Democrats denounced capitalism as exploitative and repudiated communism as dictatorial and materialistic. They proposed a reformist "third way" which would blend socialism's thirst after justice with liberal democracy's regard for freedom. Of course power must be decentralized: economic power could not be vested in the same institutions as political power, and free associations must be permitted so that individuals might have collective negotiating strength to keep the state from becoming omnipotent. Some nationalization of basic industries was advocated, but the universal seizure of productive assets by the state was ruled out. Similarly, reforms in land tenure, tax structures, administrative, educational and fiscal systems were urged; but these reforms had to be approved by voters and legislators, not imposed by an omnipotent party allegedly acting in the name of proletarian masses.[31] Frei was elected in 1964 on such a reform program. Over the next six years, notwithstanding Frei's probity, political skills, and Chile's general high level of political sophistication, his "third way" failed. Why? The reasons had nothing to do with the party's noble principles or with Frei's personal qualities: they were structural. As I have written elsewhere:

> Frei had won his mandate because enough people who wanted far-reaching change had thought they could get it from him, and simultaneously enough conservative voters who feared "the worst" (socialism and Allende) thought it was safer to accept partial change under Frei, who was quite solidly committed to parliamentary democracy and free enterprise, than to risk losing everything should a more radical candidate win. Hence Frei's seemingly noble experiment failed because, despite the appearances, it was essentially a program of palliatives. Furthermore, he could not bring himself to overstep the ideological limits of his own Christian Deomocrat model of development.[32]

I cannot here retrace in detail the reasons for the model's failure. But fail it did, as witnessed by the defection of Frei's leading Christian Democrat ideologue, Jacques Chonchol, to Allende's camp and by the election of Allende in 1970 by the same electorate which had feared to vote in a socialist president in 1964. Experiments in Christian Democracy in Venezuela—under Rafael Caldera (1969-1974) and Herrera Campins (1979 to the present) have further confirmed the limitations of Christian Democracy as a formula for developmental reform. Precisely because it is a hybrid "third way" standing midway between capitalism

and socialism, the Christian Democrat political platform wins the unqualified allegiance of almost no one. Conservatives tolerate it as the
lesser of two evils, a means of avoiding what they deem to be a "greater"
evil, namely, socialist reform. Meanwhile, progressive reformers endorse it but timidly, viewing it as the best that is realistically obtainable,
given the strength of opposition forces hostile to more fundamental
reform. In almost literal terms, the "third way" is everybody's bastard,
the object of disavowed paternity from all quarters, a political orphan
with few ardent supporters anywhere. Christian Democrat governments
in developing countries face a disturbing choice: either push ahead with
reforms consistent with their principles, thereby risking losing their
conservative or moderate supporters, or compromise with capitalistic
or semi-feudal vested interests in the name of preserving "democracy,"
thereby alienating their reformist supporters.

A painful lesson emerges here: namely, that those who would have
the best of both political worlds risk getting the worst of each. As the
Pakistani economist Mahbub ul Haq writes:

> And here we come to the second of the disastrous decisions—the
> choice of the mixed economy. In most cases, such a choice has
> combined the worst, not the best, features of capitalism and so-
> cialism. It has often prevented the developing countries from
> adopting honest-to-goodness economic incentives and using the
> free functioning of the price system to achieve efficiency in a
> capitalistic framework, if not equity. In reality, there have been
> too many inefficient administrative controls and price distortions.
> At the same time, the choice of the mixed economy has prevented
> these societies from pursuing their goals in a truly socialistic
> framework, since mixed economy institutions have often been more
> capitalistic than not. The end result, therefore, has often been that
> they have fallen between two stools, combining weak economic
> incentives with bureaucratic socialism. Neither the ends of growth
> nor equity are served by such confusion in social and political ob-
> jectives within the framework of a mixed economy.[33]

Haq explains that political constraints which dictate the choice of a
mixed system prevent leaders from implementing policy measure capable of generating success on either front. Echoing Martin Luther's "If
you must sin, sin boldly", Haq concludes:

> that the days of the mixed economy are numbered. The develop-
> ing countries will have to become either more frankly capitalistic
> or more genuinely socialist. The capitalistic alternative is work-

able only in those situations where the society is willing to accept income inequalities over a long period of time without exploding or where extremely high growth rates (10 to 15 percent) can be financed with a generous inflow of resources from Western friends. Otherwise, the only alternative is a genuinely socialist system, based on a different ideology and a different pattern of society. But this does not mean bureaucratic socialism; it means a major change in the political balance of power within these societies and drastic economic and social reforms. Whether the developing countries can manage such a change without violent revolution is a critical question of our time.[34]

In the real world impoverished masses are rarely "willing to accept income inequalities over a long period of time without exploding;" these inequalities are imposed upon them.[35] Even achieving high growth rates financed with "a generous inflow of resources from Western friends" does not guarantee social peace. A critical reading of Brazil's economic miracle[36] undermines Haq's optimism. Moreover, if the alternative is a socialist system which can be obtained only through violent revolution, can one be optimistic? If we are to believe Robert Heilbroner's dismal *Inquiry Into the Human Prospect*, not at all! Waging a violent revolution does not guarantee that either sound development or less human suffering will ensue. Kampuchea's destiny under Pol Pot's fanatics invites us to sober skepticism here.[38]

Where, then, are we left standing in the wake of these reflections on the past history of "third ways?" If we stand anywhere at all it is on a thin, and perhaps shrinking, sliver of intellectual and political space.

The history of "third ways" warns us against any naive, ahistorical exegesis of Pope John Paul II's exhortations on the subject. Most searches for "third way" paradigms in recent years take the form of a quest for alternative development strategies. A brief look at the dynamics of this quest sheds light on the policy implications of new societal models.

Alternative Development Strategies

Growing numbers of strategists reject conventional development models.[39] With few exceptions growth policies have not led to material well-being and jobs for the masses, or greater social and political freedom. Even where high aggregate growth has been achieved, distribution of benefits has been grossly inequitable,[40] and sacrifices imposed on populations in the form of economic hardship, political coercion, and violations of personal rights have often been excessive.[41]

After three decades of "rational" resource planning within nations and international resource transfers, the gaps between rich and poor countries, regions, and social classes have widened.[42] Wealth has been highly concentrated in cities at the expense of the countryside. Michael Lipton correctly denounces the built-in urban bias to development efforts in most parts of the world.[43]

Third World industrialization has bred more, not less, dependency. Hopes nurtured by earlier strategists that "self-sustaining" economic growth would follow once a certain income threshold was reached, have proven illusory.[44] A dependency sequence is in operation, with new technological, managerial and market servitudes replacing vulnerabilities founded on the shortage of capital or skilled people. Financial interdependencies, in turn, have grown so complex that one is hard pressed to know who has greater leverage: banks lending to uncreditworthy clients or nations which, like Zaire and Poland, borrow beyond their means.[45] Very few countries, capitalist or socialist, have combined economic growth with distributional equity, minimal protection of human rights, and respect for political liberties. This is why strategists search for other than traditional ways of gaining development.

Alternative developers stress three components: meeting BHN's, promoting self-reliance, and minimizing cultural damage.[46] Notwithstanding the optimistic rhetoric surrounding most discussions of alternative development strategies, serious political obstacles stand in the way of their implementation. As a result, the values underlying the alternative model play only a modest role in shaping planning priorities and resource allocations. More importantly, few countries have formulated successful "strategies for the transition" away from distorted development toward comprehensive human well-being. Although hopeful initiatives abound at the level of local projects or programs, these cannot be extrapolated to the level of national strategies. In short, "third way" strategies are more easily praised than practiced, more readily designed than implemented. And, truth to tell, few countries have seriously tried to implement true alternatives to capitalism or socialism. Most national experiments are more accurately characterized as variants of capitalism or socialism than as genuine alternative pathways to development.

Measures taken by one non-governmental grass-roots movement in Sri Lanka, however, provide a helpful lesson. I refer to the Sarvodaya Shramadana Movement,[47] whose leaders state that the goals of development must be borrowed neither from countries already "developed" nor from pre-existing theories, but drawn from a critical assessment of latent dynamisms found in traditional values and institutions. A.T. Ariyaratyne, Sarvodaya's founder, considers that "a poor country like Sri Lanka would have gone 99% down the road to development if development goals were properly defined and understood by the people."[48]

In its first decade (1958-1968) Sarvodaya centered its efforts on the total personality awakening of participants in volunteer work camps performing tasks useful to their community. A second phase aimed at the total awakening of villages. Yet, as Arliyaratne explains:

> the awakening of a village community is closely linked up with the national environment of which the villages are an integral part. Therefore, as the number of village communities participating in Sarvodaya activities increased, concepts of national development as relevant to village people's traditions, experience and aspirations also developed among them. Thus *Deshodaya or the awakening of the nation also became a Sarvodaya ideal.*

> In the present day world no community or nation can pursue a path to development without influencing and being influenced by what is happening in other countries . . . as the Movement took national proportions it also had to develop its own concepts on world development. In other words *Vishvodaya or the awakening of the world* community as a whole became a fourth ideal to strive for by the adherents of the Movement.

> Thus the Sarvodaya Movement in Sri Lanka works towards the integrated ideal of the development of Man and Society as persons, families, village and urban groups, nations and one world community.[49]

Sarvodaya draws its answer to the central question "Awakening to what?" from classical doctrines of Theravada Buddhism which counsels a middle way between all extremes: indulgence and abnegation, absorption in the world or total flight from it, atomistic salvation or collective deliverance. In Theravada Buddhism each person is summoned to awaken fully to the nature of reality's inter-related evils — suffering, death, old age and impermanence. These evils have a common underlying cause, namely, the stubborn persistence in individuals of craving, that immoderate desire which renders them acquisitive, exploitative and violent. All satisfactions born of desire are ephemeral, however, and doomed to corruption. What is worse, they addict one to further desires which are themselves condemned to futile repetition in a Karmic cycle of endless births, deaths, rebirths, and new deaths. The key to human deliverance, therefore, lies in breaking out of this vicious circle of interconnected evils, thereby putting an end to the radical *cause* of human suffering. Hope rests on Buddha's achievement, twenty-five centuries ago, of enlightenment as to the meaning of life, nature, and history. Buddha was no god but a mere mortal, distinguished from others only by his successful attainment of supreme enlightenment. After reaching full understanding, however, Buddha did not withdraw to blissful *Nibbana*, the serene and total absence of suffering and craving, but remained instead in this perishable flesh to teach others the way, the *eightfold path* to deliverance.

For Theravada Buddhism, the goal of historical existence for all individuals is to progress toward full enlightenment. Social conditions should favor such progress. This is why Sarvodaya relativizes all "goods" held out by capitalist or socialist conceptions of development, refusing to treat them as absolutes. It also relativizes the manner in which they must be sought: Benefits must not be pursued violently, in a mode which alienates men and women in craving after illusory satisfactions, in ways which exclude participation of the masses in favor of political despots.

Ariyaratne insists that:

> Development should start from the grass-roots, from the village up. People should fully participate in planning for development and in the implementation of such plans. The technological knowledge prevailing at the people's level and the available local resources should be used initially. Progressively and appropriately it could be upgraded with advanced knowledge. National development plans should be based, not partially but totally on this broad-based people's participation. It should first strive to satisfy the basic needs of the people and not artificially created wants that are a blind imitation from materialistic cultures . . .
> The ideal of Sri Lanka being a "Dharma Dveepa" (Land of Righteousness) and "Chanyagara" (Land of Plenty) is always foremost in the minds of the Sarvodaya workers.[50]

Sarvodaya treats *all modern visions of development instrumentally.* The conventional goals of modernity—material well-being, technological efficiency, and institutional modernity—are tested to see if they foster what Sarvodaya calls genuine development, namely, the full awakening of the human personality in all its dimensions. This ap-

could wish Cambodia's fate on his own country? We may have won in Vietnam after all.

What Toynbee did not foresee, because technology did not advance enough to make this possible until the 1960s, was that the West would come up with a third way to modernize: the rapid transfer of farm science, made possible by new discoveries in tropical plant genetics, to bring about the kind of agricultural revolution on which its own wealth and industrial power was originally based. . . .

If the Green Revolution had not come along precisely when it did, I think it quite possible that Toynbee's prophecy would be a lot closer to fulfillment.[62]

Whether or not one accepts Critchfield's reading of the transition to modernity, he is correct, I think, in holding that dyadic conceptions of social evolution do not exhaust available alternatives.

Conclusion

Readers of John Paul II's encyclical do well to recall this as they search for "third ways." Ideologues of every stripe are displeased by this document. A recent *FORTUNE* magazine piece complains that "Judging from the general tenor of *Laborem Exercens*, the Church remains wedded to socialist economics and is increasingly a sucker for Third World anti-imperialist rhetoric."[63] Liberation theologians, on the other hand, "wish he would give a little on his ideas about the person and about freedom, since these, they say, may have to be bent somewhat in order to achieve a just society."[64] Richard Neuhaus defends John Paul because,

As leader of a universal community, the pope cannot overtly take sides in the many-faceted conflicts between East and West, between capitalism and socialism. In his public announcements, John Paul appears to criticize evenhandedly atheistic totalitarianism and capitalism consumerism.[65]

Ours is not the first generation of Christians tempted to design societies according to Gospel lights. The existence of medieval Christendom as an imperial polity gives the lie to Chesterton's barb that "Christianity has not been tried and found wanting, but found difficult and left untried." In fact Christendom proved to be a quite viable form of social organization for several centuries. It broke down, however, because it could not guide societies through the passage from post-feudal commercialism to industrial capitalism. More significantly, as the recent history of Christian Democracy in Germany, Italy, Chile, and Venezuela suggests, that particular variety of Christian "third ways" holds out little promise to contemporary societies.

Does this mean that Christian values cannot inspire new paradigms of social construction as we enter the post-industrial age? Perhaps not, but successful paradigms will not resemble the aborted "third ways" of the 1960's.

Although facile readings of the encyclical are ruled out, many valuable themes highlighted in the document can inspire innovative social policy. Both capitalism and socialism, the Pope notes, fail to treat human beings as *subjects* of work, seeing them merely as *objects* in a production cycle. John Paul II invites manager and workers to a lofty vision of shared responsibility for promoting human welfare in society. He insists on the right of weak and disabled workers to a dignified livelihood, even though the spirit of the age favors a utilitarian calculus which ignores their intrinsic value as persons. John Paul II calls for change in the world's economic structures to assure equitable development for all. He condemns statist patterns of "socialization" of productive property as spurious. Finally, he demands that Christianity reject all forms of materialism and economicism.

In reading this letter on the dignity of human labor, one is reminded of Sarvodaya's conception of "right livelihood." In opposition to most development experts, Sarvodaya judges that a paid job is not a basic human need, but merely one possible means of providing a right livelihood. The essential value and basic need is a right livelihood. As Sarvodaya's founder explains it,

> Lord Buddha in His Noble Eight-fold Path leading to perfect enlightenment has included Right Livelihood as its fifth factor. In one of His discourses Lord Buddha mentions the four characteristics of a right approach to economic action, namely, (i) diligence in efficient productive activity, (ii) preservation of what is produced and conservation of nature, (iii) the right social milieu in which one should work, and (iv) a balanced approach to consumption.[66]

This normative view of labor embraces several broad human values:

(i) the joy of personality awakening through constructive and creative labour,
(ii) harmonious social integration by working as a member of a group and
(iii) satisfaction of the needs of life through productive work. In this economic philosophy there is an in-built motivation for self-aggrandizement that activates both the employee and the employer. Instead of productive work debasing their human relationships, they are lifted up to higher human levels and relationships. There is no alienation of the human being from his essential self or his work.[67]

Marx cursed capitalism because it alienates human beings from their deeper selves and the very fruits of their work. And popes have condemned Marxism because, they argue, it violates the true vocation of human beings to be co-creators of a humane world. John Paul II's encyclical *On Human Work* is the latest in a line of heartfelt pleas issued by socially conscious Christian leaders NOT to treat workers as mere workers. He adds his voice even to those whom he condemns when he insists that "it is through man's labor that . . . human dignity, brotherhood and freedom must flourish on earth."[68]

NOTES

1. Raissa Maritain, *Histoire D' Abraham ou Les Premiers Ages de la Conscience Morale* (Paris: Desclée de Brouwer, 1947).

2. United Nations, *Multinational Corporations in World Development* (New York: United Nations Publication ST/ECA/190, 1973); Thomas J. Biersteker, *Distortion or Development? Contending Perspectives on the Multinational Corporation* (Cambridge, Mass.: MIT Press, 1981); Raymond Vernon, *Storm Over the Multinational, The Real Issues* (Cambridge, Mass.: Harvard University Press, 1977).

3. Denis Goulet, "Goals in Conflict: Corporate Success and Global Justice," in *The Judeo-Christian Vision and the Modern Corporation*, ed. Oliver Williams, CSC and John Houck (University of Notre Dame Press, 1982).

4. Cited by John Kenneth Galbraith in the Frontispiece to *The Affluent Society* (London: Hamish Hamilton, 1958).

5. Clarence G. Walton, "Overview" in, *The Ethics of Corporate Conduct*, ed. Clarence G. Walton (Englewood Cliffs, NJ: Prentice-Hall, 1977), pp. 28-9.

6. Hershey H. Friedman and Linda W. Friedman, "Ethics: Everybody's Business," *Collegiate News and Views*, Vol. XXXV No. 2 (Winter 1981-2), pp. 11-13.

7. Examples of such advocacy are found in Richard N. Farmer, *Benevolent Aggresion* (New York: David McKay, 1972) and George Gilder, *Wealth and Poverty* (New York: Basic Books, 1980).

8. Severyn T. Bruyn, *The Social Economy, People Transforming Modern Business* (New York: John Wiley and Sons, 1977); cf. Severyn T. Bruyn, Norman J. Faramelli, and Dennis A. Yates, *An Ethical Primer on the Multinational Corporation, IDOC*, Number 56 (October, 1973), 46 pp.

9. Jacques Ellul, *Presence of the Kingdom* (New York: Seabury Press, 1967), and Jacques Ellul, *L' Homme et L' Argent* (Paris: Delachaux et Niestle, 1953).

10. "Advice from Admiral Rickover," *The New York Review*, Vol. 29, No. 4 (March 18, 1982), pp. 12-13.

11. *Ibid.*, p. 12.

12. *Ibid.*, p. 13.

13. *Ibid.*

14. Simone de Beauvoir, *Ethics of Ambiguity* (Citadel Press, 1962).

15. Denis Goulet, "Beyond Moralism: Ethical Strategies in Global Development," in *Theology Confronts a Changing World*, ed. Thomas M. McFadden (West Mystic, CT: Twenty-third Publications, 1977), pp. 12-39.

16. This typology grows from conversations with the Argentine political scientist, Marcos Kaplan, author of such works as *Estado y Sociedad* (Mexico: Universidad Nacional Autonoma de Mexico, 1978); and *Sociedad, politica y planificacion en America Latina* (Mexico: Universidad Nacional Autonoma de Mexico, 1980). Cf. Roderic A. Camp, "Intellectuals, Agents of Change in Mexico?", *Journal of Inter-american Studies and World Affairs*, Vol. 23, No. 3 (August, 1981), pp. 297-320.

17. Goulet, "Goals in Conflict,"

18. Pope John Paul II, *On Human Work* (Washington, D.C.: U.S. Catholic Conference, 1981), p. 15.

19. *Ibid.*, p. 14.

20. See, *e.g.*, Paul Oestreicher (editor), *The Christian Marxist Dialogue* (New York: The Macmillan Company, 1969); Adam Schaff, *A Philosophy of Man* (London: Lawrence and Wishart, 1963); Leszek Kolakowski, *Toward a Marxist Humanism, Essays on the Left Today* (New York: Grove Press, 1968); special issue of *Tri Quarterly*, "A Leszek Kolakowski Reader," No. 22 (Fall, 1971); Ernst Bloch,*Man on His Own, Essays in the Philosophy of Religion (New York: Herder and Herder, 1970); Ernst Fischer, Art Against Ideology* (London: Allen Lane, Penguin Press, 1969); Jan Lochman, *Encountering Marx: Bonds and Barriers Between Christians and Marxists* (Philadelphia, PA: Fortress, 1977); and, Lochman, *Reconciliation and Liberation: Challenging a One-Dimensional View of Salvation* (Philadelphia, PA: Fortress, 1980).

21. John Eagleson (editor), *Christians and Socialism, Documentation of the*

System for Meeting Basic Needs," *The Review of Politics*, Vol. 43, No. 1 (January, 1981), pp. 22-42.

47. On Sri Lanka, see Gamani Corea, *The Instability of an Export Economy* (Colombo, Sri Lanka: Marga Institute, 1975); *Welfare and Growth in Sri Lanka* (Colombo: Marga Institute, 1974); and Satchi Ponnambalam, *Dependent Capitalism in Crisis, The Sri Lankan Economy, 1948-1980* (London: Zed Press, 1981). On Sarvodaya, see Detlef Kantowsky, *Sarvodaya: The Other Development* (New Delhi: Vikas Publishing House, 1980). Cf. Denis Goulet, *Survival With Integrity: Sarvodaya at the Crossroads* (Colombo: Marga Institute, 1981), Goulet, "Development Strategy in Sri Lanka and a People's Alternative," paper prepared for the McGill University Centre for Developing Area Studies Seminar Series, February 15, 1981 and to be published in 1982; and Goulet, "Development as Liberation: Policy Lessons from Case Studies," *World Development*, Vol. 7, No. 6 (June, 1979), pp. 555-566.

48. A.T. Ariyaratne, Address to the Society for International Development, Sri Lanka Chapter, on "Integrating National Development with the Rural Sector," November, 1979 at Bandaranaike Memorial International Conference Hall, Colombo, Sri Lanka, p. 2.

49. A.T. Ariyaratne, *Sarvodaya and Development* (Moratuwa, Sri Lanka: Sarvodaya Press, n.d.), p.1.

50. A.T. Ariyaratne, *Collected Works, Volume I* (Dehiwala, Sri Lanka: Sarvodaya Research Institute, n.d.), p. 134.

51. Denis Goulet, "An Ethical Model for the Study of Values," *Harvard Educational Review*, Vol. 41, No. 2 (May, 1971), pp. 205-227.

52. Roy Preiswerk, *Mal-Développement, Suisse Monde* (Geneva: Le Centre Europe-Tiers Monde (CETIM), 1975).

53. On this see, Denis Goulet, "In Defense of Cultural Rights: Technology, Tradition and Conflicting Models of Rationality," *Human Rights Quarterly*, Vol. 3, No. 4 (1981), pp. 1-18.

54. Denis Goulet, "I Valori Tradizionali e il Loro Ruolo Vitale Nello Sviluppo," in Roberto Gritti and Eleonora Barbieri Masini (editors), *Società e Futuro*, (Roma: Città Nuova Editrice, 1981), pp. 189-204. Cf. special issue of *Development, Seeds of Change, Village Through Global Order* (1981: 3/4), entitled "Culture, The Forgotten Dimension."

55. Erich Fromm, "Introduction", in, *Socialist Humanism*, ed. Erich Fromm (New York: Doubleday, 1966), p. ix. Italics Fromm's. Cf. Georges Perec, *Les Choses* (Paris: Julliard, 1965).

56. Rodolfo Stavenhagen, *Problemas Etnicos Y Capesinos, Ensayos* (Mexico: Instituto Nacional Indigenista, 1979), p. 17. Translation mine.

57. Denis Goulet, "Socialization and Cultural Development," *Interchange*, Vol. 10, No. 3 (1979-80), p. 5.

58. Donald Hodges and Ross Gandy, *Mexico 1910-1976: Reform or Revolution?* (London: Zed Press, 1979), pp. 177-67.

59. *Ibid.*, p. 166.

60. *Ibid.*, p. 167.

61. *Ibid.*

62. Richard Critchfield, *Villages* (New York: Doubleday, Anchor Press, 1981), p. 333.

63. Daniel Seligman, "Unfair to Capitalism," *Fortune* (November, 1981), p. 63.

64. Richard John Neuhaus, "The Mind of the Most Powerful Man in the World," *Worldview*, Vol. 24, No. 9 (September, 1981), p. 13.

65. *Ibid.*

66. A.T. Ariyaratne, *Collected Works, Volume II* (Dehiwala, Sri Lanka: Sarvodaya Research Institute, 1980), p. 71.

67. *Ibid.*

68. Pope John Paul II, *op. cit.*, p. 60.

PART THREE

Strategies for Renewing Capitalism

The disproportionate distribution of wealth and poverty and the existence of some countries and continents that are developed and of others that are not call for a leveling out and for a search for ways to ensure just development for all.

Laborem Exercens, Para. 2

It is a fact that in many societies women work in nearly every sector of life.

Laborem Exercens, Para. 19

It is characteristic of work that it first and foremost unites people. In this consists its social power: the power to build community. In the final analysis, both those who work and those who manage the means of production or who own them must in some way be united in this community.

Laborem Exercens, Para. 20

The essays in Part One examine from a theological perspective the idea of co-creation as a new way to look at the ingenuity and creativity of the last two or three centuries. The three papers of Novak, Hauerwas and Hollenbach might be characterized as dialectical in their interconnectedness: the thesis is Novak's enthusiastic acceptance of the achievements and potential of capitalism and therefore the appropriateness of co-creation; the antitheses is Hauerwas' severe rejection of co-creation because of the dangers of misinterpretation which can lead to sin and idolatry; and the synthesis is Hollenbach's acknowledgement of the technical virtuosity of humans along with an equally strong cautionary note about human and organizational arrogance.

The four essays in Part Two polarize around two themes: a celebration of the achievements stemming from human freedom and creativity (Murchland and Pichler) and a wariness, even a fearfulness, about the loss of our critical capacities to judge industrial and post-industrial societies (Hehir and Goulet). In fairness to all four writers though, themes from opposing views can be found in each essay.

In Part Three, Strategies for Renewing Capitalism, there are five essays which share a common theme: capitalism, while flawed, is a *reformable* economic system which could benefit from the vision and challenge suggested by the concept of co-creation. For corporations and their managers, being inbued with this perspective means a new recognition of power and its uses. As a result, in business policy-making, certain options are ruled out as inconsistent, while, by advancing the biblical vision, others are given added weight. Co-creation provides, then, an antidote to our inability to perceive in economic and business affairs a larger theme than material acquisitiveness, competition, technical sophistication, and just plain greed.

Chapters eight and nine deal with two immensely difficult challenges to the capacity of corporate capitalism to reform itself. The economist Ernest Bartell questions whether reformed capitalism, using the rubric of the middle way, will be germane to the hundreds of millions in the Third World who do not have market power:

> The practical criticism being made is simply that, given the present distribution of ownership and control of the world's productive resources, the poor nations of the world and especially the poor within those nations simply don't have adequate opportunity to participate and compete . . .

Equally difficult is the problem of sexual equality, as seen by the writers, Sisters Andrea Lee, I.H.M., and Amata Miller, I.H.M., who have observed too much in business and in the churches to be glib about *quick* reforms.

The last three papers deal with problems of the organizational size, the technology, and the bureaucracy which are found in capitalism today. (These problems are present in socialist regimes as well.) Each paper addresses the situation which the philosopher Bernard Murchland, in chapter four, saw emerging: "complex, immensely powerful and largely incomprehensible . . . not easily amenable to human control." But the writers develop practical programs to confront this situation, and they are optimistic about the future. George Lodge sees old business habits being changed: "The 1980's may be one of those rare times when moral behavior is harmonious with what practitioners in the rough and tumble of industry find to be efficient and effective." The labor-management expert, Mark Fitzgerald, analyses several industrial reforms in Europe and the United States that for him are *both* idealistic and realistic. Elmer Johnson examines a new type of business leader: "The source of inspiration . . . is his compelling vision of a just community in which each employee and officer has the opportunity to realize his full potential as a purposeful, moral agent in rich interaction with his fellow workers." For Johnson, the notion to be a co-creator in business life is a vision that clearly outruns all competitors!

CHAPTER 8

Laborem Exercens:
A Third World Perspective

by Ernest Bartell, C.S.C.

A CERTAIN FASCINATION WITH AND EVEN SEARCH FOR A MIDDLE WAY HAS engaged the attention of followers of papal social teaching since the appearance of Leo XIII's *Rerum Novarum* almost a century ago. In part this has been due to the heuristic framework of discussion of economic systems established in that first labor encyclical, retained in its successor, Pius XII's *Quadragesimo Anno*, and still evident in *Laborem Exercens*. In each encyclical, capitalism in some form is contrasted with socialism in some form, and both are found ethically wanting, especially in their treatment of workers. The gap between the depictions of the two systems is large and the insights leading to something better are sufficiently provocative, so that the reader is easily led along a quest for a Middle Way.

In the context of economic systems established by its predecessor encyclicals, *Laborem Exercens* is significant not for the additional clues it gives for the discovery of a Middle Way but for the manner in which it extends the geographic and methodological scope of the discussion. The setting of the early labor encyclicals was very obviously western industrial civilization and into the 1960's so was most of the commentary on papal social teaching.[1] The fact that *Laborem Exercens* was greeted with great celebration among the workers of Poland and that the word "solidarity" occurs nine times in a single section on the rights of workers might suggest the same cultural bias.[2] But the fact is that the same word was used earlier by John Paul II in *Redemptor Hominis* referring to a much broader context of international justice, and still earlier by John XXIII in his labor encyclical, *Mater et Magistra*.[3] It is *Mater et Magistra* which first develops seriously the international dimensions of social justice with some reference to the Third World. The social encyclical of Paul VI, *Populorum Progessio* then developed more fully the theme of Third World development as its principal focus.

A Papal Synthesis

What John Paul II has done is to draw together more integrally these two threads of his predecessors, the condition of workers in industrialized societies and the development of Third World societies. The unifying pattern on which these two threads are woven is the theological treatment by the Pope of the worker as human person, that is as the subject of all economic activity, not simply as the object or beneficiary of an economic process. As subject of economic activity the worker shares in the creative activity of God himself.

To establish this point theologically, John Paul II interprets the first chapter of the book of Genesis with a somewhat different emphasis than his predecessors. For Pius XI "work made its appearance in the world under the sign of sin—a truth which is too often forgotten."[4] For Pius XII there was the "profound thought . . . that, after the Fall, God imposed work upon the first man so that he would have to gain his bread from the soil in the sweat of his brow."[5] For John Paul II, however, "man, created in the image of God, shares by his work in the activity of the creator and . . . in a sense continues to develop that activity, and perfects it."[6] For John Paul II the first chapter of the Book of Genesis with its divine mandate for man as co-creator "is also in a sense the first 'gospel of work.' "[7] This more positive interpretation of human work in the Book of Genesis is apparently consistent with Jewish tradition as understood by the talmudic rabbinate.[8]

John Paul II acknowledges the effects of sin upon human work in "the sometimes heavy toil"[9] that has accompanied human work since man's fall. However, the mandate that he draws from Genesis for human effort applied to work is clearly more positive and materially productive than that of his predecessors. Pius XII, for example, refers to creation in relation to human work, but that reference does not pertain to the intrinsic value of work nor to a productive mandate for human work applied to the resources of nature. Work, he says, "should remind you always of the creative hand of God; it should raise your souls towards him, the sovereign Lawgiver, whose laws ought thus to be observed in the life of the factory."[10] For John Paul II, however, "man is the image of God partly through the mandate received from his creator to subdue, to dominate, the earth,"[11] and "man's dominion over the earth is achieved in and by means of work."[12] Moreover, John Paul II explains that "the expression 'subdue the earth' has an immense range. It means all the resources that the earth . . . contains" and for him the phrase embraces "the whole of modern reality and future phases of development."[13]

John Paul II goes further in his interpretation of Genesis. If man's mandate is to subdue and dominate the earth as "co-creator" in the image of God, then the criteria for moral evaluation of human work are to be found much more in the dignity of man as active creative subject of work than in the content of the work itself or in its material results. Whatever the content or outcome of man's work, the activities of his work effort "must all serve to realize his humanity, to fulfill the calling to be a person that is his by reason of his very humanity."[14] If man is, as the Pope says, a "subjective being capable of acting in a planned and rational way, capable of deciding about himself and with a tendency to self-realization,"[15] then his work must fulfill his self-interest in the deepest sense of that word.

From this starting point John Paul II is able to weave a fabric that not only extends the thread of Leo XIII's social teaching about labor within the major economic systems of the industrialized northern nations of the world, but also unites it to the newer threads of papal social teaching about Third World development introduced by John XXIII and Paul VI. John Paul II himself makes clear the importance of the Third World to his central thesis about human work when he says:

> . . . the analysis of human work in the light of the words concerning man's "dominion" over the earth goes to the very heart of the ethical and social question. This concept should also find a central place in the whole sphere of social and economic policy, both within individual countries and in the wider field of inter-

national and intercontinental relationships, particularly with reference to the tensions making themselves felt in the world not only between East and West but also between North and South.[16]

Moreover, it was over two and one-half years prior to the issuance of the encyclical that John Paul II used the same approach to human work in an address to about 100,000 low-income workers and their families in Guadalajara, Mexico. "Work," he said to the Mexicans in early 1979, "is not a curse, it is a blessing from God who calls man to rule the earth and transform it, in order that the divine work of creation may continue with man's intelligence and effort."[17] The clear attempt by John Paul II to interweave the concerns of the Third World with the historical thread of papal social teaching on labor has not excaped unnoticed in the less affluent areas of the world, expecially within the Catholic culture of the developing areas of Latin America. In his recent commentary on the encyclical, Gustavo Gutierrez, the Latin American liberation theologian, writes that:

> . . . it is not sufficient to underline the fact that the Pope situates himself in an international perspective; it is equally necessary to emphasize that his considerations in this respect are marked by the problematic of the Third World. The first social encyclicals were situated above all in a European context. *Populorum Progressio* then clearly intended to take a different position. The present encyclical reinforces this latter point of view. Therefore, it should not be strange that *Laborem Exercens* has been less well received in Europe than in the Third World.[18]

What Gutierrez says about European response may well apply to much of the response in the United States, and at least one reviewer, Daniel Seligman, writing in *Fortune*, appears to be in agreement, albeit backhanded, when he writes that "judging from the general tenor of *Laborem Exercens* . . . the Church is increasingly a sucker for Third World anti-imperialistic rhetoric."[19]

The encyclical has also received relatively wide coverage in Latin America, e.g., no less than 17 articles and commentaries in three newspapers and a newsmagazine within the limited and controlled press of Santiago, Chile. This coverage, along with the issuance of guides and aids by dioceses of the Church to facilitate reading of the encyclical by the Catholic public, suggests much wider popular dissemination of the document than in the United States.

In addition to expanding the geographic scope of papal social teaching on work, the emphasis which John Paul II gives to the human person as the creative subject of work has methodological implications that help distinguish *Laborem Exercens* from the earlier labor encyclicals. The focus on the human person as subject of work at once draws attention to the empirical, observable effects of work, and by extension, of all economic activities, structures and systems. In so doing *Laborem Exercens* is at once more experimental in its methodology than its predecessors. Ethical judgments are made about work, other economic actions, about economic institutions and systems, not simply on the basis of conclusions reached in logical discourse, but through the application of normative criteria to descriptive analysis of observable human experience. Consistent with the pastoral thrust of much of the teaching of John Paul II, the ethical evaluation of work in *Laborem Exercens* is not simply derived from abstract consideration of natural law with a legal definition of the nature of man and the rights of man, but from the concrete experience of the human person as subject. "Work is a good thing for man—a good thing for his humanity . . ," says the Pope, "because through work man not only transforms nature, adapting it to his own needs, but he also achieves fulfillment as a human being and indeed in a sense becomes more a human being."[20]

The social value of work is determined not simply by reference in earlier labor encyclicals and the subject of considerable philosophical discussion among commentators on those encyclicals.[21] For John Paul II the social value of work emerges also from the point of view of man as the subject of work and is therefore much more experientially observed and measured, because the social value "that emerges from this point of view—that of the subject of work—concerns the great society to which man belongs on the basis of particular cultural and historical links."[22]

What John Paul II has done methodologically is to combine ethical principle and theological anthropology in making his moral judgments, linking the two in his vision of the human person as subject of work, The combination of diverse human experience and ethical principle allows him to make some contemporary judgments of economic life while retaining continuity with the philosophic thought of his predecessors.

John Paul II acknowledges the significance of such diversity when he discusses the historical development of relationships between labor and capital:

The interaction between the worker and the tools and means of
production has given rise to the development of various forms of
capitalism—parallel with various forms of collectivism—into
which other socioeconomic elements have entered as a consequence of new concrete circumstances . . .[23]

However, the admisssion of historical and cultural diversity to the
methodology of papal social teaching on labor when coupled with a
broadened scope of concern to include Third World development
strategies appears to remove distinctive meaning from the analytic
quest for a so-called Middle or Third Way between opposing models
of economic life affecting the worker. There ought to be as many "middle" ways as there are possibilities for improving the performance of
specific local, national and international economic systems with respect
to the development of the human person as both subject and object of
work. What the encyclical offers are principles for making moral
judgments and the application of those principles to specific examples
of economic behavior, institutions and systems. The strength of this approach lies in the possibility of flexible interpretation of the encyclical
within particular historic and cultural settings. The weakness lies in the
ease with which the encyclical can be used to justify particular ideological commitments. Both the strength and the weakness of the encyclical are apparent in the application of papal social teaching to the Third
World.

Economic Systems: Growth vs. Distribution

Despite the expansion in scope and methodology, much of the teaching in the encyclical is developed around comparisions of capitalism
and socialism in the tradition of *Rerum Novarun* and *Quadragesimo
Anno*. The treatment of these perennial adversaries by John Paul II
benefits in its application to the issues of Third World development
from its openness to observable experience while remaining vulnerable
to partisan interpretation in the debates over alternative ideologically
inspired models of Third World development.

One of these debates in its simplest form pits the importance of
economic growth and the creation of new and technologically more
productive wealth against the importance of the distributional problems
and issues that arise in the development process. These latter include

the problems and issues of equity or justice in the distribution of income and wealth, both domestically and internationally; they include questions of access to self-actualizing economic opportunity and broad-based participation in economic decision-making at every level of society from the individual firm upward; they include concern for the relationship between economic wealth and political power as well as for representative participation in the determination of public policies affecting economic life; they include also the challenges of national self-determination and self-reliance in an interrelated global economy.

At one rudimentary, but basic, level the debate between so-called capitalist and socialist models of development in the Third World has been a debate between the relative priorities of growth vs. distribution. Of course, no model places exclusive emphasis on either priority. If capitalist models tend to emphasize the importance of free markets to stimulate economic growth, still there is room for an interest in "growth with equity." If socialist models tend to emphasize government intervention in the economy and public ownership of the means of production, still there is concern for savings and capital accumulation for economic growth. Although virtually all development models deal in some way with both growth and distribution, it is the relative weights or priorities given to each set of objectives in development strategies that separate them. And it is the ideological commitments of the adherents of the models that set the priorities of the models and help give them their labels of capitalist or socialist.

Those who argue for the primacy of economic growth over distribution in meeting the challenge of Third World development like to point out that the most spectacular examples of modern-day Third World development have occurred in capitalist countries where free markets, private property and the economic incentives they generate have stimulated the human effort, creative initiative and willingness to assume risks that are necessary for the creation of new productive wealth. Taiwan, South Korea, Hong Kong and Singapore are familiar examples. Indeed, Milton Friedman used Hong Kong rather than any United States setting in the public television adaptation of his popular best-seller, *Free to Choose*, to illustrate the positive relationship between rapid economic growth and the workings of a competitive free enterprise system with minimal government interference in economic life.

Examples such as these are easily contrasted with the comparatively poor growth performance of many socialist Third World economies. A collection of independent analyses of development in Third World socialist economies, including North Korea, Cuba, Guyana, Tanzania, Angola, Iraq and Syria, in a recent issue of *World Development* weaves a common thread of unimpressive growth performance, whatever the other merits of the disparate development models, e.g., in meeting basic human needs of the population. After reviewing data on development performance of advanced as well as Third World countries, Jameson and Wilber in their introductory article conclude that "if an attempt is made to compare two groups of roughly similar countries, one socialist, the other capitalist, average growth in GNP is higher for the capitalist countries."[24]

Obviously, a number of factors contribute to growth performance: the political circumstances surrounding the establishment of a socialist regime; economic resources and social preconditions for development; the development strategies chosen by the socialist government; and the organizational structures introduced by a socialist government, especially those pertaining to planning and to incentives.[25] Still, for those who defend capitalist approaches to development on the basis of the overriding importance of growth to the attainment of development objectives, the theological starting point of the encyclical offers support and encouragement. Growth in capitalist models is driven by individual self-interest, human initiative, discovery and technological invention, by entrepreneurial risk-taking and hard work. And all of this is compatible with John Paul II's definition of co-creation, of man's call to subdue and dominate the earth, and with John Paul's emphasis on man as the creative active subject of his work.

Moreover, John Paul II's critique of socialism relies more on experience and observation than upon abstract principle. Like his predecessors, John Paul II allows for both private and public ownership of productive property. However, whereas Pius XI spoke in rather abstract terms about rights of ownership and about the state or the larger society as legitimate owners of productive property when necessary for the common good, John Paul II attempts to be more concrete in adding a lesson from experience, that is, the danger of bureaucratic control of productive property in the name of public ownership.[26] Moreover, except for a strong endorsement of labor unions[27] the encyclical contains no radical proposals for a reorganization of work. Even unions are urged not to succumb to class selfishness in pressing their demands, and they are urged not to play politics or even to have too close links with political parties.[28] Suggestions for sharing by workers in profits, ownership and management of enterprises are sufficiently general to be consistent with conventional western models of profit sharing, stock purchase plans and the newly fashionable team approaches to improve productivity in heavy industries such as automobiles.[29]

Consequently, it is not surprising that *Laborem Exercens* has been well-received by advocates of capitalist systems in both the economically advanced and less advanced countries. Michael Novak, writing in the *National Review* imagines John Locke, Adam Smith, Montesquieu, Madison and Jefferson, among others, "cheering John Paul II along."[30] The same is true of policymakers in Chile, which has been noted during the administration of General Pinochet for its reliance upon private industry and the free play of the marketplace to achieve economic growth despite relatively high unemployment as well as for a labor policy considered one of the most restrictive in all of Latin America. In a country in which labor unions are allowed to bargain only at the level of the individual firm and are forbidden to engage in political activity, the Minister of Labor, Miguel Kast, delivered a lecture at the National University of Chile soon after the appearance of the encyclical and identified it with the social policies and labor policies of the Pinochet government.[31] General Pinochet himself, at the end of a speech to 2,500 Chilean labor union members produced a copy of the encyclical and commented that after a first look, "the Pope is saying to me, 'Mr. President, you are doing well, the government is doing well by its workers.' "[32]

However, after making this comment the general added with a smile, "Now I must see what a second reading tells me."[33] And well he might. For, despite the emphasis in the encyclical on the biblical mandate of co-creation, John Paul II simply fails to follow up with any explicit statements about the importance of wealth creation or economic growth to development, especially to development of the economically less advanced countries. There are many references to the Third World, to the condition of labor there, particularly in the agricultural economies; to the distribution of income within Third World countries and between the Third and First worlds; to the political and social relationships between workers and employers; to the role of multinational corporations and the working of the international economy, all in reference to less economically advanced countries. But none of these references is in relation to growth and the creation of new wealth. The common theme in all is the theme of distribution—distribution of income, wealth, economic opportunity and political power.

Instead of following his biblical treatment of work as co-creation with at least an expression of support for the potential and historical record of capitalism as a vehicle for the exercise of creative human initiative, John Paul II offers an indictment drawn from the analysis of his predecessors. At the heart of the indictment is the traditional papal condemnation of materialism, which John Paul II, like his predecessors, identifies as a corrosive danger of both capitalist and socialist systems. However, there is both a practical materialism and a theoretical materialism in the thought of John Paul II.[34]

In his brief treatment of theoretical materialism, "which professes to reduce spiritual reality to a superfluous phenomenon," John Paul II is fairly evenhanded in his criticism of capitalism and socialism. That kind of materialism in either system simply violates "the primacy of the person over things."[35]

However, it is in his assessment of practical materialism, "a particular way of evaluating things"[36] which simply gives too much weight to the attractiveness of material things in the hierarchy of human priorities, that the Pope comes down hard on capitalism, especially on its emphasis on profit maximization and its treatment of labor. In perhaps his only explicit acknowledgement of the wealth-creating accomplishments of historical capitalism John Paul II prefers to focus on the distributional effects of the process, especially the human costs imposed upon labor. The resulting historical conflict between labor and capital, he emphasizes,

> did not originate merely in the philosophy and economic theories of the 18th century; rather it originated in the whole of the economic and social practice of that time, the time of the birth and rapid development of industrialization, in which what was mainly seen was the possibility of vastly increasing material wealth, means, while the end, that is to say man, who should be served by the means, was ignored. It was this practical error that struck a blow first and foremost against human labor, against the working man, and caused the ethically just social reaction . . .[37]

The conflict between capital and labor that emerged in the period of early industrial development of the economically advanced countries of the world is for John Paul II not a philosophic conclusion, but an actual struggle against exploitation:

> between the small but highly influential group of entrepreneurs, owners or holders of the means of production, and the broader

multitude of people who lacked these means and who shared in the process of production solely by their labor. The conflict originated in the fact that the workers put their powers at the disposal of the entrepreneurs and these, following the principle of maximum profit, tried to establish the lowest possible wages for the work done by the employees.[38]

The Pope is careful to point out that looking at human work as "merchandise" was an especially widespread phenomenon in the first half of the 19th century and that since then explicit expressions of this sort "have almost disappeared and have given way to more human ways of thinking about work and evaluating it."[39] However, the Pope is quick to add that the danger of treating work as a commodity and the labor force as an impersonal economic input still exists. Further on, he asserts that the conflict and exploitation in labor markets characterized by profit-maximizing entrepreneurs and capitalists on the demand side and unpropertied wage earners on the supply side "is by no means yet over."[40]

The Third World Application

For some commentators on Catholic social teaching from the more economically advanced nations these traditional descriptions of capitalist development from papal social teaching are mostly irrelevant to contemporary capitalist achievements and potential, and reflect an unwarranted anti-capitalist bias in Catholic social teaching.[41] In fact, however, labor markets in much of the Third World, including the Catholic countries of Latin America, can and do reflect the central characteristics of the classical capitalist models.

On the demand side are the employers who own or control productive capital, a large component of which in less developed countries consists of land and natural resources. For reasons rooted in colonial history, especially in Latin America, ownership of those productive resources has been, and in many countries continues to be, highly concentrated. Latin America among the three continents with the largest number of less-developed nations still has the highest concentration of productive land in the hands of a few owners according to the Food and Agriculture Organization.[42] Capital for industrialization in less-developed countries dependent upon private sources of capital must come from those with existing wealth or from outside the country. Either way, total domestic ownership of capital remains highly concentrated, so much so that even public markets for equity and loan capital are typically underdeveloped or non-existent.

On the supply side of labor markets in less-developed countries there is for all practical purposes an almost unlimited number of workers who for lack of educational or even nutritional resources, or lack of access to capital, are relatively unproductive. Under these circumstances the normal profit-maximizing behavior of employers will require them to pay no more than the subsistence wages dictated by the marketplace. The resulting distribution of income is as concentrated as the distribution of wealth that generated it, and so the poor remain poor.

In the capitalist model, the owners of capital might well reinvest their property income and entrepreneurs their profits to create new productive wealth, thereby increasing employment, and eventually productivity and wages of workers. However, there is no inherent or external rule in capitalist systems that requires such textbook behavior. Affluent families in Latin America and elsewhere have learned through many generations that their discretionary incomes can also be used for expensive consumer goods, usually imported from the developed countries, or can be invested more conveniently in investment opportunities already created in the developed world, or can simply be invested speculatively in land and other non-productive goods. Democratic institutions might moderate the distributional effects of labor markets functioning under conditions such as these, but there is nothing inherent in the working of capitalist development to provoke democratic political remedies for initially maldistributed endowments of productive capital of the kind associated with colonial Latin America.

If anything, history in Latin America has favored the reverse. The high concentration of ownership of productive wealth and income has in most nonsocialist nations favored a corresponding concentration of political power and social status. Nor are workable democratic solutions imposed easily from the outside as recent events in Central America have demonstrated.

And so it is not surprising that commentators on the encyclical in Latin America have found the critical anaylsis of capitalism in *Laborem Exercens* relevant, even to suggesting that it is directed specifically to Latin America. Alberto Maguiña Larco, writing in Peru, has observed that an address of John Paul II announcing the encyclical and scheduled two days before the original publication date of the encyclical (subsequently postponed because of the attempt on the Pope's life) explicitly stressed Latin American antecedents. He notes that John Paul II quoted liberally from his own pronouncements about the rights and liberation of the working poor and the identification of the Church with the poor, enunciated previously in a speech to workers in Sao Paulo, Brazil, and at the synod of Latin American bishops in Puebla.[43]

Moreover, there is no doubt in the minds of Latin American commentators that the analysis of the relationships between private capital and labor in *Laborem Exercens* is Marxist. "John Paul II uses in his *Laborem Exercens* Marxist analysis, categories and concepts with pleasure, lavishly and advantageously," says Maguiña.[44]

Similarly, for Gustavo Gutierrez the "structural conflict" between capital and labor is "in a certain way the theme of the entire encyclical, wherein the confrontation between capital and labor is considered the 'great conflict' of our times."[45] The chairman of the ecomonics department at the Catholic University of Peru in his commentary on the encyclical finds it significant that, in his historical analysis, John Paul II might have identified any number of conflictive relationships in the production process:

> For example, he could have distinguished between owners, managers, employees, administrators, skilled and unskilled workers, scientists, engineers, etc., etc. Correspondingly, he could have dealt with the conflicts that occupy the attention of many intellectuals, above all in the industrialized countries. For example, conflicts between owners and administrators, between professionals and managers, between skilled and unskilled workers, etc., etc.[46]

But instead the Pope chooses a "cross section more profound, more essential. The relevant social relation is that of the capitalists on one side and wage earners on the other."[47]

For these authors the source of the essential conflict is in the distribution of ownership of the means of production that permits the existence of labor markets which reduce labor to an impersonal instrument of production and leave unpropertied workers as powerless suppliers of labor in a labor market completely dependent upon production decisions made by those who own and control productive wealth. So long as private ownership of productive property permits this separation of the worker from the means of production and allows a division in society whereby those without property are left defenseless against the economic, political and social decisions of those who own and control productive property, then private ownership is contrary to the primacy of man over things as defined by John Paul II in his interpretation of man's universal mandate in Genesis to dominate the earth.

In calling for a positive relationship between capital and labor and in establishing the moral justification for ownership of productive property, public or private, John Paul II establishes a criterion grounded in production rather than in consumption. The means of production according to John Paul II:

> cannot be possessed against labor, they cannot even be possessed for possession's sake, because the only legitimate title to their possession — whether in the form of private ownership or in the form of public or collective ownership — is that they should serve labor . . .[48]

What John Paul II has done is to define a criterion of social justice that links the questions of distribution to those of production or economic growth. For him equity in distribution is justified not simply by the consumption needs of workers, e.g., in the living wage, though these are of course morally legitimate. Rather, equity in distribution is judged also by its contribution to the productive potential of a society's workers. A concentration of ownership and control of productive resources in the hands of those whose savings, investment and consumption decisions do not enable the realization of the productive potential of the population of workers violates the principle of co-creation in the interpretation of Genesis by John Paul II. Moreover, the same criterion applies to public as well as private ownership.

The operational link between the distribution of ownership of productive capital, with all that this implies for the distribution of economic opportunity, political power and social status, and the production or growth possibilities of a developing country is acknowledged by John Paul II to be stronger than in the developed countries and is understandably stressed in Latin American commentary on *Laborem Exercens*.[49] This is not surprising in light of the fact that the success stories of sustained economic growth in the free-enterprise capitalist economies of Taiwan and South Korea have been accompanied by a reduction in the inequalities of income distribution, while the painful boom-and-bust experiences of capitalist developing economies in Latin America like Argentina and Chile have been accompanied by increases in the inequalities of income distribution.

Linking distribution to production and growth possibilities also permits a more integral ethical evaluation of unemployment in papal social teaching on economic systems and of the relationship of technology to unemployment.[50] Both of these issues have relatively great significance in Third World countries with high rates of both underemployment and open unemployment. The allocation of scarce productive resources to industries that require heavy capital investment while creating few jobs in order to produce expensive high-technology products for the lucky few with sufficiently high incomes from property, profits or professional service to afford them, may well not meet the test of the primacy of man over things in a Third World society with 20 percent unemployment and 30 percent underemployment, despite the efficiency of its markets for capital, labor and final products.

Certainly it is clear that John Paul II finds little justification for a distribution of income based solely on the workings of the marketplace to set wages, profits and returns on property. For John Paul II the "gospel of work" with man at the center as the active subject of work means that "the basis for determining the value of human work is not primarily the kind of work being done, but the fact the one who is doing it is a person."[51] For John Paul II it is not a question of work being evaluated by the economic system, but quite the contrary:

> the justice of a socioeconomic system and, in each case, its just functioning, deserve in the final analysis to be evaluated by the way in which man's work is properly remunerated in the system . . . in every case a just wage is the concrete means of verifying the justice of the whole socioeconomic system . . .[52]

It is not clear what reward is morally justifiable for the exercise of individual human initiative in the creation of new wealth and economic growth according to the teaching of John Paul II. But it is clear that his statements in *Laborem Exercens* are scarcely more compatible than those of his predecessors with statements of contemporary economists like P.T. Bauer who decry redistributive taxation as unjustifiably stifling to individual freedom and initiative in less developed countries,[53] or like Nobel prize-winning Frederich Hayek who, in a published interview in Lima, Peru, condemned all income taxation and dismissed social justice as subjective opinion irrelevant to the natural law of the marketplace.[54] In any event it is true that the rights of entrepreneurs or employers receive no mention in *Laborem Exercens* as one Latin American commentator has duly noted.[55]

Nevertheless, the criticism by John Paul II of entrepreneurial behavior in a capitalist system is neither a historical nor a theoretically absolute condemnation of the rationality, efficiency and growth potential of a free market system. It is rather a criticism of the uneven distribution of the necessary economic, political and social preconditions for equity combined with a condemnation of the practical materialism that can distort men's perceptions of their ultimate self-interest. Without the necessary preconditions and without an operational hierarchy of personal values compatible with the Gospel vision of man, the material achievements of capitalist growth will simply be outweighed by the social and moral costs in the form of waste and degradation of the human person and potential through unemployment and lack of meaningful participation by great numbers of people.

The International Economy

These same principles apply to the limited analysis of the international economy in *Laborem Exercens* when John Paul II acknowledges the importance of international trade and the interdependence of nations.[56] In his earlier encyclical, *Redemptor Hominis*, he affirms that "the laws of healthy competition must be allowed to lead the way" but at the same time he calls for a redistribution of wealth and control on behalf of the development of economically less advanced nations.[57] In *Laborem Exercens* he acknowledges the tensions that exist between "the North and the South" and calls attention to the teaching of John XXIII in *Mater et Magistra* and of Paul VI in *Populorum Progressio*.[58]

As he might have done in his treatment of domestic development, John Paul II could also have stressed those aspects of free markets in international trade and finance that favor wealth creation as a social example of man's efforts to carry out the creative mandate to dominate the earth. He is explicitly conscious of the role of technology[59] in economic development and might have noted the possibilities for technology transfer from rich nations to poor nations made possible by the activities of multinational firms in the international economy. Instead, as in the analysis of domestic development, John Paul II prefers to stress the occasions for "exploitation or injustice" that are the result of the workings of an interdependent international economy:

> For instance the highly industrialized countries, and even more the businesses that direct on a large scale the means of industrial production (the companies referred to as multinational or transnational), fix the highest possible prices for their products, while

trying at the same time to fix the lowest possible prices for raw materials or semimanufactured goods. This is one of the causes of an ever increasing disproportion between national incomes. The gap between most of the richest countries and the poorest ones is not diminishing or being stabilized, but is increasing more and more to the detriment, obviously, of the poor countries. Evidently this must have an effect on local labor policy and on the worker's situation in the economically disadvantaged societies. Finding himself in a system thus conditioned, the direct employer fixes working conditions below the objective requirements of the workers, especially if he himself wishes to obtain the highest possible profits from the business which he runs . . .[60]

These harsh words about the working of the international economy, and especially about the behavior of multinational firms, when taken in the context of the scope and pastoral methodology of the encyclical as well as his statements elsewhere about healthy competition, do not represent a philosophical condemnation of the system of international markets or of the businesses that operate in it. The practical criticism being made is simply that, given the present distribution of ownership and control of the world's productive resources, the poor nations of the world and especially the poor within those nations simply don't have adequate opportunity to participate and compete creatively to the extent of their human potential.

Multinational investors do create jobs and transfer technology. But in a competitive world economy positive effects of job creation are often tentative and dependent upon comparative labor costs and returns to capital available elsewhere. The local contribution of multinationals is also dependent upon the behavior of local employers, owners and controllers of capital, who are often the intermediaries, partners or suppliers of the multinationals. Without access to the education, health and other forms of human and physical capital that characterize the many generations of accumulation within the developed nations, the poor nations and especially the poor within those nations have little to offer except their cheap labor and the kinds of agricultural and semi-industrial products that occupy a shrinking part of the budgets of the industrialized countries. Even oil is no longer the cure-all for the lucky few it once was. Moreover, the transfer of inappropriate technology, the convergence of special investment and consumption interests of local commercial and political elites with the objectives of mulitinational firms undermine potential benefits of multinational activity to the poor within developing countries. What John Paul II is saying here is simply that the social costs of profit-maximizing multinational activity can outweigh the benefits.

Nevertheless, given his focus on the creative potential of man, John Paul II is careful to avoid discounting the importance of self-reliance in order to place all the blame for the failures of Third World development on its dependence upon the industrialized world. In fact, there is less emphasis on international dependency as a source of the problems of the Third World poor in *Laborem Exercens* than in *Populorum Progressio* of Paul VI and much less attention to international dependency as a source of oppression of the Third World poor than in the writings of Latin American liberation theologians. There is no mention, for example, of the discriminatory effects of trade policies of advanced countries towards exports of the less developed countries, though there is some mild criticism of immigration policies in economically advanced countries.[61]

Attempts to place the principal blame for the failures of Third World development upon the behavior of the economically advanced nations, the oppression of the so-called periphery by the center, have been controversial within the Latin American Church.[62] They have also been rejected elsewhere in the Church of the Third World, e.g., in a strongly worded pastoral letter of the Catholic bishops of Uganda in 1981.[63]

At the same time it is difficult to deny the adverse consequences of recent phenomena in international markets upon the development of the less advanced countries, regardless of their own internal efforts. Between 1950 and 1980, for example, the six relatively unendowed countries of Central America enjoyed rapid growth which included an 1800 percent increase in exports, an increase of industrial production from 11 percent to 18 percent of total output, diversification in export agriculture, rising wages, a growing middle class and the emergence of more democratic institutions. As a result, however, of the two OPEC oil crises in the last decade and the increases in interest costs for foreign loans, along with declines in world prices for most tropical agricultural products, the same Central American countries have suffered a dramatic reversal. Average industrial growth dropped by 60 percent in the last half of the 1970's compared to the previous decade, and since then growth in total output has averaged only 1-3½ percent in most of the six countries while government deficits and inflation continue to escalate.

Although it can be argued that the two countries with relatively democratic governments have fared better than authoritarian regimes, both socialist (Nicaragua) and capitalist (El Salvador and Guatemala), all have been more adversely affected by changes in international markets than industrialized countries. Moreover, the burden of unemployment and inflation is distributed unequally, as was the growth, and the impression is that it is the poor who are most vulnerable.[64]

The combination of high oil prices, high international interest rates and soft world markets for primary products has had comparable adverse effects on the struggling economies of black Africa. So, it is not surprising that, as pastor, John Paul II, without succumbing to the excesses of international dependency theory, is on balance critical of the impact of profit maximization in world markets on the less developed countries of the world, and especially upon the poor within those countries. For John Paul II, in the international economy as well as the domestic economy, it is the total results of an economic system on the working lives of all the people that constitute the criterion by which the system is judged.[65]

As noted earlier, the analysis of John Paul II has been called Marxist, and at least one Latin American commentator has pointed out that the experimental criticisms of historical socialism in *Laborem Exercens* are much milder than the ideological characterizations of "atheistic materialism" in the conservative Catholic press in Latin America.[66] And it is true that the majority of the criticisms of socialism in *Laborem Exercens* are directed at the negative effects of socialist bureaucracies. However, bureaucratic authoritatianism is not limited to socialist societies, as an entire literature on the regimes of countries like Brazil, Argentina, Uruguay and Chile has demonstrated.[67]

Nevertheless, for those looking for radical or revolutionary remedies for the deficiencies and excesses of capitalist experience, *Laborem Exercens* is a disappointing source. The Pope eschews violence and seeks a peaceful elimination of the conflicts between capital and labor, or perhaps better, between those who own and control capital and those who do not. As mentioned earlier, his recommendations of profit-sharing and employee participation in ownership and management are scarcely novel in industrialized countries, though surely scarce in Third World capitalist economies. At the international level, his references in *Laborem Exercens* to the work of the International Labor Organization and the Food and Agricultural Organization of the United States are less sweeping than this earlier call in *Redemptor Hominis* for "the indispensable transformation of the structures of economic life" with "economic development . . . constantly programmed and realized within a perspective of universal joint development of each individual and people."[68]

Conclusion: A Delicate Balance

In *Laborem Exercens* John Paul II tries not to engage in the intellectual exercise of creating and destroying abstract models of extreme and incompatible economic systems, but simply acknowledges the actual diversity of competing systems, not only in the industrialized world, but especially in the less developed nations. And so his recommendations are neither radical, nor revolutionary, nor do they logically point to a single "Middle Way." Rather, his recommendations are reformist, of both predominantly capitalist and predominantly socialist systems. Acknowledging the wealth of existing scientific analysis and proposals covering the vast global array of existing economic institutions, policies and systems, John Paul II tries always to strike a delicate balance, avoiding single-minded endorsement of specific programs, policies and development strategies. He might have followed up on the implications of his teaching on co-creation favoring the creative potential of the human person with a systematic endorsement of policies and programs favoring free enterprise. But he did not. He might have followed up the implications of his teaching on co-creation favoring the primacy of man over things with an endorsement of a revolutionary restructuring of the world's economy and a radical redistribution of the ownership of the world's resources. But he did not. He might have been explicitly harsh on either private ownership or public ownership of productive capital. But he was not.

Instead in the cautionary balanced style of *Laborem Exercens* John Paul II offers criteria and examples for evaluating and reforming both the institutions and structures that govern economic life and also the personal behavior that shapes and is shaped by those institutions and structures. As pastor and theologian he is concerned about the worker as human person and especially about the poor of the Third World, the poor nations and the poor within those nations. In a phrase that resonates with the language of liberation theology and the 1979 document of the Latin American bishops at Puebla, he refers to the Church as "the church of the poor."[69]

As investigator and teacher he justifies and emphasizes the importance of the interrelated distribution issues, that is, the distribution of income, wealth, social status, political power, opportunity, and participation to the creative productivity of the human person. And this may be one of the most significant contributions of *Laborem Exercens* to the tradition of papal social teaching. The distributional criteria in *Laborem Exercens* are not simply a matter of the justice that is akin to charity, whereby the "haves" are morally obligated to share with the "have-nots" of the world. Instead, social justice is defined as well by the imperatives of growth that demand a distribution of the fruits of man's economic, social and political efforts that will come closest to realizing the creative potential of all persons, not just the few who have the means and ability to play a particular game, capitalist or socialist in emphasis. In linking distribution to growth in his teaching on co-creation John Paul II has also linked two principal and ongoing themes in the social teaching of his predecessors, namely, the rights of workers and the development of peoples. In doing it pastorally and experientially, at least in part, he has not tried to define the parameters of a Middle Way. Instead, his criteria for ethical evaluation are presumably applicable to the mechanisms of international markets as well as to individual small-scale grass-roots experiments in culturally integrated economic and sociopolitical development.[70]

It may well be argued that the format of an encyclical letter is simply inadequate to a task that is global in geographic scope, eclectic in its methodology and vast in its ambitions for synthesis and for balance. For those seeking clear and specific guidance for concrete and practical situations the inevitable generality and brevity of the elaboration of the themes in the encyclical are likely to be disappointing, if not confusing and frustrating. The notion of "indirect employer" for example is so broad as to include everything from local governmental agencies and individual multinational corporations to the impersonal workings of an entire international market economy.[71] The phrase becomes a convenient catch-all for all the elements of national and international interdependence affecting the lives of workers.

Similarly, the brief treatment of a broad range of issues in the encyclical inclines towards raising questions that are nowhere acknowledged. The link between distribution and growth, for example, raises questions of intergeneration equity, i.e., how much should the present generation sacrifice for greater returns to future generations? There are also innumerable sensitive, but unaddressed trade-offs, e.g., between the welfare of workers in advanced societies and those in the Third World. How much unemployment and dislocation, for example, should workers in advanced countries accept to create opportunities for those in less developed countries? Or, what is the appropriate trade-off between the welfare of rural workers and that of urban workers in the typical dual economy of many Third World countries, where a rise in farm incomes means a rise in urban food prices? And the entire question of optimal rates of population growth, if any, for fulfilling the biblical mandate of co-creation is nowhere mentioned.

Given the mismatch between the scope of the encyclical and its size, the list of unaddressed issues might continue endlessly. But that would be unfair. *Laborem Exercens* has extended the tradition of papal social teaching one more step towards the universal reality that is the responsibility of those who would live the Gospel fully. The encyclical may finally be just one more small step for co-creation, but that is better than none.

NOTES

1. See, for example, Jean-Yves Calvez, S.J. and Jacques Perrin, S.J., *The Church and Social Justice* (Chicago: Henry Regnery Co., 1961), esp. Chs. XVI through XIX, and John Cronin, S.S. and Harry Flannery, *The Church and the Workingman* (New York: Hawthorn Books, 1965), esp. Part II.

2. *Laborem Exercens*, Para. 8. All citations are to the text published by the United States Catholic Conference: Publication No. 825, Office of Publishing Services.

3. *Redemptor Hominis* (RH) 16 and *Mater et Magistra*, 157. It is interesting to observe the emphasis given to the section on worker solidarity (8) in *Laborem Exercens* by Latin American commentators. See, for example, CEP, *Sobre El Trabajo Humano* (Lima, Peru: Centro de Estudios y Publicaciones, 1982), especially the articles by Gustavo Gutierrez and Rolando Ames.

4. Pius XI, address, Sept. 18, 1938 cit. in Calvez and Perrin, *op. cit.*, p. 227.

5. Pius XII, address, June 13, 1943, *cit. in.* Calvez and Perrin, *op. cit.*, p. 227.

6. Para. 24.

7. *Ibid.*

8. Seymour Siegel, "A Jewish View of Economic Justice," in *This World*, Number One, Winter/Spring 1982, pp. 70-78.

9. Para. 9.

10. Pius XII, address, June 13, 1943, *cit. in.* Calvez and Perrin, p. 229.

11. Para. 4.

12. Para. 5.

13. Para. 4.

14. Para. 6.

15. *Ibid.*

16. Para. 7.

17. John Paul II, address in Guadalajara, Mexico, January 30, 1979, reprinted in Daughters of St. Paul (eds.) *Servant of Truth: Messages of John Paul II* (Boston: St. Paul Editions, 1979), p. 304.

18. Gustavo Gutierrez, "El Evangelio del Trabajo," in CEP, *op. cit.*, p. 19.

19. *Fortune*, Nov. 2, 1981, p. 63.

20. Para. 9.

21. Cf. Calvez and Perrin, "The pre-eminence of the common good," *op. cit.*, pp. 114-118.

22. Para. 10.

23. Para. 7. See also Para. 8, where John Paul II attributes to worker solidarity many of the changes that have occurred in both capitalist and communist systems.

24. Kenneth P. Jameson and Charles K. Wilber, "Socialism and Development," in *World Development*, Volume 9 Number 9/10, September/October 1981, p. 804. See also Crawford Young, *Ideology and Development in Africa* (New Haven: Yale University Press, 1982), esp. Ch. 4, "The African Capitalist State."

25. Jameson and Wilber, *loc. cit.*, p. 805.

26. Para. 14. Cf. *Quadragesimo Anno* 49.

27. Para. 20.

28. *Ibid.*

29. Para. 14.

30. *National Review*, October 16, 1981, p. 1210.

31. "Enciclica Coincide Con Metas Nacionales," in *El Mercurio*, (Santiago, Chile), October, 1981.

32. *El Mercurio*, September 17, 1981, pp. 1, 14.

33. *Ibid.*

34. Para. 13.

35. *Ibid.*

36. *Ibid.*

37. *Ibid.*

38. Para. 11.

39. Para. 7.

40. Para. 11.

41. See, for example, Michael Novak, *The Spirit of Democratic Capitalism* (New York: Simon and Shuster, 1982), Ch. XIV.

42. Food and Agricultural Organization of the United Nations, *Agriculture Toward 2000* (Rome: FAO, 1981), p. 87 and passim.

43. John Paul II, address (undelivered because of assasination attempt) published in *L'Osservatore Romano*, No. 20 (646), May 17, 1981, cit. in Alberto Maguiña Larco, "Enciclica Laborem Exercens: Radical Novedad," in *Que Hacer* (Lima, Peru) November, 1981, pp. 66-69.

44. Maguiña, *loc. cit.*, p. 65. Some U.S. commentators would agree: "Judging from the general tenor of *Laborem Exercens*, the Church remains wedded to socialist economics," writes Daniel Seligman, *loc. cit.*

45. Gutierrez, *loc. cit.*, p. 53.

46. Javier Iguiñiz, "Conflicto entre Trabajo y Capital en la Presente Fase Historica," in CEP, *op. cit.*, p. 122.

47. *Ibid.*

48. Para. 14.

49. Para. 8 and Iguiñiz, *loc. cit.*, pp. 124 ff.

50. Para. 18. For a Latin American commentary see Carlos Chipoco, "Los Derechos de los Hombres de Trabajo," in CEP, *op. cit.*, pp. 142-3.

51. Para. 6; Cf. Para. 8.

52. Para. 19.

53. See, for example, P.T. Bauer, "Ecclesiastical Economics is Envy Exalted," in *This World, loc. cit.*, pp. 56-69 and *Equality, The Third World and Economic Delusion* (Cambridge: Harvard University Press, 1982.)

54. Interview in *La Prensa* (Lima, Peru), February 5, 1981, p. 10.

55. Chipico, *loc. cit.*, pp. 132-3.

56. Para. 17.

57. *Redemptor Hominis*, Para. 16.

58. Para. 7.

59. Para. 5.

60. Para. 17.

61. Para. 23. Cf., for example, Gustavo Gutierrez, *The Theology of Liberation* (Maryknoll: Orbis Books, 1973)

62. See, for example, Joseph Ramos, "Reflections on Gustavo Gutierrez's Theology of Liberation," and "Dependency and Development: An Attempt to Clarify the Issues," in Michael Novak (ed.) *Liberation South, Liberation North* (Washington: American Enterprise Institute for Public Policy Research, 1981), pp. 50-67.

63. *Be Converted and Live, Pastoral Letter of the Uganda Hierarachy* (Kampala: St. Paul Publications, 1981), esp. sections 18-19, titled "To Blame Others."

64. See "Central America's War," *The Economist*, 27 March-2 April, 1982, pp. 17-23, esp. p. 18.

65. Para. 17.

66. Rolando Ames, "El Trabajo y El Hombre, "CEP, *op. cit.*, p. 97.

67. See, for example, David Collier (ed.) *The New Authoritarianism in Latin America* (Princeton: Princeton University Press, 1979) esp. A.O. Hirschman, "The Turn to Authoritarianism in Latin America and its Economic Determinants," pp. 61-98 and Guillermo O'Donnell, "Tensions in the Bureaucratic Authoritarian State and the Question of Democracy," pp. 285-318.

68. *Redemptor Hominis*, Para. 16. Since *Laborem Exercens* John Paul II has subsequently spoken of the need for "constant revision" of the world's political and economic systems to promote human dignity. See the *New York Times*, Sunday, April 4, 1982, p. 13.

69. Para. 8.

70. See, for example, the analysis of the Sarvodaya experiment in Sri Lanka by Denis Goulet in *Survival with Integrity: Sarvodaya at the Crossroads* (Colombo, Sri Lanka: Marga Institute, 1981), esp. Part I.

71. Para. 17.

CHAPTER 9

Women in the Workplace: Challenges and Opportunities

by Andrea Lee, IHM and Amata Miller, IHM

THE SCOPE OF A SYMPOSIUM ON THE RECENT ENCYCLICAL OF JOHN PAUL II ON human work, *Laborem Exercens*, is likely to be sweeping and diverse given the centrality of work in human experience and its multiple facets. From the myriad of possible areas of analysis, we have chosen a micro-analytic one which not only springs from our own identity and experience as women, but also reflects the evolution of a phenomenon which has already wrought significant change upon world economic, social and political structures—the increasing presence of women in the world of work outside of the home. Some analysts claim that this phenomenon embodies the potential for changes equal in degree and scope to those evident during the transition from an agricultural to an industrial society.[1] The reality and implications of an exponential growth in the number of women who work outside the home are of immediate concern and interest to economists and social scientists, as well as to the controllers of work environments. Eli Ginzburg, chairman of the National Commission for Manpower says:

> This (women working outside the home) is the single most outstanding phenomenon of this century. It is a worldwide phenomenon,

an integral part of the changing economy, and a changing society. Its secondary and tertiary consequences are really unchartable.[2]

It is our conviction that bringing the feminist lens to bear upon the discussion at this predominantly male symposium will raise some useful questions about the realities of women in the workplace, the intersection of thought themes in feminist theory and the encyclical and, in the original language of the symposium title, to pose a "religious challenge to corporate power."

It is our hope that by focusing on the centrality of economic issues within the women's movement and the seriousness of the economic injustices facing women in the workplace, we may contribute toward a more full understanding of the true nature and societal implications of women's struggle at this time in history. (Too often, Catholic Church members and leaders dismiss the women's question as trivial or focus on the particular areas of dissonance between the feminist struggle and Church teaching, e.g., ordination or abortion issues, rather than on the fundamental areas of agreement between feminist principles and Catholic social teaching.)

Our topic then will be to explore the implications of the encyclical, *Laborem Exercens*, in terms of its congruence within feminist principles on work and its implications for the humanization of the world of work for women as well as for men. Some limitations in scope and design are presented in order to clarify the dimensions of this paper. Our discussion has evolved as a reflection on data and informed experience rather than as a formal research treatise. This reflective stance is built upon several years of monitoring the experience of women at work from our particular disciplines. We have attempted to outline the most pertinent themes without concluding that these are the only themes which might be developed. Our focus is on women as a marginalized group, but this focus is not meant to signify any less concern for workers in other marginalized groups. In addition, our emphasis on women working outside the home in no way lessens our regard for women's work within the home.

Finally, it is acknowledged that, for many feminists, a Church built on patriarchal exclusivity can have nothing credible to say to women or to other social institutions in need of reform of their treatment of women. There is sharp disagreement on this point, and it must be acknowledged that the authors are not in full agreement on whether the Church can speak credibly to corporations in this regard. However, our

Christian hope encourages us to search for possible linkages, to point out alliances in thought and to place trust in the growing congruence of thought among diverse groups. While acknowledging that a defensible focus on the points of divergence could be quite reasonably drawn, our emphasis is rather on the points of intersection.

The perspective of any writer has a significant impact on the outcome of an exploration and analysis. The authors of this paper share a sociopolitical perspective which places credence in the possibility and desirability of an evolutionary transformation of social realities from within institiutions and other social organizations. The two disciplines of economics and organizational theory offer at least the possibility that our reflections will transcend a single focus or mode of analysis. We will also address the question of women's work—what the encyclical says or does not say about it, and the implications for corporate powers were the encyclical vision to become reality for women—from a feminist perspective, a point of view which will be more thoroughly developed in the first major section of this paper.

Another perspective which, because of its ties with the design and theme of this symposium, must be discussed more fully at the outset is our view concerning the role, scope, and power of corporations within contemporary society. It is presented here as a prelude to our discussion of our selected topic and as a framework within which that discussion can occur.

Perspective on Corporations

We are not among those who see corporations as the incarnation of evil, solely responsible for all society's ills, incapable of any good. Rather we count ourselves among those who see corporations as key institutions exercising social, economic, and political power within our society and thus also extending their influence to many other parts of the world.

Though corporations originated as primarily economic structures, it can no longer be maintained that they have solely an economic function in our society, so central have many corporations and groups of corporations become to the life of local communities, individual states, and indeed, the whole nation. Thus, they can no longer hide behind the view that their sole responsibility is to their stockholders. With the increasing scope of their influence has come an increased scope of responsibility. The economic function of corporations now extends far beyond the provision of the products they produce. Because of the magnitude of the employment and income effects of their activities, the fate of local, regional, national and international economies is dramatically influenced by decisions made in corporate board rooms. In some cases these linkages are very clear—as in Youngstown, Ohio, or in Flint, Pontiac or Detroit, Michigan. In other cases the linkages are more obscure. But there is no escape from the responsibilities of power.

Another aspect of our view is that corporations are *one* institution among many in our society, thus they are part of the system which expresses the cultural values and the historic experiences of the American people who have, over time, created the economic system we have today. Economists describe it as a "Mixed Economy." (Some might perceive it today as a "Mixed-up Economy!") This connotes a combination of market and political decision-making processes to mobilize our resources in order to satisfy our needs and wants and to allocate the outcomes in accord with our societally determined standards of what makes a "good society."

Among the participants in this symposium, as among the American population, there are varying views of whether our present degree of "mix" is the preferred one to accomplish our purposes. Nevertheless it seems clear that social, economic, and political power are in fact shared, however uneasily, among private and public institutions today. The continual effort to develop societal processes which embody our deepest democratic principles in effective decision-making within all aspects of our communal life is one of the most challenging of pursuits. Corporations cannot by themselves create the "good society" as envisioned by the encyclical, but they *can* hinder its realization insofar as they seek to maintain myopic and antiquated views of their responsibility—views which do not reflect today's reality.

From the perspective of the authors, Catholic social tradition calls for a view of society as more than a collection of individuals whose pursuit of their own goals will realize the "greatest good for the greatest number." Our tradition as described once again in *Laborem Exercens* sees society as more than the sum of its parts, rather as having a life of its own which must be nurtured and guided by institutions with societal scope, seeking the *common good*. Corporations are called by Catholic social teaching, as are individuals and other ecomonic institutions, to help to develop democratic means whereby the good of *all* the people can be achieved. It calls for specific recognition that the market is not democratic in its allocation of either resources or products, and so must be complemented by other socio-economic-political institutions.

A third aspect of our view of corporations which we would like to present at the outset is that we view corporations as cross-cultural institutions with vast resources, experience, power, and capability which can be used as instruments for building community world-wide. In international circles multinational corporations are usually called "transnational enterprises" (TNE's). This connotes a broader perspective on their influence and their potential for constructive contributions to the building of a new world order—a perspective which the authors share.

Finally, it is important to state that we recognize the variety among corporations in their style, structure, policy, practice, and philosophy. Since they are human institutions there is rich diversity among them. Some are enlightened in their approach to human and societal concerns, while others seek to retain a nineteenth century "Robber Baron" perspective of management prerogatives and responsibility. The data presented here is the result of the operation of corporate structures as a whole and, as in any aggregation, individual variations are masked.

The remainder of this paper will be organized in three specific sections:

1. The Vision: An outline of feminist themes and threads of congruence and dissonance between selected themes in *Laborem Exercens* and the feminist principles.
2. The Reality: Current issues for women in the workplace.
3. Closing the Gap between Vision and Reality: Toward a transformed world: Areas for action.

These three sections will attempt to delineate the parameters and suggest some approaches to answers for the following questions: Where are the points of congruence between the feminist principles elucidated and those gleaned from the encyclical? Are there points of divergence and, if so, do they carry the capacity to neutralize the strength derived from points of congruence? If the discovery of congruent themes related to work in feminist theory and the encyclical, *Laborem Exercens*, suggest a credible vision of a preferred future for women in the work world, what are the dimensions of the present reality and the challenges they pose which look to this vision as worthy of our best human striving? If we have a glimpse of the vision and a clear grasp on our present reality, what concrete steps are possible in order to reduce the gap between vision and reality? Does the strength derived from the discovery of congruent themes offer any real hope for the transformation of the work realities of women? What is the "responsible response" of corporate powers to the growing convergence of value frameworks and principles among diverse social groupings?

The Vision: An Outline of Feminist Themes and Threads of Congruence and Dissonance Between Selected Themes in *Laborem Exercens* and Feminist Principles

Despite some initial anxiety that attempting to uncover points of congruence within a papal encyclical and the body of feminist ideology would prove to be an ill-advised procrustean adventure at best, there appear to be some areas of thought congruence as well as a few notes of stark dissonance. While the specific focus of this symposium, as well as the limits of space and time, do not permit a thorough analysis of themes in both, several surface as fruitful areas for exploration.

If one searches within the encyclical for a prescriptive plan of action toward transformation of the work world, disappointment is the most probable result. In the same way, a hope that feminist ideology will reflect undeniable unanimity, such that it embodies a single well-defined political strategy, is likely to go unfulfilled. The most that can be hoped for — and this is not necessarily an inferior outcome — is an heuristic guide for action and decision-making.

Most recently, the papal encyclicals have been precisely that — less pietistic, more prophetic; less a prescriptive or algorithmic approach to human activity than a statement of broad principle and a framework within which responsible action may occur and which is open to divergent descriptions for a preferred future. It could be argued successfully that the encyclical's "success" might be measured in terms of its force and power in guiding decisions, initiating positive change and innovation, and encouraging attitudinal and behavioral shifts. By avoiding inappropriate expectations of specificity and prescriptive accuracy, the reader encounters the freedom to explore the encyclical themes and their relevance as guides for action within particular nations, cultures, communities, and work environments.

A similar statement may be made with respect to feminist ideology. The prospect of condensing the complex and nuanced reality of feminism into a manageable set of principles is an unwieldy one. Even in the inner circles of the women's movement, there is no concise, thoroughly accepted definition for feminism. Even the word itself sparks a disparate pool of responses.

Somewhere in the blur of elementary school, most of us learned that suffixes were little syllables tagged onto the end of words. They created subtle rather than substantive changes in meaning and certainly held no capacity to evoke strong emotion, crystallize beliefs, spawn political activity, or separate persons into "we's" and "they's." It soon became apparent, however, that "ism" or "ist" added to "femin" connoted a vastly different meaning than did "ine." In traditional circles, *feminine* was acceptable, desirable, and appropriate—a truly proper adjective; *feminist* and *feminism* raised eyebrows, stirred up unrest, and muddied the waters of social acceptability, having quickly become somewhat suspect nouns.

As an expression of human struggle, feminism is simultaneously a subject for rich description and sparse definition. Reflecting this as ideological diversity in their book, *Feminist Frameworks*, Jagger and Rothlenburg-Struhl outline four basic feminist perspectives:

> 1) *liberal feminism*—seeks opportunities for the advancement of women within the existing society through substantive changes in the worlds of education, work and other social and political structures.

> 2) *Marxist feminism*—centers the source of women's oppression in the single, evil core of a capitalist economy and regards the remedy as its dissolution.

> 3) *radical feminism*—locates the source of women's oppression in the socio-economics of gender and not in a particular economic system.

> 4) *socialist feminism*—a synthesis of radical and Marxist feminism which looks to both economic systems and gender peculiarities (childbirth) as the root causes of structural misogyny.[3]

In reality, the delineations may not be so neat and the majority of feminists view the roots of women's oppression as a complex aggregate of social, political, economic and religious realities. It is true, however, that the transformational perspective adopted in the introduction to this paper would suggest that the liberal feminist perspective is most closely identified with that of the writers.

Feminist Themes

Even within the diverse pool of what stands in the shade of the "feminists umbrella," several themes surface and dominate. These themes become more focused and compelling when viewed in a Christian context. If space constraints lead us to put forth these themes with the verbal austerity of axioms, it must be left to the rich stores of women's collective history to flesh out these abstract principles. The selected themes are outlined here:

1) Feminism is one of the fundamental movements toward human liberation. In that sense, it both derives strength from other primary struggles against classist and racist oppression and enters the energizing stream of solidarity with its own particularized focus and perspective.

2) If feminism is a primary movement toward human liberation, Christian feminists approach the struggle from a critical stance of awareness, analysis, and action amid enduring beliefs about the action of God in human life, and the meaning of the Gospel in the light of human experience (in this case, women's experience).

3) Feminism is not of "recent design;" it has spanned centuries of both conscious and unconscious struggles of women to achieve full personhood. Feminism has embodied the exhilaration of victory and the numbing effect of defeat; it has experienced periods of paralysis and of apparently boundless energy and drive. Viewed as a continuous, although diversely expressed, whole, feminism lays claim to a rich heritage despite the obliteration of its history by socially induced amnesia. Viewing feminism as a fad or isolated pockets of activism distorts and shrinks a bigger reality which embraces a startling continuity of issues and themes.

4) The feminist struggle centers on the right to and achievement of excellence, i.e., full personhood, by women in their private and professional lives, in political, social, religious, and economic spheres.

5) Systemic and systematic devaluation of women's abilities and aspirations has seriously diluted the potential of humankind to create a just and humane earth.

6) Feminists struggle against systemic economic oppression of women, pointing to the sharply disproportionate number of

women and children among the world's poor. Across generations of feminist activity, the ruts which trap women in poverty have engaged the compassion as well as the creative energies of feminists. They regard poverty as a systemic, and indeed epidemic, "social disease" affecting primarily women. As a result, eradication of the roots of economic oppression assumes a position of primacy in the feminist movement.

7) Social institutions embody a source of power able to effect social change, i.e., institutionalize emerging or shifting norms, and therefore are a logical target for action by feminists.

These are several of the most predominant feminists themes, ones which span at least several of the ideological perspectives outlined earlier. They establish a context within which to examine the rich variety of feminist thought and some points of congruence with selected themes in the encyclical *Laborem Exercens*. Certainly they pivot on the axial premise of the struggle for quality of life for women and, indeed, for all human persons.

Selected Encyclical Themes

Quality of life and its pursuit through work is also a theme which threads through John Paul II's encyclical. In addition, several other predominant themes relevant to our discussion here may be mentioned:

1) The dignity of the human person is what gives value to work and, conversely, the work of human persons should contribute to the development of quality of life[4] (6,9,10,15,26).

2) There is not a hierarchy of types of work, i.e., the varying kinds of work do not carry different degrees of worth or value. There is no hierarchy of work in terms of intrinsic value (6,12).

3) Organizational styles of decision-making should reflect, in a positive manner, the eradication of value being assigned to work on the basis of position in the hierarchial structure (14,15,18,20).

4) Human persons deserve work environments wherein they can conceive of themselves as co-creditors or partners in the total human effort toward wholeness and excellence (24,25,26,15).

5) Compensation is a pivotal issue in the world of work—both the level and the mode of determining it; a level of support equal to need is demanded by justice principles (19).

Intersection of Ideas in Feminist Theory and Encyclical Themes

1. Centrality of Work in Human Experience

The search for points of congruence between the selected themes from *Laborem Exercens* and the pivotal feminist principles yielded some serendipitous results. From the outset it seems appropriate to view feminist ideology as a vital subset of the great movements of human struggle toward liberation. Within organized efforts to shrink and obliterate classist, racist, and sexist oppression of human beings in order that they may be free to stretch to the edges of their God-given potential for human excellence, there may be derived critical and primary relationships between these struggles and the struggle of human persons within the common and unifying arenas of human work. Certainly the encyclical reinforces the primacy of work within the domain of human experience, not only as a means of maintenance and survival, but also, ideally, as a means by which human persons participate in the ongoing creative activity of God in the universe. As clearly as John Paul II stated that "the Church finds in the first pages of the Book of Genesis the source of her conviction that work is a fundamental dimension of human existence on earth" (4), feminists focus a remarkable percentage of their efforts on transforming or revolutionizing the workplace for women, so central is it perceived to be within the reality of human existence.

During the 1970's, the feminist focus on the workplace, and other centers of economic reality, intensified. The proliferation of economic themes in women's liberation circles—feminist literature highlighting the Equal Rights Amendment as an economic or 'bread and butter' issue; the now-famous 59¢ button blitz (women in the United States make an average of 59 cents for every dollar a man makes); disturbing data on the feminization of poverty; the principle of equal pay for work of comparable value; the sharp increase in the number of households headed by women and in the number of women in the workforce—attempted to shift the public image of "women's liberation" from the faddish fancy of bored middle-class white women to one which was developing increasingly sophisticated political strategies. The feminist effort sought to force United States business, political and economic powers to come to grips with the presence, forced stagnation, and mounting discontent of women in the workplace. (Data on these and other experiences of women in the workplace will be presented in the second section of this paper.)

Work became the focus and few stones were left unturned in the effort—the under-representation of female energy and creativity in the upper echelons of corporate monoliths in both policy-making and administrative positions; the over representation of women in low-paying, dead-end support positions within corporate structures; schedule rigidity and unsatisfactory programs for child care; unequal access to training and education programs; the complex dilemmas which surface with the increase in female labor in third-world countries housing U.S. corporate enterprises—all these areas have engaged feminist energies.

2. The Value of Work is Derived from the Dignity of the Person

In outlining a "gospel of work," John Paul II establishes a framework of analysis wherein these and similar problems of working persons may be examined when he says that the "basis for determining the value of human work is not primarily the kind of work being done, but the fact that the one who is doing it is a person" (5). He also makes reference to the collective reaction to work conditions which do not permit the attainment of full personhood or even, in some cases, the minimal needs for survival which ". . . gave rise to a just social reaction and caused the impetuous emergence of a great burst of solidarity between workers," and that this reaction "united the working world in a community marked by great solidarity" (8). Perhaps unknowingly hinting at the escalation of efforts on behalf of women workers, John Paul II asserts that "movements of solidarity in the sphere of work . . . can be necessary also with reference to the condition of social groups that were not previously included in such movements" (8). He goes on to state that "this solidarity must be present whenever it is called for by the social degrading of the subject of work, by exploitation of the workers and by the growing areas of poverty and hunger" (8).

All of the above appears to lend credence to the delineation of links between recent feminist efforts in the domain of work and the pivotal themes of the encyclical, *Laborem Exercens*, regarding the integral worth of the human person as the value qualifier of work, a qualifier which equalizes the value of work by upgrading the social worth of all human labor to a discernible and dignified level rather than by equalizing downward to a common level of mediocre acceptability.

It appears, then, that viewing work within the full scope of the human struggle toward liberation, i.e., the unleashing of opportunities for development of full human potential, holds meaning both within the context of feminist frameworks and the encyclical, *Laborem Exercens*.

3. Appropriateness of Action on Behalf of Self and Others

The feminist principles which address the struggle and activity of women within a Christian context call for an approach which embodies a critical stance of awareness, analysis, and action within the context of deeply-held beliefs about the action of God in human life and the Gospel imperatives for a contemporary world. Certainly this approach is proactive rather than reactive and would seem to suggest that responsible action on one's own behalf, as well as that of others, is appropriate for women in the work force. In his discussion on workers' rights, John Paul II reiterates this principle regarding collective and worker-initiated action as was suggested in the above mentioned quotes from the encyclicals. This emphasis on self-initiated action, decisive movement toward the attainment of human rights, and social organizing in order to achieve these goals suggests a departure from the traditional mode of "suffering servant Christianity." It stands in contrast to a mode of Christianity which deceives persons into believing that strong action toward achievement of liberation or quality of life, or, in a more limited sense, the achievement of a just and humane work environment is somehow incongruent with the model of Jesus Christ as the "lamb led silently to slaughter." Feminist refusal to bear such a burden which replaces creative energy with guilt is congruent with the papal affirmation of legitimate (in light of Christian principles) social action toward justice in the workplace, where justice is defined as the creation of an environment where all workers have an opportunity to attain the social fruits of the God-given human dignity. "This entirely positive and creative, educational and meritorous character of man's [woman's] work must be the basis for the judgments and decisions made today in this regard in spheres that include human rights" (11).

4. Significant History of Feminist and Church Involvement in Labor Issues

The encyclical reinforces the establishment of the dignity of human labor within the framework of divinely-bestowed intrinsic human worth. If Leo XIII's *Rerum Novarun* introduced a new player into the drama of social criticism of the world of work, it was surely not a player who dramatized an as yet undiscovered theme. John Paul II's repeated return to the "Genesis roots" of work as a human activity and his assertion that the Church has always been an advocate for the vision of work as co-creation would lend credence to this statement. In the same way as some look to the Church's involvement in the social aspects of labor as a nineteenth and twentieth century phenomenon, there is a prevailing social perception that feminist activism is of recent origin.

There is clear evidence to the contrary. The women's suffrage movement is known to many; a fewer number are aware of the strong feminist presence in the nineteenth century abolitionist movement and the strong history of female presence in labor struggles. A sampling of quotes points to a persistent thread of feminist concern for justice in the world of work:

> The flour merchant, the house builder and the postman charge us no less on account of our sex; but when we endeavor to earn money to pay all these, then indeed, do we find the difference. (Lucy Stone, 1855)[5]

> Wherever, on the face of the globe or on the pages of history, you show me a disenfranchised class, I will show you a degraded class of labor. Disenfranchisement means inability to make, shape or control one's own circumstances. The disenfranchised must always do the work, accept the wages, and occupy the position which the franchied assign to them. This is exactly the position of women in the world of work today. (Susan B. Anthony)[6]

> Working women, throw your needles to the winds; press yourselves into employments where you can get better pay; be conductors in our cars; drive hacks. If your petticoats stand in the way of bread, virtue, and freedom, cut them off. (American Equal Rights Association, 1868)[7]

> Women, you must work out your own deliverance with fear and trembling, and with the direction and blessing of God, you can do it. (Angelina Grinke, 1842)[8]

5. The Talents and Abilities of Women are Underutilized

The impact which a transformed work reality for women would have may be viewed from several perspectives. Were the papal call toward the value of work being determined by the intrinsic worth of the person accomplishing it to be transplanted into practice, compensation levels for millions of women in low-paying service and support positions would rise, at considerable cost to the employing agencies. There are not a few corporate critics, including some feminists, who believe that corporate profit is built on a foundation of a cheap, available labor pool, frequently female, which has been socialized to the point that barriers to promotion, low pay, and lack of voice in determining policy do not surface as stimuli which engender dissent and action in the direction of change. There is evidence of congruence between the encyclical's echo of the Church's teaching on the rights of workers to organize, although feminists have adopted a more aggressive stance in raising the consciousness of women to recognize their plight and act to change it.

This struggle of women and other marginalized groups to improve their status and levels of compensation is the most visible focus of organized action. It is equally possible, however, to view the underutilization of female energy and abilities within corporate endeavors as both related to compensation and promotion inequities and, more importantly, as an unfortunate and unprofitable waste of human resources.

Feminist effort to document the magnitude of this reality has been both consistent and frustrating. One wonders what the result might be if the full scope of women's potential were made available in the workplace. Even the most sterile fiscal analysis by a corporation addressed the question: "What resources have we not tapped which are available to us?" In nearly every area of human endeavor, the feminist response would be "women's resources:" their intellectual capacity, ingenuity and creative energy, their perspective and outlook. Certainly in the competitive marketplace effective use of available resources is a principal consideration. One can only conclude that the full spectrum of women's potential has not yet been viewed as an undeveloped resource by corporations bent on leaving no "profit-generating" stone unturned or that the price or risk of turning this stone over is still too high. This point bears an interesting relationship to the Pope's focus on co-creation or "work as a sharing in the activity of the Creator" (25).

In the same paragraph, John Paul II continues with an assertion that:

The word of God's revelation is profoundly marked by the fundamental trust that man, created in the image of God, shares by his work in the activity of the creator and that, within the limits of his own human capabilities, man in a sense continues to develop that activity, and perfects it as he advances further and further in the discovery of resources and values contained in the whole of creation (25).

Even if we concede that the papal reference to "man" is generic and inclusive, the marginalized experience of women leads to the unfortunate conclusion that, in the world of work, the papal "man" is both sex-specific and exclusionary, to the mutual detriment of women and the world. God's creative work is stifled and limited; our ability to create a just and humane earth is weakened. Pifer comments on this reality in a recent article: ". . . more and more Americans are beginning to see full employment of women's abilities as a social and political imperative. Not only is it a national moral obligation stemming from our country's basic principles, but, more pragmatically, we are beginning to realize that the safety and prosperity of the nation will increasingly depend on the maximum use of our entire stock of human talents."[9]

6. Systemic Economic Injustices Are a Primary Stimulus Toward Transformation of the World of Work

It has been mentioned earlier that, despite public belief to the contrary, the major focus of feminist effort has been on the uncovering and eradication of economic injustices related to work. In his reiteration of the Church's teaching on the rights of workers, John Paul II points to several areas which have also been the subject of feminist attention: the right to "suitable employment for all who are capable of it" (18); the right to unemployment and other work benefits as "a duty springing from the fundamental principle . . . of the common use of goods, or . . . the right to life and subsistence" (18); the right to "just renumeration for work done" (19).

The feminist struggle for justice in the workplace is also centered on these principles of justice. Efforts to enable legislation to correct inequities; establishment of regulatory agencies (however slow-moving and ineffectual); efforts to present the facts on levels of compensation, unequal pay for equal work, unequal access to pension and social security benefits, lack of job security and unemployment statistics as well as the plight of displaced homemakers all have captured the attention and energies of feminists with a goal of transformation. A further discussion of data related to women's work and economic injustices will be developed in the next section of this paper.

Points of Dissonance

The search for points of congruence between the papal encyclical and the feminist focus on work surfaced some clear points of agreement. It would be a mistake and perhaps a curious manifestation of wishful thinking to conclude, however, that the papal documents and the feminist effort to reform the work world move in full synchrony. There are some undeniably dissonant notes. A brief mention of them will deter the inclination toward haste in making unwarranted assumptions on the practical implications of this alliance of thought. Three points appear particularly deserving of mention.

1) Most women work because of economic need. Some women, however, work because their work is a positive contributor toward the development of themselves as human persons. Many women work for a combination of the above reasons, albeit in varying proportions. With the publishing of the encyclical, *Laborem Exercens*, an immediate flurry of comment ensued realtive to what the Pope said or did not say about women working "outside the home." It is not within the scope of this paper to discuss whether or not married women should work outside the home when economic necessity does not demand it, but rather to point out that when the Pope refers to a "single salary given to the head of the family for his (in this case the "his" is clearly not intended to be generic) work sufficient for the needs of the family without the spouse having to take up gainful employment outside the home" (19), he assumes a stance in sharp contrast to that of feminists. The Pope's statements are clearly related to earlier pronouncements of his regarding the proper and principal role of women as motherhood. While the concept of a "social re-evaluation of the mother's role" would meet with agreement by feminists, few would agree that the primary "mission of a mother" is to stay at home. The feminist view holds as inviolable the principle of woman as a human person with needs, wants, rights, and responsibilities independent of her relationship to husband and children. Even as we began with the assertion that "quality of life" was a

common goal articulated by both feminists and the papal encyclical, the Pope's idea that, in most cases, quality of life for women is attained by being wife and mother is resisted by feminists. They, on the other hand, hold that while this may well be true for some women, for many others quality of life is enhanced by their working productively outside the home and sharing more equitably with their husbands the responsibilities, burdens and joys of parenting.

2) The feminist idea of "equal pay for work of comparable value" stands in uneasy juxtaposition to the encyclical focus on compensation based on need. It may be unrealistic to conceive of a marginalized group relinquishing its acquisitive striving for the same visible signs of "success" as those possessed by the power groups. There is ambivalence within feminist ranks on this point and certainly the analysis invades the socialist/capitalist debate, exceeding the scope of our discussion here. Efforts within feminist groups to "level-out" the hierarchies of position and status, to seek out and hear the stories of working women, to search for common threads of experience have been significant. No less significant, however, has been the emergence of the "queen-bee syndrome" among women who have "made it" and the prevailing feminist belief that the values of various works differ, can be evaluated, and should be asigned levels of compensation accordingly. Ellen Cantarow highlights the dimensions of this dilemma when she says that:

> Such questions are double-edged. On the one hand they have the kernel of momentous potential; redefining the value of scorned work could lead to questioning the competitive bases for valuing human worth that characterized most of American life. But they could also just advance the "me first" ethic, encouraging the thought that secretarial work is intrinsically "better" than maintenance work. (It would hardly be the first time workers near the bottom had been pitted against each other).[10]

3) Finally, the whole issue of credibility alluded to in the introduction must be addressed. There are certainly significant hurdles to be overcome before feminists could be led to believe that the patriarchal church is championing their right to develop as full human persons. If the rhetoric suggests that the striving for "quality of life" and human excellence is a proper task for all, the policy and practice of the Church demonstrates that the parameters of what determines "quality" for women is narrowly defined and carefully prescribed. The Pope appears to

counter his own logic in arguing that motherhood is what gives worth and value to women, since the original principle as stated by the Pope placed the source of worth or value within the person and not within other relationships to human persons or social institutions.

There is the clear possibility that the Church cannot speak credibly to corporations or any other social institutions on the issues of justice regarding women in the work place. While this possibility is acknowledged, our choice has been to proceed as if a productive intersection of thought is possible. We keep in mind, however, the warning of Thelma McCormack that "normative theories dignify lost causes, comfort the victims, and feed their fantasies of wish fulfillment; they touch a chord within all of us, winners as well as losers."[11]

Even with this sobering awareness, the hope for transformation encourages many women to move forward. The Women's Declaration of Sentiments (Seneca Falls, New York, 1848) urged that "facts be submitted to a candid world."[12] In order to move with greater clarity in understanding the present reality of women in the corporate world, the following section of this paper will do precisely that.

The Reality: Current Issues for Women in the Workplace

In this second part of the paper we will focus on the workplace from the perspective of the women who are counted as part of the "labor force." This does not imply uncritical acceptance of the market-determined definition of "work" as exclusively that which enters into market transactions. Within the limits of time and space and the scope of this symposium we will focus only on work outside the home, and the realities facing the women who make part or all of their social contribution in this arena.

What does the recent encyclical have to say to the corporate world, in particular, in relation to policies and practices as they affect women? In the light of current realities, what challenges do the normative principles restated by John Paul II pose to the policy makers and administrators in corporations? What guidance do they give to those who seek to influence the corporate institutions as workers or stockholders or citizens?

While there are many aspects of the economic oppression of women which could in some sense be said to be beyond the control of the corporations, as dominant economic institutions they both embody prevailing social patterns and originate or foster changes in those patterns. Thus, it *is* appropriate to look at the present realities for women and pose challenges to corporate decision-makers in their regard.

In this section the *data* will present the challenges. The facts, drawn together in one place, placed alongside the normative vision of the encyclical, contain a clear call for change. This section will present first a brief overview of the economic realities of women in the labor force. This will give a perspective on the magnitude and importance of the economic realities facing women today and thus the urgency for society of resolving these issues.

Women in the Workplace—Overview

One of the most profound societal changes in the 1970's, a decade of marked change in American society, was the increasing presence of women in the work force. Bureau of Labor Statistics data indicate that as of June, 1980, 51% of all women over 16 were in the labor force, and 42% of all jobs were held by women. In 1950, 34% of U.S. women were in the work force.[13] Focusing on married women reveals that 52% of all married women were in the work force, and that 47% of married couple families have both husbands and wife working. Only 37% have the husband only working. By 1980 almost half of the children in two-parent families had working mothers, up from 38% in 1970. Fifty-seven percent of all women with children under 18 were in the labor force in 1980.[14] Clearly, the type of family envisioned by John Paul II in *Laborem Exercens* (19) and other statements is becoming less and less typical in the United States. That the American public also is largely ignorant of the scope of change that has occurred in family patterns partially explains that failure of private and public policy makers to deal with the consequent realities.

What of the myth that women work only for "pin money" and that their labor market status is thus less significant in economic terms than that of men? Again the facts bely the myth. Bureau of Labor Statistics data show that 20% of the mothers in the labor force in 1980 (3.8 million women) were heads of their households. Analysis of data on married women whose husbands also work showed that women are most likely to work if their husbands have incomes slightly below the national median (i.e., in the $10,000 to $15,000 range in 1977). That is, women whose husbands are teachers, technicians, small proprietors, mechanics, construction workers, police, or fire fighters are most likely to be in the work force. This corroborates other data that indicate that the ability of lower income families to live at a working class standard was dependent on the earnings of the wife. In 1979, nearly two out of three women in the work force were either single, widowed, divorced or separated, or had husbands who earned less than $10,000 per year.[15] These facts should be sufficient to show that most of the women in the work force today are there because *they* are increasingly the breadwinners for themselves and others. Economic necessity born of the rising divorce rate; the recurring high levels of unemployment, national and regional; increasing consumer indebtedness; persisting inflation; and lengthening life span for women drove many women into the labor force even while others chose to pursue careers for personal reasons.

Increasing attention is being drawn to the "feminization of poverty." Again the facts attest to the reality. Bureau of Labor Statistics and Census Bureau data indicate that 79% of the poor in the U.S. today are women and children. Over 12 million full-time workers are eligible for some form of public assistance—67% of them are women. Forty-two percent of all female single-parent households with children under 18 live in poverty and 50% of all minority single-parent households with children under 18 live in poverty. Between 1969 and 1976 the entire increase in the number of families living in poverty was among female-headed households.[16] This presence of women among the poor in disproportionate numbers indicates the institutionalized sexism that permeates the socio-economic system. In the words of *Laborem Exercens* (8):

> And the "poor" appear under various forms: they appear in various places and at various times; in many cases they appear as a *result of the violation of the dignity of human work*: either because the opportunities for human work are limited as a result of the scourge of unemployment, or because a low value is put on work and the rights that flow from it, especially the right to a just wage and to the personal security of the worker and his or her family.

This brief overview gives the data base for the scope of the problem and its seriousness. It indicates the end result of the operation of the U.S. socio-economic system, of which corporations are but one part. There are some specific aspects of the economic problems of women which are particularly traceable to corporate actions, however. Data on a few of these can be presented here.

Women in the Clerical Occupations

In its 1979 publication, "Women Still in Poverty," the U.S. Civil Rights Commission observed:

> Traditional ideas of where women belong in the economy and patterns of employment discrimination have nearly excluded women from certain areas of employment . . . and from the skilled crafts, which have been traditionally male-dominated. Women have often been channelled (regardless of their inclinations) into lower paying, lower status jobs that men have not wanted, such as clerical and household work.[17]

Clerical work has the largest percentage of women in the work force — it is the largest female ghetto; it is also the lowest paid. After World War II women saw clerical work as a step-up from blue collar work. In 1950 62% of clerical workers were women; by 1979, 80% were.

Median usual weekly earnings of full-time clerical workers in 1979 show the usual gap between male and female earnings. Even in this field where women predominate so markedly their earnings are only 64% of those of men.[18]

The U.S. Civil Rights Commission found that employment agencies steer women into clerical jobs, and that they are classified by employers into jobs with little promotion potential. An example from the insurance industry cited a woman who rated "very high" on all the tests during the training period, and was assigned to be a "direct correspondent"—a clerical employee who handles inquiries from individual subscribers, while male, non-minority trainees were assigned to be "group subscribers," positions which proved to have more responsibility and much more rapid promotion.[19] Such subtle forms of discrimination are difficult to eradicate, but they demonstrate the systemic violation of the principles of human dignity and of work as a means for self-actualization outlined in *Laborem Exercens* (9,15,26).

Harris Shrank and John Riley studied a large bureaucratic corporation with 14,000 employees in home and field offices. They observed that there are certain families of jobs defined as appropriately male or female and that all jobs within large organizations tend to have some position within a hierarchy. That means that each job tends to be pegged at certain salary and status levels. Some jobs, however, such as secretarial jobs, are hierarchical only within specified limits. "There is, for example, a hierarchy of secretarial jobs, but it has an upper limit well below the highest level of jobs within the corporation."[20] They concluded,

> An occupant in the female pool of jobs has for the most part been precluded from the same sort of hierarchical movement that is found in the male pool of jobs. Of course there has been some potential for upward mobility within the female pool, but change, if it occurred, was slower and more limited in range. The upper limit for the male pool is the president's position. The comparable upper limit job within the female pool is often secretary to the president.[21]

This is but one example of what has been documented in many places. Harris and Shrank found that in the 1970's some changes were taking place which point the way to future action.

As new types of jobs were opened up gender-free pools developed in areas where there was no cultural tradition to reserve the roles to one sex or the other (e.g., computer programming, systems analyst). Also affirmative action programs have widened opportunity for women at all job levels.[22] The development of new jobs or job families may well provide the opportunity to upgrade the employment status of women within the corporate structures.

Women in Management

It is commonplace that women do not generally hold positions of power and authority in American corporations. Where women are in management they tend to be concentrated in lower-paying positions, in selected fields, and in staff rather than line positions, and in less powerful, less prestigious organizations.[23] In 1979 women were 25% of managerial/administrative workers overall, up from 14% in 1950 and 17% in 1970. The heaviest concentration was in sales managers and department heads in retail trade where 39% are women. Louise Kapp Howe notes that women tend to be concentrated in apparel areas but are rarely found in furniture departments where the pay is higher.[24]

If we look more closely at the data we find that women are only 5% of middle managment and 1% of top management in the largest companies. A 1978 FORTUNE survey of the 1,500 largest companies in the U.S. found only 10 women among the 6,400 corporate officers and directors.[25] There is evident disparity between male and female executives in salary patterns. In 1975 BUSINESS WEEK reported that only 3% of managers and administrators earning over $25,000 were women, and only 15 women (compared to 2,500 men) headed major corporations and earned more than $100,000.[26]

Some change is occurring, however, since even 15 years ago in the mid-1960's only 1% of entering managerial trainees were women, while in the mid-1970's the entry figure was 15%. Linda Kellner Brown comments on the significance of this, noting that the presence of even a few women in the executive suites reinforces women's aspirations to achieve success in a previously male field. She notes that many investigators have argued that so-called problems of women in management would evaporate if only there were more of them.[27]

The Civil Rights Commission indicated that management representatives at their hearings did not deny that women are underutilized or concentrated at low-level jobs, but they did deny any deliberate discrimination in their practices. Most large corporations have personnel practices which allow wide latitude at each supervisory level. It is here that the informal, "secondary labor market" phenomenon comes into play, where attitudes and stereotypes and personal preferences rather than objective qualifications influence promotion paths.

The penicious effect of all this is to restrict women to lower-paying jobs, contributing to the phenomena of economic distress outlined at the beginning of this section. Enlightened corporate policy and attitudes on the part of managers responsible for personnel at each level can be significant in upgrading the positions of women in the corporate hierarchy. As corporate executives encounter managerial couples each with their own career goals, the old resistance will tend to break down. Interestingly it has been found that older executives are less likely to have stereotypes about managers than are younger persons, probably because of their experiences with working wives and peers.[28] Principles regarding dignity of persons and work like those outlined in *Laborem Exercens* can provide support for more opportunity for women in the corporate structures.

Work Hazards for Women

Another area where corporate practice contradicts the principles regarding work outlined in the encyclical concerns hazardous working conditions. In specifying the rights of workers is included "the right to a working environment and to manufacturing processes which are not harmful to the workers' physical health . . ." (19). At the present time there are three particular occupations in which women are particularly victimized by corporate practice. These are the emerging occupational health and safety issues.

First, with the increasing use of word processing equipment in offices there is increasing documentation about hazards of eyestrain from watching video display screens and stress from the noise and speed of the work. There is some evidence that there are potential harmful cumulative effects of X-rays from the cathode ray picture tubes. All of these problems can be limited by relatively simple changes in work patterns and office equipment design. Eyestrain can be reduced to a significant degree by allowing hourly breaks, and installing anti-glare screens and adjustable lighting. Noise can be diminished by placing the high speed printers at a distance in soundproof enclosures. Encasing in metal rather than plastic can reduce radiation emissions.[29]

Second, in the electronics industry concentrated in Santa Clara County's Silicon Valley where 80% of the employees are women there has been recent documentation of chemical hazards. The trade uses 10% of all the chemicals in the U.S., including some of the most dangerous corrosives, toxic solvents, poisons and carcinogens. Area physicians are beginning to voice their concern over rising medical problems, and the death rate has risen 20% in the last eight years. Investigators have found that the chemicals in combination may have geometically greater impact than each of them separately. The fact that most of the employees are Asians or Mexicans who have been brought in by the corporations from successful overseas operations makes organization of the workers more difficult. In addition, some manufacturers have found it profitable to encourage home assembly of the silicon chips. Reports have been received of vats of dangerous substances boiling on the kitchen stoves of women who work without any protection of minimum wages, social security, or workers' compensation.[30]

A third area of exploitation of women is in the garment industry where the competitive nature of the assembly process gives incentive to cut costs in every conceivable way. The industry is organized into "inside shops" with production facilities of the firms that design and merchandise the garments and into "outside shops," small contractors who do the sewing and assembly of the garments for the "inside shops" whenever they have an overflow of orders and for "jobbers" who contract out all of their assembly work. Because of the vulnerability and availability of immigrant women, a new generation of sweatshops with all the conditions of the nineteenth century variety has sprung up in New York's Chinatown and in the South Bronx. It is estimated that there are 500 in each of these locations. These employ mainly Hispanic and Asian women who work at piecework rates as low as 75¢ a dress. In weekly terms it is not unusual for one of these women to work a 60-hour week and take home the equivalent of $1.30 an hour (in comparison to the $4.00-$5.00 an hour usually made by ILGWU members). In hopes of making a little extra money the women also often take work home. Again, lack of education, language barriers, and immigrant status often makes it difficult to determine the extent of violations.

Sociologist Roger Wadinger has noted that what is happening is the internationalization of production for labor as well as capital. "The same people who are making clothes abroad under conditions that violate international labor codes come here to make them under relatively similar conditions."[31]

It is difficult for consumers to identify the manufacturers and contractors involved in making the clothes they buy, since retailers sew their own labels into the clothes they sell. But corporate managers know who their suppliers are.

In these areas of blatant disregard for human health, clear responsibility is apparent and women's lives are at risk. The old battles keep returning in new forms. Perhaps enlightened corporate executives can be enlisted in the battle this time around.

Closing the Gap Between the Vision and the Reality: Toward a Transformed World: Areas for Action

It is deep in our tradition that we are called to participate in the redemptive action of God in the world. Since Vatican II the call to action for social transformation has been articulated ever more clearly as a constitutive element of living the Gospel. Thus, the vision of a transformed world, outlined in the body of Catholic social teaching (as well as in other religious and secular documents) is not only for speculatiave discussion. It is also intended to provide an action orientation—some guiding principles for concrete steps for change. Choices are made in specific decisions in the light of a fundamental value stance. Without being prescriptive, Catholic social teaching, as part of the body of ethics, is generally normative.

The key principles of Catholic social teaching, expressed anew in *Laborem Exercens*, are finding corroboration in the work of the growing interdisciplinary body of scholars and focusing on the study of the future. These are also being joined by business leaders (such as the Italian industrialist Aurelio Peccei) and diplomats such as the UN's Robert Muller who see new value bases as essential for the survival of humankind in the next century. Values such as the fundamental dignity of the human person, stewardship of resources, human solidarity, and subsidiarity in organizations are integral to religious and secular visions of a preferred future. For example, the World Council of Churches has been sponsoring scholarly dialogues among futurists since the mid-1970's investigating the contours of and paths to a "just, sustainable, and participatory" future.

Dennis Gabor, Nobel Prize-winning physicist, has called in his book, *The Mature Society*, for application of energies to "social innovations" to create a world in which each person will work according to her/his intellectual gifts and abilities and motivation toward service. James Robertson, British economist, in his book, *The Sane Alternative: A Choice of Futures* describes three scenarios: "business as usual future;" "technological-fix future;" and the "SHE" future (sane, humane and ecological). His preferred SHE future expresses in its structures the values of socio-economic balance and harmony within persons, between persons, and with nature. All of these examples are cited to show the strength and diversity in the chorus of voices calling for transformation of the workplace along the lines outlined in feminist and papal themes.

In particular, Alan Pifer, as president of the Carnegie Corporation of New York in his 1976 Annual Statement, envisaged the nation setting in motion changes needed to build a new society, creatively responsive to the increasing presence of women in the workplace. It would be based on four principles which incorporate the values common to the feminist vision and *Laborem Exercens*:

1—the right to a job for everyone who needs/wants to work
2—equal opportunity and fair rewards for everyone in all sectors of employment
3—development and utilization of the abilities of every citizen
4—maximum flexibility for each person in the organization of his/her own pattern of life[32]

What are some of the specific action areas that would lead to such a society? In particular, what are some challenges to corporate policy and power?

What if corporations joined labor unions and citizen action groups in developing strategies for non-inflationary full employment? The negotiation of new contracts in the face of economic necessity in the auto industry and elsewhere provide some bases for hope that it is possible to take joint action which is mutually beneficial in the longer run. Perhaps the current public outcry against the nuclear arms race can provide occasion for corporations also to recognize the fundamentally harmful long-term effects of the arms build-up on the economy and join the conversion effort. (According to Employment Research Associates, the $135 billion 1980 U.S. military budget cost the jobs of nearly 1.3 million women in comparison with what would have been available if comparable funds were in the hands of consumers or state and local governments.) Unless adequate employment opportunities exist, the rest of the social justice agenda will be in vain.

What if corporations became at least gender-blind in hiring and promotion practices? The developing of new job pools in new industries or new divisions of expending companies can provide opportunities for farsighted executives to introduce evolutionary change. And perhaps more visionary managers, recognizing latent talent in an underutilized female clerical force, might initiate personnel policies and educational opportunities enabling women to upgrade their positions.

What if corporate practice encouraged the development of small suppliers and worker-owned businesses? Through their purchasing patterns and contracting practices some large firms have encouraged the development of successful and viable specialized suppliers. Small businesses generate over two-thirds of the new jobs in the nation, and provide better advancement possibilities for women than do larger firms. Perhaps we might learn from the Japanese experience to encourage the strength of smaller enterprises.

What if corporate executives began to educate themselves and their constituencies to take a longer-run view, to recognize that development of everyone's potential is in the interests of all of us together? Perhaps new models of labor management cooperation might emerge. Perhaps the growing concern for improved productivity might lead to development of new forms of worker participation in decision-making which would bring the complementary gifts of women and men together in peer situations which would release new creativity in persons and organizations.

What if corporations tried to guarantee the maximum flexibility for each person in the organization of his/her own life? Perhaps the success many companies and 10% of the work force have had with flexible schedules might encourage others to experiment in ways that provide women and men opportunity to balance their home and work responsibilities more equitably. Perhaps the movement for job-sharing might lead to more fulfilled and less stress-laden workers and make it possible for women with children to carry on careers without interruption. Perhaps some creative approaches to child care might be developed.

What if corporations adopted the principles of participative decision-making consonant with feminist and encyclical principles? Perhaps adoption of some of the currently popular Japanese styles of management might lead to more humane and responsive workplaces that would also be more productive. Perhaps resistance to employee organization might give way to recognition of the realities of interdependence and the need for cooperation. Perhaps employees might respond in unexpected ways.

What if we gave a revolution and everybody won?[33]

NOTES

1. Sheila Robbotham, *Women's Consciousness, Man's World* (Baltimore: Penguin Books, 1973).

2. Eli Ginzburg, *New York Times*, November 29, 1977, pp. 1,28.

3. Alison M. Jagger and Paula Rothenburg Struhl, ed., *Feminist Frameworks* (New York: McGraw Hill, 1978).

4. Encyclical references are noted by paragraph numbers within the text, e.g. (8). Translation provided by United States Catholic Conference: Publication No. 825, Office of Publishing Services.

5. Lucy Stone, quoted in Papachristou, ed., *Women Together: A History of Documents of the Women's Movement in the United States* (N.Y.: Knopf, 1976), p. 33.

6. *Ibid.*, p. 21.

7. *Ibid.*, p. 61.

8. *Ibid.*, p. 13.

9. Alan Pifer, "Women Working Toward A New Society" in ed. K.W.

Feinstein, *Working Women and Families* (Beverly Hills, CA: Sage Publications, 1979), p. 17.

10. Ellen Cantarow, "Workers Not Wives", *In These Times*, December 9-15, 1981, p. 12.

11. Thelma McCormack, "Toward a Nonsexist Perspective on Social and Political Change" in Millman and Kanter, *Another Voice* (New York: Anchor Books, 1975), p. 4.

12. *Woman's Declaration of Rights* in Papachristou, ed., *op. cit.*, p. 24.

13. Bureau of Labor Statistics, *Perspective on Working Women: A Databook,* Bulletin 2080, October, 1980, pp. 6-7; Riley, Maria, "Women Between Work and Family: Between Myth and Reality", *Center Focus*, Issue 42, March, 1981, pp. 1-3.

14. *Ibid.*

15. *Ibid.*

16. cf. "Wealth and Women", *Dollars and Sense*, No. 71, November, 1981, pp. 12-14; "Poverty: A Women's Issue", *National Organization for Women*, 1979; Pearce, Diana, "Women, Work, and Welfare: "The Feminization of Poverty" in ed., K.T. Feinstein, *Working Women and Families*, (Beverly Hills, CA: Sage Publications, 1979).

17. US Civil Rights Commission, Clearinghouse Publication 60, July, 1979, p. 19.

18. BLS Bulletin 2080, Table 49.

19. USCRC Clearinghouse Publication 60, July, 1979, pp. 22-25.

20. "Women in Work Organizations" in ed. Juanita Kreps, *Women and the American Economy,* (Englewood Cliffs, N.J.: Prentice Hall, Inc. 1976), pp. 89-90.

21. *Ibid.*

22, Ibid., pp. 99-100.

23. Rosabeth Moss Kanter, "Women and the Structure of Organizations: Exploration in Theory and Behavior" in Millman and Kanter, ed., *Another Voice,* (New York: Anchor Books, 1975), pp. 35-38.

24. *Pink Collar Workers,* (New York: G.P. Putnam, 1977), p. 16.

25. W. Robertson, "The Top Women in Big Business", *Fortune*, July 17, 1978, pp. 58-63.

26. "Up the Ladder—Finally", *Business Week*, November 24, 1975, pp. 58-68.

27. "Women and Business Management", *Signs*, 5 Winter, 1979), p. 269.

28. *Ibid.*, p. 278.

29. "Word Processing and the Work Process", *Dollars and Sense*, no. 69, September, 1981, pp. 6-9.

30. Sue Martinez and Alan Ramo, "In the Valley of the Shadow of Death", *In These Times*, IV October 8-14, 1980, pp. 12-13.

31. Hardy Green and Elizabeth Weiner, "Bringing It All Back Home", *In These Times,* March 11-17, 1981, pp. 8-9; "Sweatshops Still Thriving", *Dollars and Sense*, no. 52, December, 1979, pp. 8-9.

32. "Women Working: Toward a New Society" in K.W. Feinstein, ed., *Working Women and Families* (Beverly Hills, CA: Sage Publications, 1979), pp. 26-33.

33. Eric Mount, *The Feminine Factor* (New York: John Knox Press, 1973), p. 178.

CHAPTER 10

Managers and Managed: Problems of Ambivalence

by George C. Lodge

POPE JOHN PAUL II'S THIRD ENCYCLICAL, *ON HUMAN WORK*, PROVIDES MORAL and religious support for many of the remarkable developments in United States labor management relations in the early 1980s. Quality of work-life programs, workers' participation in managerial decisions and employer-employee cooperation for labor cost reduction reflect the encyclical's spirit. In his assertion that "the proper subject of work continues to be man;" his warning against "considering human labor solely according to its economic purposes;" his reminder that "the right to private ownership" is not "an untouchable dogma of economic life;" his admonition that giving ownership to the state does not necessarily give man the control he needs "to know that in his work . . . he is acting for himself;" and his conclusion that "in the final analysis, both those who work and those who manage must in some way be united . . . ;" the Pope is speaking directly to the issues which leaders of American business and labor confront in 1982.[1] Furthermore, he is, it seems, saying that a lot of what those leaders are doing is good.

The current drift in the direction of the encyclical has been prompted more by the necessity of coping with the withering effects of world competition than by moral sense, but that does not make it less good.

229

Indeed the 1980's may be one of those rare times when moral behavior is harmonious with what practitioners in the rough and tumble of industry find to be efficient and effective.

The harmony, however, should not blind us to the discord and difficulty which the Pope's message carries for many in America and which need to be overcome if his call is to be acted on effectively. In weakening the idea of property rights, for example, the encyclical erodes what many still consider the source of management authority, the basis of the right to manage. And when he advises unions to forego the adversarial struggle in the name of unity with management, he threatens a strongly held conception of American trade unionism.

"I believe deeply in a conflict theory of labor relations," Thomas R. Donahue, secretary-treasurer of the AFL-CIO, told the students at the University of Massachusetts in January 1982. "Workers properly want, and are entitled to . . . a larger piece of the pie, whatever the size of the pie . . . The meek may inherit the earth, but probably not in your or my lifetime."

Such a spirit finds its counterpart among many managers whose principal purpose is to maximize return to shareholders on the grounds that shareholders are "owners," and thus have first claim on corporate earnings. The effects of shareholder gain on the work force, the community or even the long-run interests of the corporation are, according to this view, of secondary importance. These managers regard unions as adversaries to be beaten, or better still, killed. As recently as five years ago, Heath Larry, former chairman of U.S. Steel and then president of the National Association of Manufacturers, announced the formation of "a Council on a Union-Free Environment" to assist employers "to manage with sufficient skill" so that "employees will find no need to invite the services of a union to represent them."[2] In 1982 the U.S. was rife with consultants ready to teach those skills.

In these circumstances it was not surprising that Donahue felt embattled. Union membership was down to little more than 20% of the work force; its influence in Congress was at low ebb; its role and mission in many settings was unclear; and finally President Reagan, who had been elected with many labor votes, seemed to relish humiliating the labor movement. He excluded it from his inaugural ceremonies and a few months later exulted in decertifying the Air Traffic Controllers. Although the White House was sending some friendly signals in 1982, AFL-CIO President Lane Kirkland did not feel it an exaggeration to liken Mr. Reagan's economic policies to Rev. Jones' Koolaid. There was certainly no life in the idea of joint consultation among government, labor, and business for "the industrialization of America" which had been President Carter's last wish before leaving office in January 1981.

It was remarkable, however, that despite the hostile climate, there seemed to be an unprecedented degree of collaborative innovation occurring in labor-management relations, much of it in the direction of cooperation and respect for human beings which the Pope advised. In this paper I shall try to clarify this ambivalence. I shall cite examples of the innovations occurring, and consider their implications for the roles and relationships of government, business, and labor in the United States. I shall suggest that what is occurring can only be fully understood if it is seen as a radical departure from traditional American ideology, and if the implications of the new ideology, which the events reflect, are made clear.

New Departures

It was in the early 1970's that substantial departures from the traditional adversarial relations between managers and unions began to occur. In both the automobile and steel industries, as well as in other non-union settings such as IBM, Hewlett Packard, TRW, and Procter and Gamble, the contractual relationships between managers and workers were being augmented or replaced slowly and hesitantly by consensual ones, aimed at developing a sense of commitment and community between managers on the one hand and those whom they managed on the other. The process took many forms: team building, organizational development, job enrichment, and in the steel industry a no-strike pledge and compulsory arbitration. In many industries management and unions were mindful of their common interest in warding off the growing threat of foreign imports.

It was the competitive forays of the Japanese, in particular, that quickened the pace of consensual activity in the seventies. The United States, once the economic wonder of the world, was being clobbered by Japan and indeed a number of other Asian and European countries. It was not just an isolated firm or industry here and there; it was *every* industry on which Japan, for example, chose to target her sights: autos, steel, semiconductors, computers, color TVs, appliances, and more. What was most disconcerting to Americans was that the competition was systemic. We were being defeated by a set of relationships between government, business and labor, in short by a country which was capable of formulating and implementing a coherent national strategy. "Individual United States companies are competing against Japan *as a country* (emphasis added)," said Philip Caldwell, chairman of the Ford Motor Company, adding that new relationships among government, business, and labor in the United States were required if we were to recover.[3] The Japanese were making better products for less money with more modern equipment and more advanced technology. Industry and labor gradually realized that their mutual survival was at stake. The grim necessity was coming clear. The country had to consume less and invest more; to innovate and take risks for long-term gains instead of settling for short-term return to shareholders; managers had to manage more imaginatively and workers had to work more productively. Western Europe faced the same necessity. Indeed what historically has been called "the Christian world" was being formed by competition to suppress old divisions and seek a new sense of community; to follow the Pope's dictum: "In no way can labor be opposed to capital or capital to labor, and still less can the actual people behind these concepts be opposed to each other. . . ."[4]

There is growing evidence that relatively well-educated people derive a greater sense of fulfillment from their work if they have a greater sense of participation in the design and control of that work and, also, they work more efficiently. Today in America there is what Irving Bluestone, former vice president of the United Automobile Workers, called a "tidal wave" of procedures aimed at insuring participation. They vary widely from community to community, industry to industry and job to job. The procedures have many names but they are all embraced by the necessarily vague term, quality of work life (QWL). (At Ford it's called "employee involvement" [EI]). They proceed from the top of the enterprise down to the shop floor and from the shop floor up. They are found in some 1500 companies, according to *Business Week*, in many service as well as manufacturing industries, in the private sector and increasingly in the public sector. Implicit in all of them is the idea that relationships between those who manage and those who are managed are best determined by consensus rather than by conflict around a contract. Consensual procedures are not necessarily a substitute for the collective contract; rather they are aimed at problems and issues which do not conveniently fit within the contract form. It remains to be seen whether the evolving machinery of consensus will erode the contract. Certainly that possibility is there. Also there is the threat of erosion of traditional notions of corporate governance. The right to manage in QWL plants comes not so much from shareholders via a board of directors as it does from those who are managed. Indeed in many QWL plants—GM's for example—the word management has been changed to "support team," the idea being that managers serve the workers. The effective manager is the one who can assemble winning teams, the gamesman, as Michael Maccoby has called him (Let *him* also mean *her* and *he* also *she*). Consensus management not only provides the individual with a greater sense of fulfillment but it educates him about the reality in which the corporation exists. He perceives the demands of competitiveness which the firm confronts and feels the necessity of sacrificing for the good of the whole.

The idea of consensus carries with it, however, shocking implications for traditional managers and trade union leaders. If workers sacrifice for the good of the whole, so must management. QWL programs invite comparisons, for example, between the salaries of the chief executive and the lowly sweeper. QWL plants are characterized by an absence of executive dining rooms and special parking places in the company lot. Managers do not wear ties and coats. These symbols illustrate the democratic nature of the innovation. If the authority of management comes from the managed, what happens to the board of directors? What is its role? Who sits on it? How does the boss get to be the boss? And what is the role of a trade union in a consensual set-up? Accustomed to adversarial bargaining, conditioned to attracting the loyalty of membership by effectiveness on the contractual battlefield, what does the trade union leader do in a consensual arrangement? And what happens to the thousands of workers who are cast aside after labor and management have cooperated for competitiveness? These questions, which are implicit in the Pope's encyclical, are also at the core of America's troubles in the 1980's.

New Concessions, New Demands

In the winter of 1982 some 4.5 million workers faced contract negotiations which entailed the necessity of wage and benefit concessions— of foregoing "a larger piece of the pie," to use Tom Donahue's phrase. Workers and unions recognized that the pie, such as it was, had to be invested in making their companies more competitive. In return they insisted upon an unprecedented invasion of what had been management prerogatives. They needed access to the company's financial records to be able to trust the facts which management was giving them. They sought assurance that management would in fact spend the money saved from lower labor costs to benefit the corporation and its employees, and not use it to diversify into other industries or build plants in other countries. They sought a share in the company profits, and control over the investment of the billions of dollars amassed in pension funds so that those funds could contribute to the revitalization of communities in which union members lived. In short, they were seeking to participate in what had been purely managerial decision-making, to join in thinking with managers at all levels of the corporate structure about the company, and in some cases, the community as a whole.

The first big concession had come in 1979 at Chrysler where the UAW agreed to give up more than $600 million in wages, time-off, and pensions in order to keep Chrysler going and make it eligible for government loan guarantees. In return the union gained most of the rights mentioned above as well as the seat on the board of directors for UAW President Douglas Fraser. (On March 5, 1982 Pan American World Airways named Robert L. Gould to its board of directors. Gould is president of the company's Air Line Pilots Association bargaining unit. Pan Am's unions had agreed earlier to work rules concessions in order to save the ailing company money.)

Ford, which lost $1 billion in 1981, in February 1982 made a contract with the UAW which resulted in savings of $1 billion during the three-year life of the contract. In return for cuts in real wages, fringe benefits and holidays, the company promised six months' notice before any plant was closed, not to close any plant simply to buy cheaper parts from outside the country, to guarantee workers with 15 years service up to 60% of their earnings if they were laid off and unable to find another job, and to give all workers a share in profits when and if pre-tax earnings reached 2.3% of sales.[5]

The Beginning of Change

Changes in the automobile industry had begun in the late 1960's at General Motors when the company was plagued with productivity problems. Unexcused absences increased 50% between 1965 and 1969. Sometimes on Mondays and Fridays as many as 20% of the work force did not show up. Grievances and disciplinary layoffs were at unprecedented levels. Drugs, alcohol and guns in the locker rooms were symbols of the deterioration.

A local union president in 1970 said:

> Every single unskilled man in my plant wants out. They just don't like it. This whole generation had been taught by their fathers to avoid the production line, to go to college to escape, and now some of them are trapped. They can't face it. They hate to go in there.[6]

At the same time foreign automobile manufacturers were acquiring an increasing share of the U.S. market. More and more money was being piped through the collective contract in an effort to buy better performance but to no avail. "Management and the public have lately been shortchanged," complained GM Chairman James Roche in 1970. "We have a right to more than we are receiving."[7]

The union was no less frustrated. In many ways it had lost control of its members. Try as it might to persuade them that they were getting a good deal in the collective agreement—in fact their wages were about twice the national average for manufacturing workers and twice that of their Japanese competitors—many workers were dissatisfied and unwilling to respect the discipline of the contract. In short, the authority of management, rooted in membership representation, had been eroded. Their relationship, prescribed in the contract, was no longer definable or negotiable by leaders whose authority was uncertain. Both groups were wallowing.

In 1970 Irving Bluestone took over as director of the General Motors department of the UAW and a year later Stephen H. Fuller left Harvard to become vice president of GM for personnel administration and development. Fuller's was a new job for GM. The company had split its labor relations staff in two, leaving the collective contract and its adversarial negotiating process with the vice president of labor relations, giving Fuller the task of solving the problems of productivity and motivation which had become so troublesome. It was a fortuitous set of choices. During the 1970s Bluestone and Fuller, working separately in their respective organizations, forged what was to be perhaps the most extensive and one of the most successful procedures in America for involving workers in what had been management decisions.

Shortly after his appointment Fuller said:

> What we are doing is signaling as obviously and as frequently as
> we can the commitment of top management that it is interested
> in improving job satisfaction. We are trying to open the doors and
> give people an opportunity to share in improving the quality of
> what they do. [8]

Those who are accustomed to and dependent upon the contract in
both management and the union were doubtful about, if not hostile to,
the participation which Fuller and Bluestone were encouraging. Their
efforts reflected an entirely different approach, oriented toward achieving consensus between management and labor, instead of continuing
the adversarial relationship rooted in conflict.

Speaking of George B. Morris, the vice president of industrial relations, Bluestone said:

> I think George felt that any encroachment upon managerial pre-
> rogatives which would be indicated by workers participating in
> a meaningful way in making decisions on the shop floor was an
> erosion of authority and the corporation must retain for itself all
> possible authoritarian control over the workplace. [9]

Likewise shop stewards and plant managers schooled in the old contractual proceedings and in old notions of management rights felt
threatened by the change. There was backbiting, union people fearing
that they were being coopted by management and management believing that their rights were being given to the union. The charges were
obviously somewhat hollow in that both sides could plainly see that
rights and authority they might have derived in the past from the old
ideas were feeble at best.

Beginning with joint health and safety committees, new hire programs, pre-retirement counseling, and drug and alcohol abuse programs, Fuller and Bluestone drove the managers and workers throughout the GM system into joint activities which eventually would improve
product quality, scheduling and organization of work, standard setting
and more. By 1980 it was clear that to be an effective manager at GM
you had to be able to obtain and retain the support of those whom you
managed. [10] The right to manage was coming from the managed.

Although the quality of work life program at GM was begun with the
commitment of Fuller and Bluestone at the top, its particular form of
evolution was under local control and differed from plant to plant.

Said Ray Calore, president of Local 664 at GM's Tarrytown, N.Y.
plant:

> We as a union knew that our primary job was to protect the
> worker and improve his economic life. But times had changed
> and we began to realize we had a broader obligation, which was
> to help the workers become more involved in decisions affecting
> their own jobs, to get their ideas, and to help them improve the
> whole quality of life at work beyond the paycheck.[11]

This was consistent with Bluestone's conception of the mission of a
union which was "to bring democratic values into the work place."
Donald Ephlin, now the UAW chief at Ford, echoed the same notion,
"We are going to be working for the expansion of industrial democracy
in the plant."[12]

To protect union members from the feared exploitation of quality of
work life programs by management—"a stopwatch in sheep's clothing,"
William Winpisinger of the Machinists union called them—both sides
agreed to six laws governing its application: QWL could not be used
to support a speedup or reduce manpower; workers could not be forced
to participate; no agreements in the contract could be waived; the
elected union representatives had a right to attend any QWL meetings;
the program was strictly voluntary; and either party could get out at any
time.[13]

The results of QWL at GM have been a dramatic decline in absenteeism and turnover, a marked increase in the number of plants which have
reached agreement on local contracts prior to a national settlement by GM
and the UAW, and improvements in productivity and quality of work.

In 1979 the union feared that GM was using QWL as a way to avoid
unionization, especially in some of its new southern plants. After all,
if workers and managers could control the plant through discussions
among themselves, what was the need for a union? Facing the possibility of a company-wide strike on this issue in 1979, GM agreed to
automatic union recognition at all new plants opened after 1979.

There seemed little likelihood of movement away from QWL at GM.
When George Morris retired, his successor as vice president of industrial relations was one of Fuller's men, Al Warren, former personnel director at Fisher Body. "That was a signal up and down the
system," said Fuller.[14] QWL had come to stay.

In many ways, however, its future is far from clear. Can the notion
of GM vs. the UAW truly become GM/UAW? The views of a GM
sander on the assembly line are relevant. Martin Douglas had been with
the company 18 years when he was laid off in February of 1982. He
wrote in the *New York Times*:

General Motors is constantly comparing my wages to those of the Japanese auto worker, but I am sure that GM doesn't want to enter into a relationship such as the Japanese firms enjoy with their workers.

GM has never offered to guarantee me a job for life as the Japanese do, or subsidize my housing, or provide me with opportunities for low-cost vacations. Instead, GM wants to cut my pay to that of my Japanese counterpart and close the plant whenever by so doing it will maximize its profits. . . .

I don't know what the president of General Motors made last year. I do know that in good years, he made close to a million dollars. I don't know exactly what he does each day, but I am sure I have a better idea of his job than he does of mine.

So now he comes to me when times are hard and asks for sacrifices, and I say to him: "You should have come a little earlier when times are good and we could have gotten to know each other. If you had, I would now be more willing to help."[15]

Managing the Transition

How long will it take to remove the legacy of adversarialism? How quickly can the sense of participation and control implicit in Bluestone's vision of corporate democracy become a reality? The answer to these questions depends on how well management, labor, and government understand the implications of what is happening. Bluestone and other union leaders like him are ambivalent about the radicality of what they have begun. They distinguish between what Bluestone calls "managing the work place and managing the enterprise." He prefers to see QWL in terms of the former, not the latter, but he acknowledges that over time worker involvement in broader managerial questions is inevitable. "In fact," he said recently, "it's happening more quickly than I would have expected."[16]

Glenn Watts, president of the Communication Workers of America, has made QWL an essential part of his union's national strategy with AT&T and other companies in the rapidly changing electronics and telecommunications field. "Workers must be involved in planning the introduction of new technology or it won't work," he said. "We are definitely moving in the direction of consensus-building and away from the old adversarial relationship." Although, like Bluestone, he was reluctant to suggest that unions would participate in management decisions about the enterprise as a whole, he admitted that "bit by bit we're going to get there. I can't at the moment imagine how, but it seems to be absolutely inevitable. Either that or we're going to have chaos in our society, with the people that don't have fighting to get something from those that have it. It's a question of timing. It will take time." Watts continued:

> If you look at what quality of work life really means, it is a breakdown in the adversarial relationship, a breakdown in the old notion of authority rooted in property, and shareholders, and a board of directors, the old hierarchy. The manager is going to get the right to manage, the ability to manage, only so long as the people he manages are interested and involved and prepared to give it to him. The task of management is to build this consensus, and the role of the union in these circumstances is one of contributing to the creation of the consensus.

At the same time Watts was conscious of tradition:

> To the extent that the workers are not the owners of the business, they play a different role. They've got an interest in the enterprise and their interest must be protected. But I do believe it can be protected by the more traditional collective bargaining process augmented by quality of work life programs and other such innovations. I do not embrace the idea that workers ought to participate on the board of directors, for example.[17]

Some like Thomas Donahue say that the collaboration occurring today is no different from the past. Noting that there have always been committees of cooperation between management and labor, he said "our interest in quality of work life goes back to the day—probably 200 years ago—when the first trade unionists banded together in America to seek to improve the condition of their work."[18] He argues persuasively that cooperation can only work if the union is strong. Union strength derives from the contract which rests on conflict of interest between labor and management. So there can only be cooperation if there is conflict.

The crucial question seems to be: Can the union be strong if the contract becomes less important? Can the union find strength in consensualism? It is significant that the CWA is finding that its skill and experience in negotiating quality of work life programs is an important part of its competitive strategy against other unions in the communications industry as well as elsewhere. Recently, for example, it organized 35,000 government workers in New Jersey at least partly owing to its QWL capabilities. If we assume that the needs of workers, companies and the country lie increasingly in the realm of consensus-making and QWL programs, then it might be that the union that sticks to its contractual traditions will die. It might be that the strong union will be the one which learns best how to define a new role for itself in the new approach. If that is so, there is no time to waste on ambivalence. It is necessary to face squarely the new relationships and redesign the union's role accordingly. The difficulty of doing this is plain. Union leaders and shop stewards brought up in the adversarial traditions, skilled in its tactics, and familiar with its language will find the new ways baffling and troubling.

How can workers with pressing short-term needs be expected to take a long-term view of the good of the enterprise? It will take considerable education, for example, for the union leader in the automobile industry to understand that if GM is going to be able to sell cars in the growing Mexican market it must as a matter of Mexican law produce cars in Mexico. In order for such a move to be successful American workers must be in some way compensated: retrained for new jobs, relocated, given a share of the corporation's profits gained in Mexico or some such deal. Is this the stuff of contractual bargaining or does it rather emerge from wide sharing of information, from common understanding and from a spirit of partnership? The role of government cannot be separated from such questions. Public policy for trade and investment is central. A major responsibility for funding the retraining and relocation of displaced workers must fail upon government. It may well be necessary for the U.S. to have a national manpower plan whereby skill shortages and surpluses are identified and appropriate educational efforts are made to provide the skills which are needed. Again, such suggestions are greeted with ambivalence by many.

Management, like labor, is ambivalent about QWL. It contributes to a happier work environment, increased productivity and good ideas about how to do things better. It builds a sense of teamwork and loyalty and in many instances increases the worker's sense of duty. Experience for example at the Cummins Engine plant in Jamestown, N.Y., which is highly participative, shows that peer group pressure on work teams is a potent deterrent to tardiness and absenteeism. In fact consensual pressures there have from time to time been unwholesomely severe.

But managers are anxious about the loss of authority and control which they perceive as inherent in the transition. Even though there is considerable evidence that the power of managers actually increases as they learn how to derive authority from those whom they manage, those who have never done it are naturally anxious. Middle managers and supervisors are especially uneasy. They are literally in the middle. In a survey conducted by Harvard Business School professors Richard Walton and Leonard Schlesinger, one supervisor said, "I'm like one of those lizards that is always changing color, except that I don't have any control over what color I am. When the workers want me I've always got to be there. When they don't, I have to tread lightly." Another noted that workers get a good deal of attention, training, and rewards from QWL, but he said, "When things are going well, no one recognized how I've busted my butt to get the team working together. But when things go poorly, they let met know right away."[19]

Furthermore, with the greater efficiency of participative systems, it is frequently possible to make do with fewer managers so that their fear of being laid off is added to their other apprehensions. This raises an interesting question of democracy. If workers are organized for democratic participation and representation and top management has its own organization and committees of one kind or another, may it not be necessary to organize supervisory personnel for adequate participation? Perhaps they should be allowed or even encouraged to join unions.

Some innovative managers in participative systems have been disappointed that their success in a particular plant may not be recognized at corporate headquarters. Walton has documented this phenomenon at the experimental Topeka facility of General Foods. Even though the Topeka experiment was an outstanding success in every respect, its practices threatened managers at headquarters "whose leadership style was built on opposite principles." The demands of Topeka managers for autonomy and independence—for going their own consensual way—created friction among those in headquarters who "simply did not understand the Topeka system . . . The effect of this friction was to sour the career opportunities within General Foods for most of the original Topeka managers."[20]

The problem for managers is the same as for unions: if they do not understand the full implications of what they are doing pragmatically they will fail to anticipate its full range of consequences and may fall prey to some of the worst possibilities of the transition. How are we to grasp the full implications of what is occurring? The concept of ideology is helpful. It is not that the changes outlined above are occurring for ideological reasons; they are the product of necessity, of inexorable changes in the real world and of pragmatic experimentation to find a better way. *But* those changes cannot be fully comprehended unless their ideological implications are made clear. Only then can managers and union leaders fully understand what old assumptions are being eroded and what new choices are before them. Only then can they see the full panoply of change of which their particular activities are but a part.

Ideological Implications of Transition

Ideology is the hymns we sing to justify and make legitimate what we are doing or, perhaps, what we would like to do. It is the collection of ideas through which we translate *values* into action. Justice, for example, is a value every community everywhere has always cherished in one way or another. So is economy, the efficient use of resources, and survival. In this sense values are noncontroversial. But, obviously, different communities at different times mean different things by justice; they have different conceptions of economy and different requirements for survival. Ideology is the bridge of ideas for carrying values into *the real world*. This bridge gives them specific meaning and makes them live in such institutions as government, corporations and labor organizations at a time and in a place. The very function of ideology makes it controversial. Frequently, as in America today, an old one tends to linger on, uninspected, while institutional practice departs from it in many pragmatic ways so as to cope more effectively with the real world. We do not practice what we preach and we find it difficult to preach what we practice. The resulting gap causes confusion and illegitimacy. There is uncertainty, for example, about the roles and relationships of government, corporations and union. They are forced increasingly to act differently from what they are supposed to do according to the old assumptions. Their leaders lack confidence; the institutions lack purpose.

There are two general ideologies — individualism and communitarianism — and many variations of each. The traditional ideology of the United States is composed of five great ideas that first came to America in the 18th century, having been set down in 17th century England as natural laws by John Locke, among others. These ideas found fertile soil in the vast, underpopulated wilderness of America and served the country well for a hundred years or so. Although throughout U.S. history the ideas have been buffeted and eroded by communitarian practices, particularly in times of crisis, they continue to be remarkably resilient. "They are," says Prof. Samuel Huntington, "at the very core of (our) national identity. Americans cannot abandon them without ceasing to be Americans in the most meaningful sense of the word — without, in short, becoming un-American."[21]

The First Prototype — Individualism

A review of the Lockean five provides a starting point for understanding the transformation now taking place.

1. *Individualism.* This is the atomistic notion that the community is no more than the sum of the individuals in it. Fulfillment lies in an essentially lonely struggle in what amounts to a wilderness where the fit survive — and where, if you do not survive, you are somehow unfit. (This harsh interpretation of Locke followed and contrasted with that of many of the founding fathers — Thomas Jefferson, for example — for whom individual fulfillment and happiness required a "moral sense" of participation in and obligation to a community as in the ideal of "the gentleman.") Closely tied to individualism is the idea of *equality*, in the sense implied in the phrase "equal opportunity," and the idea of *contract*, the individualistic device by which persons are tied together as buyers and sellers, employers and employees. In the U.S. political order, individualism evolved into *interest group pluralism*, which became the preferred means of directing society.

2. *Property rights.* Traditionally, the best guarantee of individual rights lay in the sanctity of property rights. By virtue of this concept, the individual was assured freedom from the predatory powers of the sovereign. From this notion the corporate manager derived the authority to manage which fixed his priorities on maximizing returns to shareholder-owners.

3. *Competition-consumer desire.* Adam Smith most eloquently articulated the idea that the uses of property are best controlled by each individual proprietor competing in an open market to satisfy individual consumer desires. It is explicit in traditional U.S. antitrust law and practise.

4. *Limited state.* In reaction to the powerful hierarchies of medievalism, the conviction grew that the least government was the best. Today we do not mind how big government may get, but we are reluctant to allow it authority or focus. Keep it separated, checked, and balanced, and whatever happens the cry is, don't let it plan — particularly down there in Washington. Let it be responsive to crises and to interest groups. Whoever pays the price can call the tune. Says Huntington: "Because of the inherently antigovernment character of the American Creed, government that is strong is illegitimate, government that is legitimate is weak."[22]

5. *Scientific specialization and fragmentation.* This is the corruption of Newtonian mechanics, which says that if we attend to the parts, as experts and specialists, the whole will take care of itself.

If we consider the past 5,000 years of human history, we are struck by the extent to which this atomistic, individualistic ideology constitutes a fundamental aberration from the historically typical communitarian norm. It stands as a radical and in many ways noble experiment that achieved its most extreme manifestation in America in the 19th century. Since that time it has been steadily deteriorating in the face of various challenges — wars, depressions, new economic and political systems, the concentration and growth of both population and corporations, ecological degeneration, and a realization of scarcity. The Pope said this ideology is not "untouchable dogma." He might have a gone a good deal further.

Even though deteriorating, however, the five components of the old ideology retain great resilience. They are the assumed source of legitimacy and authority for our great institutions. The difficulty is two-fold:

> 1. The old ideas perform less and less well as a definer of values in the real world of today. It is more and more apparent that the values the old ideology seeks to achieve are not being attained.

> 2. Many of our most important institutions — notably large, publicly held corporations, some trade unions, and the federal government — have either radically departed from the old ideology or are in the process of doing so in response to needs for such things as efficiency, economies of scale, productivity, and global competitiveness.

If we were to ask, what is the ideology that would legitimize the actual behavior of our institutions, we would, it would seem, come up with five counterparts to the Lockean five.

The Second Prototype—Communitarianism

Briefly put, these are the components of the ideology that has achieved or is achieving dominance in the United States, and this is the ideology implicit in Pope John Paul II's encyclical: communitarianism; rights and duties of membership; community need; the active, planning state; and holism.

1. *Communitarianism* The community—New York City, for example—is more than the sum of individuals in it; the community is organic, not atomistic. It has special and urgent needs as a community. The survival and the self-respect of the individuals in it depend on the recognition of those needs.

There are few who now get their kicks à la John Wayne. Individual fulfillment for most depends on a place in a community, an identity with a whole, a participation in an organic social process. Further, if the community, the factory, or the neighborhood is well designed, its members will have a sense of identity with it. They will be able to make maximum use of their capacities. If the community or its components are poorly designed, people will be correspondingly alienated and frustrated. In the complex and highly organized America of today, few can live as Locke had in mind.

Equality of result or hierarchy. There has also been a shift away from the old notion of equality. It used to be equality of opportunilty, an individualistic conception under which blacks, whites, men, and women had an equal place at the starting line and each was supposed to be able to go as far as he or she was able without discriminatory obstruction. Around 1970, however, this idea was radically altered by "affirmative action." The good community—the corporation or whatever—was told to adapt itself to the inequalities in the surrounding environment so as to approach equality of result.

In the 1980's "affirmative action" is under attack in the United States for several reasons. The idea of "reverse discrimination" offends white males; it is regarded by some as demeaning to those it was designed to help; and in the school system it produced what might be called the "nobody fails" syndrome, which eroded educational standards. Ideologically, there are three possibilities in the light of these objections:

> 1. The U.S. could stay with equality of result and try to make it work. Big institutions will have a hard time doing anything else because of their current commitments, existing law, and the ex-

pectations of their employees. Managers of such institutions may well miss the forceful hand of government.

   2. The U.S. could return to equality of opportunity which requires, above all, equality of education for blacks and whites. Is this to be achieved through integration, as the Supreme Court mandated in 1954, or some other way?

   3. The U.S. could move to the idea of hierarchy—meritocracy, for example—wherein one's place is determined by knowledge and skills without regard for either form of equality. If it is hierarchy, the question becomes who is at the top, who is at the bottom, and how acceptable will these designations be?

Consensus. The idea of consensus as opposed to contract is inherent in the actions of managers and unions as they seek ways in which to restrain wages, close plants, increase productivity, improve employee motivation, and promise fairness. It was what lay behind Fuller and Bluestone's work at G.M. and that of the managers at Topeka. It depends on labor-management trust instead of arm's length antagonism.

   As Donald Ephlin, UAW leader at Ford, said of the 1982 agreement: "It was a problem-solving exercise, not negotiations in the true sense. We had problems that we wanted solved—the loss of jobs and the lack of security that our members have. The supplementary unemployment benefit plan had gone broke; payments had stopped." And on the company side, Peter Pestillo, vice president of labor relations, was equally revealing: "We make a great effort in this agreement to work toward greater participation by our work force in the business process. I think that's the wave of the future. We use the word deep in the agreement that's simply called 'governance.' "[23] It seems doubtful that Ford and the UAW could have reached their agreement if the company's "employee involvement" program had not been in place, involving workers directly in management decisions at all 65 Ford assembly plants.

   The transition to consensus is impeded by the residue of traditonal ideology. Trade unions are naturally loathe to give up the power and legitimacy that once was theirs under the old notion of the adversarial, bargained contract. Managers, too, are nervous about moving away from the old bases of authority implicity in property rights and the contract, the old notions of governance. If improved productivity depends upon the transition, the issue is clear: How much crisis, how much recession is necessary before the United States can catch up with the Japanese and others who are more able to achieve consensus?

The problem in Europe is complicated by the presence of the pre-Lockean ideas of hierarchy and class. If the union is the vanguard of the working class as it is in Europe, the idea of consensus with management as opposed to conflict is particularly repugnant.

Much as some would argue otherwise, consensual systems are not all good. There is nothing utopian about communitarianism, as history and Jonestown surely remind us. As we go to consensus it is worth remembering that the idea of contract was invented to protect the individual against the group. Groupiness jeopardizes many precious attributes of individualism. And if the trade union derives its purpose and legitimacy from the adversarial notion of contract, and if consensus is inevitable, the labor movement is in trouble. It will either adapt or it will perish. In order to adapt it must appreciate fully its new functions in a consensual set-up. Pragmatically, unions are doing just this, but pragmatic innovation without ideological renovation is insufficient. In the steel industry, for example, cooperation—consensus—at the top of the industry between companies and the United Steelworkers of America has been occurring for more than a decade. But neither companies nor union perceived the ideological implications of what they were doing. The result was estrangement within the union between the shop steward on the shop floor, who lingered with the old adversarial idea, and the union leadership which had moved to a new idea. If consensualism is to work it must be introduced simultaneously from the top down and from the bottom up. The industry is now belatedly introducing workers' participation with management at the bottom but the legacy of adversarialism dies hard.

2. *Rights and duties of membership.* For some years in America a set of rights has been superseding property rights in political and social importance. These are rights to survival, to income, pensions, health, and other entitlements associated with membership in the American community or in some component of that community, such as a corporation.

The escalating rights of members in society have strained the ability of government to raise the taxes necessary in order to pay the bill. All levels of government have placed a firm budgetary cap on rights, actually reducing some. At the same time—inevitably—came the realization that if the community assures rights it must require duties. The question is: Who decides a person's duty? In Japan the community imposes a sense of duty—it always has. But in the U.S., "liberals" and "conservatives" alike were inclined to leave the question of duty to the individual—to upbringing, religion, and conscience. The inexorabilities of communitarianism, however, are forcing government to define the duty of those who do not seem to be doing it for themselves. It is called "workfare." If everyone has a right to a job, as the Humphrey-Hawkins Act suggests, does not everyone who is able-bodied have a duty to work? If so, how does a nation implement this idea? There would seem to be three ways of coping with the idle: Government can pay them; government can employ them, or government can coerce or subsidize business to employ them. Europe and the United States have tended to prefer the first two, Japan the third. The U.S., however, appears to be moving toward the third. If so, the implications for the role of government and its relationship to business and labor are important to consider.

If the duties of the poor and the weak are to be made more explicit, does it not follow that those of the rich and powerful must also be clear? As the Reagan budget cuts made their way through Congress in the summer of 1981, David Stockman, director of the Office of Management and Budget, was shocked at the failure of government to require sacrifice from the well-organized and powerful economic interest groups. He felt that the moral premise of austerity had been eroded.[24]

Duty may also be defined by peer groups, as noted earlier. Implicit in QWL programs is the idea of duty, both managers and workers limiting their rights, conscious of their interdependency and the interests of the whole firm. The Ford-UAW agreement, for example, says that non-union salaried employees must accept the same hardships as union workers in an "equality of sacrifice" provision. Local union officials may file a grievance if they think that Ford is keeping too many managers on the rolls while union members are being laid off.[25]

Not only have membership rights become more important than property rights to many, but the utility of property as a legitimizing idea has eroded. For example, it is quite obvious that our large public corporations are not private property at all, that is they are not owned—in any real sense of ownership—by shareholders. Attempts at shareholder democracy represent heroic but naively conservative strategies to force shareholders to behave like owners and thus to legitimize corporations as property. But such action is fraught with practical difficulties. Lingering with the old idea may delay the time when managers take a long-term view of corporate interests rather than managing in the short-run interests of shareholders.

If GM and the hundreds of other large corporations like it are not property, then what are they? The best we can say is that they are some sort of collective, floating in philosophic limbo, dangerously vulnerable to the charge of illegitimacy and to the charge that they are not amenable to community control.

There is no doubt that some means will be found to legitimize the large corporation and to make it responsive to community needs. There are three possibilities: 1) control can rest with shareholders and be justified by the ability to compete to satisfy consumer desires in the market; 2) control can come from all the members of the corporation; 3) control can come from the community through government. The trend appears to be away from 1) and towards 2) and 3). Important questions of corporate governance arise: How are the workers to be represented in decision-making at various levels of the corporation? Do they want to be? After all, it takes time and effort. What if there is no organized representation of workers as is the case in most U.S. companies? Does management of the auto industry, for example, not need a union to reflect worker interests adequately in corporate decision-making and to make decisions acceptable to workers? May not AT&T want Glen Watts on its board whatever he might prefer? How does he responsibly say no? And how is the community or government to be best reflected in corporate control? Regulation is cumbersome and expensive, especially when unplanned and incoherent. Some form of partnership with government seems preferable but who is the senior partner and what are the terms of the partnership? What level of government is appropriate? Putting it another way, for any particular community need, what is the relevant community? The answers to such questions require careful thought about competence and authority and how the two are put together. Workers may have increasing authority, but not necessarily the competence to manage.[26] Business may have considerable competence to deal with toxic substances, but government has the authority to make ultimate trade-offs.

The governance problems of ailing giants — like Chrysler — pose particularly interesting ideological problems. Under the terms of the traditional ideology, such companies should die when they no longer serve the interests of their owners or consumers in the marketplace. But the politics of the real world makes death unacceptable so at the last moment they are snatched from the grave in the name of an ill-defined community need, propped up and made to continue their miserable existence. A more efficient, humane, and competitive approach is suggested by Japan's communitarian system. The sick corporation is diagnosed when its disease first appears (about 1974, most would say, in

Chrysler's case). Industry, government, and labor officials talk together; a consensus is reached about the best remedy. If Chrysler had been in Japan, for example, the remedy might have been industry consolidation through merger with retraining and relocation for displaced workers. An early diagnosis gives everyone time to manage an adjustment. It seems likely that sooner or later the United States will be forced to recognize the enormous cost of its ideological schizophrenia. Perhaps the only question is when and how the institutions involved will rearrange themselves.

3. *Community need.* Reliance upon marketplace competititon enforced by the antitrust laws as a way of defining community need no longer seems adequate. As the Justice Department has recently suggested, bigness is no longer bad. In fact it seems necessary in many cases in order to compete with the Japanese. Also, reliance upon individual consumer desires does not meet community needs for clean air and water, safety, energy, and jobs. As a consequence, the means of determining community need requires greater attention, especially when it is impossible for the community to meet all of its needs at once.

4. *Active, planning state.* This brings us to the role of the state, which is changing radically. For better or worse, it has become the arbiter of community needs. Inevitably, it will take on unprecendented tasks of coordination, priority-setting, and planning in the largest sense. It will need to become far more efficient and authoritative, capable of making the difficult and subtle tradeoffs that now confront us — for example, between environmental purity, energy supply, economic stability and growth, rights of membership, and global competition.

Ironically, President Reagan's breathtaking 1981 economic program to cut taxes, increase defense spending, balance the federal budget, increase productivity, cut inflation, and attain full employment may well turn out to mark the beginning of an explicit recognition that the U.S. economy requires government planning — if not a planned economy.

If the role of government were more precisely and consciously defined, the government could be smaller and more efficient. To a great extent, the plethora of bureaucracies today is the result of a lack of focus and comprehension, an ironic bit of fallout from the old notion of the limited state. With more consciousness we could also consider more fruitfully which issues are best left to local or regional planning and which, in fact, transcend the nation-state and require a more global approach.

In the face of serious pressures from Japanese and European business organizations, which emanate from ideological settings quite different from our own, there will be more and more reason to set aside the old idea of domestic competition in order to organize U.S. business effectively to meet world competition. Managers will probably welcome if not urge such a step; they may, however, be less willing to accept the necessary concomitant: If, in the name of efficiency, economies of scale, and the demands of world markets, we allow restraints on the free play of domestic market forces, then other forces will have to be used to define and preserve the public interest. These "other forces" will amount to clearer control by the political order, in some form or other.

If the United States is being beaten by government-business-labor systems, which are more effective than our own, as Mr. Caldwell and others have said, we either must raise tariff walls to protect ourselves from these alien systems, or we must assemble our own tripartite apparatus in order to compete successfully. Since tariff protection cannot be effectively maintained in an increasingly interdependent world, the only choice is a tripartite system assembled in the name of community need. The labor movement has favored this since 1980; business and government have been ambivalent about it. A great deal of the ambivalence derives from traditional ideological assumptions about the roles and relationships of government and business. These need inspection.

5. *Holism—interdependence.* Finally, and perhaps most fundamentally, the old idea of scientific specialization has given way to a new consciousness of the interrelatedness of all things. Spaceship earth, the limits of growth, the fragility of our life-supporting biosphere have dramatized the ecological and philosophical truth that everything is related to everything else. Harmony between the works of man and the demands of nature seems an absolute rule of survival. It is thus of profound ideological significance, subverting in many ways all of the Lockean ideas and raising an important question about the Pope's use of the biblical passage, *subdue the earth*, which can lead to ecological irresponsibility—in place of ecological harmony which, I am sure, he espouses.[27]

Conclusion: A Cautionary Note

The ideas in the papal encyclical support the new departures in labor management relations occurring in the United States. They also challenge traditional ideological assumptions in America. These assump-

252 **Strategies for Renewing Capitalism**

tions go well beyond business and labor and inevitably involve a conception of the individual and his place in the community, the role of government and a conception of science and reality. If the innovations upon which the United States has embarked are to be successful, the ideological implications of the changes must be observed, old assumptions examined, new ones put in place and ambivalencies managed. Otherwise labor unions, corporations, and government will be weak and uncertain about their missions, their roles, and their relationships. The community as a whole will suffer.

NOTES

1. All references to *On Human Work* will give the paragraph number in the text of the paper. I am using the translation provided by the United States Catholic Conference: Publication No. 825, Office of Publishing Services. Para. 5,6,13,14,12.
2. NAM press release 77-17, December 1, 1977, mimeo, Washington, D.C.
3. "The Automobile Crisis," *Harvard Business Review*, January-February 1981, pp. 77 and 81.
4. Para. 13.
5. *The Economist*, February 20, 1982, p. 16.
6. Bert Spector and Paul Lawrence, *General Motors and the United Automobile Workers*, Harvard Business School case service, President and Fellows of Harvard College, 1981, p. 2.
7. Ibid, p. 3.
8. Ibid, p. 5.
9. Bluestone Interview, Detroit, Michigan, September 8, 1981.
10. Bluestone Interview, op cit.
11. Spector and Lawrence, op cit, p. 9.
12. *Harbus News*, April 20, 1981, p. 1.
13. Bluestone Interview, op cit.
14. Spector and Lawrence, op cit, p. 16.
15. Martin Douglas, "G.M. vs Its Workers," *New York Times*, op ed page, Feb. 15, 1982.
16. Bluestone Interview, March 17, 1982.
17. Watts Interview, Washington, D.C., November 23, 1981.
18. University of Massachusetts, speech, January 1982, mimeo., p. 2.
19. "Do Supervisors Thrive in Participative Work Systems?", *Organizational Dynamics*, Winter 1979, p. 26.
20. Richard Walton, "The Topeka Work System: Optimistic Visions,

Pessimistic Hypotheses, and Reality." Harvard Business School Working Paper, 1982, p. 22.

21. Samuel Huntington, *American Politics: The Promise of Disharmony* (Cambridge, Mass.: Harvard University Press, 1981), p. 63.

22. Ibid., p. 39.

23. The MacNeil-Lehrer Report, Feb. 15, 1982, transcript, pp. 2 and 4.

24. William Greider, "The Education of David Stockman," *The Atlantic Monthly*, December 1981, pp. 50-54.

25. *Business Week*, March 1, 1982, p. 91.

26. See John F. Witte, *Democracy, Authority, and Alienation in Work* (Chicago: University of Chicago Press, 1980).

27. Para. 9.

CHAPTER 11

Focus on Labor

by Mark J. Fitzgerald, C.S.C.

IN THIS ESSAY I PLAN TO CONSIDER SOME OF THE PRACTICAL IMPLICATIONS OF *Laborem Exercens* as they relate to the labor scene. To this end it is my intention first to set forth certain basic premises of the encyclical and then endeavor to relate them as closely as possible to current trends in labor-management relations, both here and abroad, trends which may approximate "the many proposals put forward—by the highest magesterium of the Church—for joint ownership of the means of work, sharing by the workers in the management and/or profits of business."[1]

First of all it might be noted that Pope John Paul II has a somewhat different concept of the factors of production than conventional economic wisdom classifies as land, labor, capital and management. As one instance, John Paul II defines capital as including "not only the natural resources placed at man's disposal, but also the whole collection of means by which man appropriates natural resources and transforms them" to his needs. Such means include, "machines, factories, laboratories and computers."[2] Thus, for John Paul II, land (or natural resources) and capital come under the same treatment. Here one may recall the statement: "The expression 'subdue the earth' has an immense range."[3] In actuality *Laborem Exercens* indicates that capital which comes out of the earth through the work of man is within this "range."

Further, capital "remains a mere instrument" in providing the means of production for the worker as the "primary efficient cause" in developing and transforming the resources of the earth for his own use.[4]

Moreover, the biblical term "subdue" in the mind of John Paul II, has no element of ruthless exploitation, but refers to the use of land and capital in a planned and rational way toward the realization of one's humanity and for the benefit of all mankind, in keeping with the will of the Creator of "nature," the source of land and capital.[5] Further, the Pontiff states that the whole collection of instrumental factors, no matter how faultless they may be in themselves, are nevertheless, over generations, the result of work and are "subordinate to human labor."[6] John Paul considers the observations just stated to be the theological basis for the sphere of man's labor in the process of production[7] and "the guiding thread," of his encyclical.[8]

In light of these considerations, the same document maintains that instruments of production only condition human work and are not to upset the primacy of the person over things by placing the worker in a state of dependence which reduces him to secondary importance.[9] In this regard, the Pontiff points out that the priority of labor has been violated by laissez faire capitalism, which has held as an untouchable dogma the exclusive right to private ownership of the means of production and has rejected Christian teaching that the right to private property "is subordinated to the right to common use" of "the goods of the whole of creation."[10]

However, John Paul, as did his predecessors, likewise rejects Marxist collectivism, which denies the right of a person to the private ownership of property, "when it is a question of the means of production."[11] In effect he recognizes the legitimate role of those who function as entrepreneurs and who own the means of production or act in place of the owners.[12] The Marxist program for eliminating the class owning capital goods is thus foreign to Catholic teaching.

Nevertheless, John Paul noted that property, particularly the means of production, is to "serve work" and that it is contrary to the nature and legitimate possession of capital to set it up as a separate entity in opposition to workers or to exploit them.[13] Even more strongly, the Pontiff holds that the only legitimate title to the possession of capital, whether privately or publicly owned, is to serve workers and thus achieve the "universal destination of goods and the right to common use of them."[14] Obviously, here is a restatement of traditional Christian teaching on the responsibility for stewardship over the goods of the earth. Moreover, John Paul also observes that if this duty of stewardship is not being performed, socialization of certain means of production cannot be excluded from consideration.[15]

Further, the Pontiff observes that under any form of ownership of the means of production, care must be taken to avoid a threat to the right order of values by regarding work as an impersonal force to the extent that the worker himself is seen in the dependent role of "an instrument of production," rather than "as the effective subject of work and its true maker and creator."[16] To safeguard against this threat, John Paul urges that every country should have as its central principle for social and economic policy that the human being is the purpose of production.[17]

The Dignity of Work

To emphasize the dignity of work, the encyclical points out that it is the will of the Creator that through work the individual should be able to achieve the dominion over the world that has been entrusted to him.[18] Moreover, rather than degrading him, work should make him more of a human being, provide the foundation for family life and enable the individual to enjoy human rights permitting him to derive creative, educational and other meritorious benefits through his labors.[19] By contrast, when a low estimate is placed on the dignity of work and the rights related to it, substandard wages, unemployment and family insecurity become a scourge.[20]

In the view of John Paul, a sound labor system will result from the overcoming of the opposition between the "small but highly influential group of entrepreneurs" who own or manage the means of production and the vast number of employees who only contribute their labor.[21] Here he stresses again the need to recognize the real priority of labor over the instruments of production by encouraging workers to share in the whole production process.[22]

Unlike the Marxists, the Pontiff denies that opposition between the parties above springs from the existing structure of the production process. In fact, he holds that those who run or manage the means of production and those who provide the labor in the process "are inseparably linked."[23] Nevertheless, John Paul stresses that the worker wants not only proper renumeration for his labor, but also desires that within the process of production provision be made for him to realize that in the work he is doing, "he is working 'for himself'," and does not feel because of excessive top down control that "he is just a cog in a huge machine moved from above."[24] The encyclical points out that if such provision is not made "incalculable damage" results not only for the economy, but especially for the worker as such.[25]

While such warning had apt reference to work on the typical assembly line, it takes on even more significance during the present development of new processes such as "the electronics and the microprocessor technology" of more recent times.[26] One might add other areas, including telecommunications, computerization and robotics. Here the Pontiff observes that although these developments of technology can serve as a useful ally in one's work, there is still the possibility that such mechanization can supplant the individual, depriving him or her, if not of employment, very possibly of "all personal satisfaction and the incentive to creativity and responsibility," putting the worker in subservience to the machine.[27]

On an even more grim note, with respect to a large segment of modern technology and its potential impact on mankind, John Paul urged that consideration be given the "prospect of worldwide catastrophe in case of nuclear war, which would have almost unimaginable possibilities of destruction."[28] One might observe that in such an event technology would not stop at being the industrial master, but would become the apocalyptic destroyer.

Returning to the principle of the common use of goods, which John Paul sets forth as "the first principle of the whole ethical and social order,"[29] he regards wages as a practical form to enable the great portion of mankind to have access to goods intended for the use of all, whether goods of nature or fabricated goods.[30] For a just wage, which he regards as the key to a proper relation between worker and employer, John Paul declares that an adult responsible for a family should through his wages be able not only to maintain his family but also be able to provide security for its future, "without the spouse having to take up gainful employment outside the home . . . . "[31] The Pontiff notes that this amount of renumeration could come either through a family wage from the employer, or also through family allowances to mothers "devoting themselves exclusively to their families."[32] He regards the achievement of this amount of renumeration per family as the test of "the justice of the whole socioeconomic system."[33]

The State and Labor

John Paul assigns a prominent role to the State in regard to conducting a just labor policy, namely one which assures that "the objective rights of the worker are respected." While the employer has the responsibility concerning concrete terms for "the actual work contract and labor relations,"[34] he considers it a function of the state to condition the conduct of the employer in general terms, without freeing him from his own responsibility to assure the rights of his workers and not let them be left to the vicissitudes of economic systems.[35]

To this end the Pontiff holds that the state should concern itself with "the issue of suitable employment for all who are capable of it."[36] Government action is therefore seen as appropriate in time of general unemployment or regional unemployment and he notes that at a certain level unemployment "can become a social disaster."[37] Of particular regret to Pope John Paul is the situation confronting young people who after appropriate technical and professional training are unable to find work and thus cannot become actively responsible for the economic and social development of the community.[38]

In any event, John Paul notes that it is a moral duty of the state "to make suitable grants indispensable for the subsistence of unemployed workers and their families."[39] He derives this duty from the basic principle of the moral order, namely, the common use of goods, or "the right to life and subsistence."[40]

As a preventive measure for the dangers of unemployment, John Paul urges that the state, in cooperation with various intermediate groups between government and the parties at the work place, "make provision for overall planning with regard to the different kinds of work" which shape economic life. He notes that by making use of the initiative of individuals, groups and the local work complex, a "one-sided centralization by the public authorities" will be averted and a more rational coordination will result.[41]

On the international scene the Pontiff notes that to safeguard the objective rights of workers of every type whether "manual or intellectual, industrial or agricultural,"[42] channels of communication should be maintained with such multi-national bodies as the United Nations and its affiliated organizations, including the International Labor Organization and the Food and Agriculture Organization. John Paul considers it their task to be guided by a precise diagnosis of complicated world problems, taking into account the influence of natural, civil and historical circumstances.[43] By rational planning for the organization of work and mindful of the needs of individual states, the Pontiff believes there is more likelihood of arriving at "the right proportions between the different kinds of employment," namely, industrial, white-collar, scientific and services.[44] To supplement such planning, need was expressed for a proper system of education and instruction to enable workers to perform at best advantage in occupations appropriate to them.[45] Here John Paul calls world attention to the vast numbers of people presently unemployed or underemployed, and even beset by hunger, as ample evidence that currently the organization of work and employment is critically at fault in major areas.[46]

The Role of Unions

Mindful that workers themselves must shoulder the greater part of the effort to defend their rights mentioned above, John Paul acknowledges that this situation gives rise to another right, the right of association to form unions. He further points out that associations "are an indispensable element — in modern industrialized societies," not only for workers in industry, but for every occupation, including employers.[47]

However, the Pontiff urges that workers should stress a positive, constructive role for their unions by promoting issues which are in harmony "with the needs and merits of working people" in the various occupations and even in times of controversy or opposition they should always be mindful that workers and employers must remain united in a producing community.[48] Avoiding any tendency to follow a policy of narrow group self-interest, unions according to John Paul, should aim at correcting, for the sake of the common good, whatever may be defective "in the system of ownership of the means of production or in the way these are managed."[49]

Nevertheless, John Paul stresses that while "union activity undoubtedly enters the field of politics" in the sense of having a prudent regard for the common good, unions do not have the nature of political parties seeking civic power, nor should they be the pawns of political parties, or be too closely linked with them. He notes that otherwise they can be deflected from their proper role of safeguarding the just rights of their members and be used for ulterior purposes.[50]

The encyclical recognizes the legitimacy of the strike or work stoppage by unions to obtain the just demands of their members when it takes place "under proper conditions and within just limits."[51] Here John Paul notes that the strike remains an "extreme means" and its use for political purposes is not warranted. Moreover, he points out that a strike must not put at risk "essential community services" and observes that "abuse of the strike weapon" could lead to the stoppage of all socioeconomic activity, a condition contrary to the common good.[52]

We might turn now to a passage in the encyclical where John Paul II spoke approvingly of "proposals for joint ownership of the means of work, sharing by the workers in the management and/or profits of businesses" as recognition of the workers' proper position in the production process.[53] This passage has close relevance to John Paul's views on the purpose of production, the role of work and the worker's share in the economic process.

As an indication of how great is the variance between the main thrust of *Laborem Exercens*, regarding the respective roles of labor and capital (and conventional economic thinking), it is appropriate to reflect for a moment on what has long been accepted as the proper function for these two factors of production. It has been held that the key characteristic of private enterprise in capitalist economies is the control of production decisions by owners of capital and the managers who represent them. As a consequence the control of work remains separate from the work as such. In effect those who operate the machinery to produce goods do not decide what types of machinery or technology should be installed nor the manner in which they should be used. According to conventional economies, efficiency requires that decisions on matters pertaining to methods of production, investment policy, pricing and the like must be the exclusive prerogative of those whose capital is at risk in the enterprise.

According to this view, to maintain growth in profits, the owners of capital and their managers must retain the function of decision-making and use it in the most efficient way or else the enterprise will succumb to market forces. Accordingly, this arrangement has meant the selection of capital-intensive programs with decreasing employment per unit of production. It follows therefore that efficiency in this context embraces worker well-being, increased employment and greater output only if in accord with greater profits for capital. Thus, the individual who is employed to operate the machinery owned by another is largely controlled by decisions of others concerning his work.[54]

Consideration will now be given to various trends in labor-management relations in several industrial nations to determine the extent, if any, they indicate progress toward reaching the goals set forth in *Laborem Exercens*. First consideration will be given to collective bargaining.

Collective Bargaining

This device in the United States has been mainly relied on by unions to affect corporate policy.[55] As one prominent union official has pointed out, through it grievance procedures are now firmly established which protect the employee's right to be heard and to be represented in case of disciplinary action. Moreover, through collective bargaining workers have achieved higher wages, reduced hours and improved working conditions. Further, through negotiation between management and unions additional benefits, once thought beyond reach of workers, are part of collective bargaining contracts; they include paid sick leave, holidays, vacations with pay, health insurance, pension plans, unemployment benefits and adjustments for cost of living.[56]

Yet collective bargaining has brought about no significant change in distribution of wealth or income from owners of capital to workers. A study based on the U. S. Bureau of the Census, Statistical Abstract for 1976, shows that from 1947 to 1975 the shares of earned income by families, from the top fifth to the lowest fifth, have undergone no significant change. However, family income has risen in absolute terms for all five groups, thus greatly reducing the number of families who were in poverty in the 1960's.[57] Moreover, management control has not been shifted to workers to any great extent. Key decisions on what is to be produced, location of plants, plant closures and mergers are usually the exclusive prerogatives of management.

Further, even some of the recent benefits gained under collective bargaining are now in the process of "giveback" renegotiations.

Even as late as 1976 the traditional attitude of the AFL-CIO on not challenging the decision-making jurisdiction of management was restated at an international conference in Montreal to the effect that unions had no desire to become partners with management by confusing in any way "the distinctions between the respective roles of management and labor in the plant."[58] Strong preference for sturdy independence and aggressive collective bargaining was espoused instead.

As an indication that management has been in accord with keeping this distinction intact, a vice president of the United Autoworkers recalled that "when Walter Reuther many years ago talked about what we would accept at the bargaining table, if prices were reduced, we were told that was none of our concern. When we asked the companies to improve the quality of the product, we were told that was none of our concern."[59]

Nevertheless, in recent months, as a trade-off for possible "giveback" concessions, the United Automobile Workers have requested some form of profit-sharing proposals from the automotive companies. Moreover, in early 1981 the UAW advocated that workers should demand "input into decision-making, corporate accountability, and democratic national planning so that rebuilding America's auto industry will benefit us all."[60]

Edward L. Cushman, former vice president of American Motors, Inc., observes that the basic desires of employees to achieve "security, recognition, opportunity for change and improvement" and belief that the employer cares for them have often been frustrated because management has not been properly sensitive to the role of the corporation as a social institution. Cushman points out that the worker expects and is in need of job and income security. Further, it is his desire to have the ability to "predict what is to happen to him on the job." Moreover, he wants assurance that he is a member of a continuing group with regular work assignments, who enjoys recognition and respect from his employer and can feel confident that he is making his due contribution to the general production effort.[61] Cushman urges that long-range planning to secure this objective is an unfulfilled need to be met by employers and must be put into effect if management is to gain the worker's maximum contribution to the corporation.[62]

He notes, moreover, that efforts to achieve "union participation in management decisions on plant location, plant closings and production scheduling," have not met with much success in the United States. At best, he observes, there has been some progress through collective bargaining agreements in placing limits on "contracting out" work formerly done in a union plant.[63]

Cushman acknowledges that unions have an impressive history of achievement for their members and for society as a whole. He believes that through collective bargaining a more equitable sharing of corporate income has resulted not only through wages, but from benefits, including pensions and health insurance. He notes that, through unions, rules have been devised to prevent capricious managerial decisions on matters of "job assignments, job security and working conditions." Cushman points out that by means of "the grievance procedure and arbitration," a body of "private jurisprudence has been established to enforce these rules" and "the dignity of the worker as a human being has been enhanced."[64]

Worker Representatives on Boards of Directors

A trend more noticeable in European countries than in the United States is the appointment of representatives from workers to serve on the boards of directors of major coporations. As rationalization for this development is the assumption that the governing body of last resource for the corporation is the board of directors and that employees of the company should be recognized as a group deserving of representation in such a body, namely, by individuals of their own choosing. As board members it would be their function to present views markedly different from the conventional position of directors representing the sectors of management and finance.[65] This rather sanguine expectation of the role for worker-directors has not been borne out from the findings of an extensive study of their performance in European countries.

The final report of the Bullock Commission in England noted a conclusion in a study by the National Swedish Industrial Board of three years of experience with minority representation by worker-directors. The Swedish Board observed that while one could question whether this type of representation had thus far caused any notable increase of the influence exerted by employees, it had nevertheless facilitated opportunities for insight and in the long run could increase employee influence as well.[66] For the present it appears that minority directors have little opportunity to alter the character of board decision-making because they bring about no actual shift of power from shareholders and management to the worker group and are really fully dependent on the other directors who reflect the controlling influence.

Another factor disadvantageous to the worker-director is his dissimilarity to the other board members because he lacks demonstrated managerial ability and ownership rights. Accordingly, he tends to remain in the background and only raises issues directly affecting workers such as plant closures or job security and acquiesces to other management positions.[67]

A number of suggestions have been formulated which could make the influence of worker-directors to some degree more effective regarding corporate operations. It has been held that they should have full participation on all corporate committees in which board members take part. Further, worker-directors should include a substantial representation from local union plant officials who thus have direct links and accountability to local unions.

In contrast to the situation in West Germany, it has been suggested that compensation for a worker-director not be paid to the individual himself, but be deposited in a union fund so as to lessen the status gap between the worker-director and other union members. It has been noted that board compensation both in Europe and the United States is frequently equal to the income of a full-time worker for a whole year.

Further, it is recommended that worker-directors should have adequate staff and research facilities, preferably provided by their unions, at their disposal to aid in their analysis of information presented to them. In this regard it is urged that worker-directors are entitled to receive more information, by having company books available for their examination. It is also said that worker-directors at present are handicapped by legal and customary restrictions concerning the particular topics at board meetings which they can discuss with their union members.

A significant recommendation of the Bullock Commission in England, in addition to urging parity representation, is the provision of government funds to be used for the training and education of new worker-directors. Further, Carnoy and Shearer observe that with the advent of worker-directors in Sweden in 1973 the Swedish Trade Union Confederation has maintained a training school for their use with a curriculum including courses on the basics of finance, accounting and planning.

According to European experience, any disadvantage from the use of worker-directors is not that they might present a subversive threat. Rather, it is the possibility they could be of no relevance whatever and even be a deception. Unless their function can really be demonstrated as part of the total effort to bring about industrial democracy, such an unfortunate outcome will not be avoided. Further, because of the limited role played by corporate boards, other strategies need also be followed to achieve democracy in the economy and the workplace, including broader issues in collective bargaining and new trends in labor legislation.[68]

Co-Determination

With respect to worker representatives on company boards, it is appropriate here to comment on the development of German co-determination which began in 1950 in the iron and steel industries, and provides for supposed parity representation by worker-directors for all major companies since 1976. Early fears that this type of worker representation would jeopardize policies advocated by management or stockholder representatives have been found to be without warrant. A study done by the Biedenkopf Commission and sponsored by the German government, indicates that worker-directors have demonstrated little inclination to affect general business policy of a given company and have given their attention to social and personnel factors during board sessions. In consequence there has been slight indication that worker-directors have had any impact on decisions relating to investments, dividends or other matters of concern to stockholders. Nevertheless the Biedenkopf Commission did find that worker-directors have brought about a greater stress on social issues, but in no instance did they challenge the acceptance of the canon of profitability as the basis of managerial planning and policy.[69]

In the conclusion of his study of German co-determination, Alfred Diamont states that it has served more to maintain the character of an industrial system than to transform it and represents an evolutionary trend from the Workers Council Movement in post-1918 Germany, now stripped "of its broader political aims and of its radical political ambitions." Moreover, he notes that it is still "far removed from full-parity codetermination," and even doubts that, if the latter is ever achieved, there would be a radical transformation of society and economy in the Federal Republic of Germany. Nevertheless, Diamont observes that one result has been a much greater tendency by management to engage in worker consultation on an extensive range of issues.[70]

Returning to the assumption that boards of directors are the ultimate source of decision-making for corporations, there are a number of factors which cause one to doubt this assumption. It appears more likely that these boards tend to serve as ratifying bodies for decisions already made by management. By the very fact of their infrequent meetings they must depend on management for information and counsel in order to reach realistic decisions. Outside directors, for the most part busily engaged as heads or representatives of other corporations, are especially dependent on management for specific information regarding board meetings. Needless to say, inside directors are the management people themselves who, in separate sessions, have already formulated the decisions for the board as a whole. The worker-director, without corporate connections, remains an outsider who is easily out-voted if he is inclined to challenge majority views.[71]

Works Councils

Following World War II, works councils came into being in many Western European countries. They consist of plant-level committees with elected worker representatives who consult with management on various work issues. However, actual negotiations still take place at the top level between national unions and national employer associations.[72] This latter circumstance, which keeps the works council in merely an advisory role and thus deprived of any actual decision-making power, has brought about a widespread disillusionment in terms of the initial expectations held for the works councils.[73]

In Italy, however, because of extensive strikes in 1969, a more meaningful type of worker participation has been put in effect. Through floor and factory assemblies and councils, elected workplace representatives have control of plant-level negotiations and have replaced the old former consultative works councils. Moreover, they have broadened the scope of bargaining and established permanent negotiations at the workplace with no restriction on issues to be brought to the bargaining table.[74]

As instances of new confrontations with management because of the changed form of worker participation, challenges have related to organization of work, and the power of management relating to planned investments. In exchange for a commitment by the Fiat Company to place investments in southern Italy, the workers agreed to extend a reduction in working hours over a longer time zone. The agreement concerning the southern investment was no vague promise, but actually included detailed provisions for Fiat's expenditures on social infrastructure in the south. A similar gain by workers through negotiations took place in regard to investment plans at Alfa-Romeo, a government-owned automobile company. Slater notes that the significance of these Italian in-plant worker councils is not only in the unrestricted range of issues for negotiations, but also in the worker initiative in defining their scope.[75]

New Labor Legislation in Sweden

Carnoy and Shearer point out that Sweden, to a greater degree than all other countries in Western Europe, has made the most progress through legislation toward increasing workers' control both at the workplace and in broader company decision-making. They note that a series of laws passed since 1971 has substantially modified the structure of authority within Swedish corporations, by reducing managerial prerogatives and subjecting to the collective bargaining process an entirely new area of managerial decisions. While many of these laws are too recent for adequate appraisal of the practical results they will bring, it is believed they nevertheless represent a distinct break with Sweden's past methods in the field of industrial relations.

As one instance, the revision of the 1949 Work Safety Law, passed in 1973, authorizes the in-plant health and safety steward to halt any work process the steward regards as dangerous until a judgment has been rendered by a government health inspector. Moreover, the law stands as guarantor of the steward's job security, training and time off with pay to discharge his duties. Moreover, this law shifts from the union to the employer the burden of instigating a court challenge and presenting evidence. Further, the company is legally bound to provide the safety steward and the plant safety committee information in advance regarding scheduled changes in plant layout, equipment and new construction. Such planned changes can be delayed by union representatives on the grounds of safety and health under the law, including psychological as well as physical well-being.

With respect to job security, employers under the Security and Employment Act must give notice of dismissal from one to six months in advance; the variation as determined by length of service and age. All "unreasonable" terminations are illegal and this term for older workers is given a legal definition. If a dispute arises, the affected person remains on the job with full pay until a labor court resolves the matter, with the employer assuming the burden of proof.

The Swedish Law on Employment Promoting Measures provides for tripartite committees composed of union, company and government employment office representatives, which have for their purposes to alter personnel policy and redesign jobs in order to fit local demand for labor to the existing labor supply. Further, this law requires employers to give notice both to the local union and the local employment office of projected layoffs up to six months in advance in order to provide greater opportunities for older employees and others who also have some kind of handicap.

The law on the status of union officials confers on them all the legal protection enjoyed by safety stewards under the Work Safety Law. In addition they are given the right to information and the right to time off for training for union work at company expense. As a means of providing even more information to the unions for collective bargaining, a 1976 law requires that all firms with at least twenty-five employees must have two worker representatives on the board of directors.

A rather sweeping law on co-determination passed in 1976 states that unions can negotiate contracts for co-determination rights in all areas relating to hiring and firing, work organization, as well as management of the firm. Moreover, management must initiate negotiations prior to initial changes in operations, including expansion, mergers and reorganization of the firm. Further, if the union so demands, the company is required to negotiate on all other changes as well. The law specifies that information from company books, as well as other data, must be supplied to the union, and even particular studies are to be conducted if considered necessary to provide information requested by the union.

Carnoy and Shearer regard these new pieces of legislation as constituting a "major transformation of the structure of authority in Swedish enterprise" and "the most far-reaching labor legislation reform in any Western mixed economy." However, they note that the significance of this body of laws will depend on how these newly conferred opportunities for democratic participation in industry for unions and their members will fare under practical application.[76]

Quality of Work Life Programs

In recent years a number of firms in the United States have instituted worker participation programs designed to overcome various productivity problems. Quite usually the changes at the work site are planned by such experts as technical specialists and industrial psychologists who redesign jobs to reduce boredom and improve safety and health conditions. The entire work flow of a plant may be revamped in some instances.[77]

A notable instance of the use of greater worker participation at the job level is General Motors' Buick plant in Flint, Michigan. There enhancement of quality and productivity has been achieved by delegating greater responsibility to laborers at the work site. As one indication of such delegation a laborer in that plant can shut down a main production line at the push of a button on a control panel whenever a problem is encountered which warrants it. This worker is one of 2500 employees at the Buick plant who have been trained in Quality of Work Life principles.

Along with hundreds of other Buick production line workers, Mrs. Eddo Brantley makes decisions in regard to rejecting defective raw materials, adjusting machine settings and even moving machinery to step-saving locations. In recognition for assuming this type of responsibility these workers are freed from being accountable to foremen, punching time-clocks or from always working at the same repetitive job. Of course, in addition they receive higher pay.

While such on-the-job practice has been used in Japan with astonishingly good results by a number of its leading companies, it is only beginning to spread throughout the United States and Buick remains one of the most outstanding pioneers. The impetus that persuaded Buick to seek a better quality of product by enhanced worker participation was the pressure for change after many years of labor unrest and frequent strikes. Both management and union local officials realized that company sales and jobs were at risk unless a brighter day dawned for industrial relations. The joint efforts by UAW Union Local 599 and Buick management to design worker participation programs has borne fruit in terms of a 77% increase in sales in 1980 from the 1975 low and an absence of strikes since 1974.

It is acknowledged that the training programs for the workers are costly, but management is confident that the payoff is there in better quality, reduced scrap and greater productivity. The training program includes development of listening skills, resolving conflicts in groups and establishing goals. Work groups range from eight to fourteen people and they are expected to produce only high quality parts. To this end, when a worker discovers that rods are not fitting properly into a torque converter core, he consults with other members of his work unit and then shuts down the production line. The next step is to call in a machinist who makes an adjustment on a different production line and output resumes. One worker recalled that under the old system pressure from the foreman to meet the production schedule caused employees to let the faulty parts stay on line and they left the responsibility for finding them to the quality inspector. Because of the trust and cooperation between union and management and the resulting high quality of production, Buick is now winning contracts in bidding for production of parts for other GM divisions.

Comments on the program by rank and file employees are most revealing. One worker who elected to remain on the job, though eligible for retirement, observed that after 32 years of "never having any say in how my job is done," the program is "fantastic." Another worker declared that "I'm no longer a job rat under this concept. . . ." Having been trained for a half-dozen jobs in the line, he now rotates positions with his team members. Another worker, presently a member of the Quality of Work Life Training staff, recalled that his "union was founded 40 years ago on the principle of dignity on the job." He then stated that "there is dignity—and involvement—now at Buick."[78]

Nevertheless, from a study of QWL programs in the United States five or six years after their installation, Paul S. Goodman has found that at least 75 percent of the programs were no longer functioning. He noted that of the programs studied they initially enjoyed a modest degree of success. However, he observes that most of the projects under study were only experimental in nature and lacked expert guidance because of no organizational theory behind them.

Factors that may have contributed to lack of endurance of these projects, according to Goodman, were departure of an internal sponsor or a deflection of his initial commitment; failure to maintain for new workers the thorough initial training program; lack of adequate follow-up communication to determine if QWL standards were being maintained; conflict between QWL and non-QWL segments of an organization whether company or union; ambiguous initial goals and consequent controversy over results. In some instances doubts arose on the part of unions as to whether traditional collective bargaining procedures and grievance handling could be maintained by local union officials with increasingly close interaction with management.

Factors which Goodman believes will point to a declining trend for QWL projects in the 1980's are: a decrease in the major government subsidy for these programs which had existed in the early 1970's and a lack of continuing support for QWL projects by organizations which were active initially. Apart from such internationals as the UAW and the Steelworkers, no substantial growth of union interest has developed in these programs.

To provide better guidance for these programs in the 1980's, Goodman advises that specific rather than vague goals should be set at the start of these projects and definite but longer-range timetables for reaching them (at least five years rather than about two years as was common in the 1970's). He also urges total organization commitment by both union and company rather than divisions of attitude within the structures.[79]

Labor-Management Committees

Douglas Soutar in a speech at Notre Dame in June, 1981, observed that in the past two years it has become fashionable to encourage more labor-management cooperation by means of labor-management committees either by contract or by unilateral action of the employer. He found nothing new in labor-management committees as such and recalled they were widespread during World War II, promoted by the War Production Board, and he observed for the most part that they disappeared almost as rapidly as they sprang up.

Nevertheless, he believed that with worsening economic conditions, pressures may again find the parties functioning together on these committees to seek a better understanding of each other's problems and to give more attention to employee motivation in order to improve productivity. According to Soutar, a recent study by the General Accounting Office indicated that about 1000 productivity-sharing programs exist in the United States and, of the 54 plans studied in depth, 80% reported that improved labor relations had resulted in addition to better worker performance and attitudes, as well as reduced absenteeism and turnover.

On a national scale, Soutar noted that under several administrations labor-management committees have been called into existence, but observed that most of them broke up because of opposing philosophical views relating to the interests they represented. Moreover, these national committees tended to deal with issues rather far removed from typical questions discussed during collective bargaining. At least such committees offered opportunities for face-to-face confrontations by leaders of both unions and managements.[80]

A number of Western European governments now exercise control over some managerial decisions by negotiating tripartite agreements, with unions as the third party. Extensive control by this arrangement has taken place in regard to plant location. In West Germany no relocation or transfer of work may take place unless approved by the government and until it has been submitted to a works council composed of elected employees. If the latter opposes the planned shift, the matter goes to mediation. Moreover, no plant closure may take place without obtaining a permit from the state labor exchange which is empowered to reject the tentative action if it finds that substantial unemployment is present in the area concerned.

In France the local government employment agency has authority under the nation's federal labor code to reject plant closures following consideration of the rate of employment in the area and the company's economic justification for the shutdown. Moreover, it is illegal under French law to terminate employees in a plant closure or relocation in order to avoid wage increases under collective bargaining. As in Germany there must also be consultation with factory worker committees. To proceed with a closure, without complying with these conditions, brings on a reversal of the action as well as cash damages for the affected employees. It has been said that union pressure has brought about these types of planning restrictions in order to lessen the impact of industrial hardship, but have not eliminated it as such.[81]

Profit-Sharing and Pensions

Usually such programs result in workers owning but a small percentage of their company's total shares and they would therefore have to vote as a block and quite unanimously in order to have even a modicum of influence over company policy. What is more, worker stock options permit managers to have a convenient source of direct investment capital in workers' wages with no need to yield control of the firm to the employees.

It is true that productivity may increase if the employees feel they will have a share in the company's profits and it may even persuade workers to pass up wage increases in favor of increased profits and greater stock dividends. Nevertheless, because of their minority stock shares, workers continue to remain without meaningful ownership and without rights to take part in management decision-making.[82]

Worker pension funds when invested in the employer firm also can be considered a possible avenue to worker participation in management. However, practical experience indicates that while such funds have become a significant source for capital investment, they have not increased employee participation in managerial decision-making. Very frequently pension funds, through banker trustees, have beome legally separated from their owners, who thus yield control over investment policy. In some instances, even without such trusteeship, legal barriers may prevent workers' pension funds from being invested in the same company where the workers are employed.[83]

New Technology and Employment

The Yamazaki plant in Japan today has enormous computerized equipment which grinds, bores and fashions parts for a high-technology machine similar to itself, a process described as robots producing robots. A scattering of human workers are present who operate cranes which place metal castings on fixtures for automatic wheeling to a storage area. During the night shift the machines work on with no human assistance, other than a night watchman. The computer orders a machine to cease one task, begin another, increase speed or decrease it, all according to the programmed schedule.

While American companies are moving ahead with similar types of technology, the Japanese are still in the vanguard and excel with machines that can receive electronic instructions from a main computer and can execute the orders. The Japanese see the result to be reduced costs and greater output and freedom from labor problems.

Moreover, the Yamazaki Company now is in the world market to sell such manufacturing systems, complete with equipment, programming and engineering expertise at prices ranging up to $50 million. The company acknowledges that 300 serious inquiries have been received from the United States and more than 600 foreigners have visited the Yamazaki plant in recent months. The whole development indicates the facility of the Japanese in applying existing technology of microelectronics and computerization to the manufacturing process more quickly and smoothly than is done in other countries.

As one instance, in the early 1970's Japanese industry was producing up to 3 million cars annually with a work force including subcontractors of 450,000. By 1980, though production had reached over 10 million, the work force had not increased numerically because of the extensive use of industrial robots, estimated at more than in all the rest of the world.

It is said that large companies in Japan maintain systems of life-time employment and workers therefore have no fear of being replaced by robots. This sense of job security supposedly has induced a ready willingness on the part of Japanese workers to accept labor-saving technologies. Further, because of the high level of technical education on the part of the average worker in Japan they are eager to adapt themselves to industrial change. Another favorable factor is that Japanese companies carry on extensive training programs for their workers.[84]

This roseate picture of "contented labor" in Japan has been sharply criticized recently to the effect that the Japanese work system exacts a heavy sacrifice from all industrial workers, especially from the vast majority who work in small firms where there are no so-called lifetime jobs. In fact it has been found that many small companies in Japan depend heavily on non-union, lower paid, temporary workers who can be readily laid off if costs increase.

The group in Japan which bears the brunt of the sacrifices are women who comprise 40 percent of the work force. They are trained only for menial tasks and are presumed to be in industry only temporarily and they usually do leave after a few years. It is said that women in Japan earn on the average less than 60 percent of men's earnings.

Concerning the minority of industrial and white collar workers who have lifetime jobs, their situation appears less impressive when it is realized that because of early retirement policies, most workers must leave such jobs between the ages of 55 and 60. In effect under this policy, older workers are then terminated when they reach high wage levels and are replaced by younger, more recently trained workers at lower pay. Moreover, instead of a pension, the retired worker receives a lump sum payment, usually equivalent to three years' pay. Inevitably, the terminated worker must seek another job, often a menial, poorly paid one.[85]

It is of significance to note that of all American corporations, General Motors has the largest robot program and it is predicted that by 1990 GM may have 14,000 robots in operation.[86] This circumstance gives substance to the estimate that when automobile production returns to normal there will be far fewer employees in the industry than before the recession. Mindful that already over 27 percent of the U.S. automobile market has been taken over by foreign imports,[87] a widespread use of robots for assembly lines, loading machine tools, foundry work, spot welding and spray painting may project a grim picture of technological unemployment in the 1980's for the automobile industry.

Harley Shaiken, a research associate at the Massachusetts Institute of Technology urges that UAW workers endeavor to obtain some control over the new technology in the automobile industry by seeking a voice regarding what the new equipment will be designed to do. Further, he urges increased wage income for the fewer workers who will be producing the greater output. It is his belief that by 1990 robot production in this country could reach 200,000 annually.[88]

Reference has been made in *Laborem Exercens* to another form of modern technology far more devastating in its effects than depriving workers of employment. Nuclear technology is capable of "world wide catastrophe" by destruction of human life on a genocidal scale. Should a single 20-megaton explosion occur over the New York metropolitan area the loss is estimated at "close to 10 million people killed or seriously injured. . . ."[89] Such a nuclear weapon is in the arsenals of the superpowers today and is equivalent to 1,400 Hiroshima bombs.

In several countries, thousands of people of varied skills and training are engaged in designing, producing and maintaining nuclear weapons capable of virtually wiping out the human race. The question must be asked whether the tasks they are doing in any way resemble the role of work set forth in *Laborem Exercens*, where mention is made of the "entirely positive and creative, educational and meritorious character of man's work. . . ."[90] , and that work should make one more of a human being and serve as the foundation for family life.[91]

Wages

As noted above, John Paul II observes that a family head by means of wage income should be able to maintain his family and provide for its future security without the mother being required to engage in gainful employment outside the home. It is appropriate here to examine the content and dollar figure for an intermediate annual urban budget for a four-person family as complied by the Bureau of Labor Statistics of the U. S. Department of Labor and issued on April 22, 1981.

The dollar amount of the budget was $23, 134.[92] It provided for food, housing, transportation, clothing, personal and medical care and other consumption items and also covered social security and personal income taxes. However, no provision was included for savings and for education beyond high school. Nevertheless, the U. S. Department of Commerce reports that for the year 1980 the median family income was below this budget, at $21,023.[93]

Further, it is commonly assumed that automobile workers in the United States are among the most highly paid wage earners in the country and are even considered as overpaid by some. Here it may be noted that according to the "pattern" contract for 1979 of the United Automobile Workers, the average autoworker's income, assuming a 40-hour-week for 52 weeks, was $19,157. That year the U. S. Department of Labor estimated that for a "modest but adequate" annual budget for an urban family of four an income of $20,517 was required.[94] It should be pointed out, however, that a survey revealed that in 1979 "less than a third of UAW members" lived in families where the head worked full-time. Thus it appears that most UAW members in 1979 did not have take-home income of $19,157, unless they had other sources of compensation.[95]

In Retrospect

After this discussion on efforts in a half dozen countries to move in the direction of industrial democracy, it must be concluded that the goal expressed in *Laborem Exercens* whereby capital should be at the service of labor, rather than labor at the service of capital, is far from becoming a reality in the near future. It is true that government as the "indirect employer" in a number of nations has enacted legislation to enable unions to share to some degree in the decision-making process of industry. However, it appears that unions in those countries have not yet brought about any basic change in the balance of power exercised by corporations over the economy. One might recall here the consequences from co-determination in West Germany and the presence of worker-directors on corporate boards in other countries.

Nevertheless, in the past year in the United States, there have been some significant concessions by management in exchange for heavy "give backs" by unions. To gain wage freezes, easing of restrictive work rules and deferral of benefits from unions, corporations in depressed industries have agreed to guarantees against plant closings, consultative rights to unions regarding capital investment plans, access to confidential information on costs and greater worker participation in

the decision process on plant and production problems. These nego-
tiated settlements have taken place in certain companies engaged in the
rubber, steel, meat packing and printing industries. Extensive wage and
benefit reductions have been conceded to the Ford Company by the
United Auto Workers Union in exchange for lifetime union guarantees
for senior employees, greater job security and more of a share in
decision-making by workers.[96] It must be noted that opening of company books to unions and consultation in decision-making with workers
have taken place in the past in times of economic crisis, but were
discontinued with the return of prosperity.

John Paul II's advocacy of "workers sharing in management and/or
profits of business" as "recognition of the proper position" of "the
worker in the production process"[97] stands in sharp contrast to a 1978
decision by an industrial magistrate in Western Australia who declared
in nineteenth-century common law fashion "that the defendant had the
power to direct the worker not only as to the work he did, but in the
way, place and time in which it was done.—The defendant was the
master and the worker the servant."[98] In the United States the heading
"Master and Servant" is still used in indexes to legal journals referring
to such issues as discharge cases, employee inventions under the patent
acts, and enforcement of employee non-competition agreements.[99] We
can all hope that this is nothing more than an historic anachronism.

NOTES

1. Pope John Paul II, *Laborem Exercens* (Washington, D.C.: United States
Catholic Conference, 1981), Para. 14, Work and Ownership.

2. Para. 12, The Priority of Labor.

3. Para. 4, In the Book of Genesis.

4. Para. 12, The Priority of Labor.

5. *Ibid.*

6. *Ibid.*

7. *Ibid.*

8. *Ibid.*

9. Para. 13, Economism and Materialism.

10. Para. 14, Work and Ownership.

11. *Ibid.*

12. *Ibid.*

13. *Ibid.*
14. *Ibid.*
15. *Ibid.*
16. Para. 7, Threat to the Right Order of Values.
17. *Ibid.*
18. Para. 9, Work and Personal Dignity.
19. Para. 11, Dimensions of the Conflict.
20. Para. 9, Work and Personal Dignity.
21. Para. 11, Dimensions of the Conflict.
22. Para. 13, Economism and Materialism.
23. *Ibid.*
24. Para. 15, The "Personalist" Argument.
25. *Ibid.*
26. Para. 5, Work in the Objective Sense: Technology.
27. *Ibid.*
28. Para. 12, The Priority of Labor.
29. Para. 19, Wages and Other Social Benefits.
30. *Ibid.*
31. *Ibid.*
32. *Ibid.*
33. *Ibid.*
34. Para. 17, Direct and Indirect Employer.
35. *Ibid.*
36. Para. 18, The Employment Issue.
37. *Ibid.*
38. *Ibid.*
39. *Ibid.*
40. *Ibid.*
41. *Ibid.*
42. Para. 17, Direct and Indirect Employer
43. Para. 18, The Employment Issue.
44. *Ibid.*
45. *Ibid.*
46. *Ibid.*
47. Para. 20, Importance of Unions.
48. *Ibid.*
49. *Ibid.*
50. *Ibid.*
51. *Ibid.*
52. *Ibid.*
53. Para. 14, Work and Ownership.
54. Martin Carnoy and Derek Shearer, *Economic Democracy* (Armonk, New York: M. E. Sharpe, Inc., 1980), pp. 128-130.
55. Milton Derber, *The American Idea of Industrial Democracy, 1865-1965* (Urbania; University of Illinois Press, 1970), p. 462.

56. William Winpisinger, "An American Unionist Looks at Co-Determination", *Employee Relations Law Journal*, Autumn, 1976, p. 139.

57. Robert B. Carson, *Economic Issues Today*, (New York: St. Martin's Press, 1980), p. 148.

58. Milton Derber, "Collective Bargaining: The American Approach to Industrial Democracy", *The Annals, AAPSS*, 431, May 1977, p. 92.

59. *Proceedings of the Conference on: Are Changes Ahead in Labor Relations?*, Notre Dame, Indiana, 1981, p. 25.

60. "The Myth of the Affluent Auto Worker", *Solidarity*, Detroit, February 13, 1981, p. 7.

61. Edward L. Cushman, *Cooperation or Conflict*, Wayne State University, Detroit, 1981, p. 17.

62. *Ibid,* pp. 3, 4.

63. *Ibid,* pp. 15, 16.

64. *Ibid,* p. 14.

65. Carnoy and Shearer, *op. cit.*, p. 250.

66. *Report of the Committee of Inquiry on Industrial Democracy*, Chairman Lord Bullock (London: Her Majesty's Stationery Office, January 1977), p. 93.

67. Carnoy and Shearer, *op. cit.*, p. 251.

68. *Ibid,* pp. 255-257.

69. *Ibid,* p. 254.

70. Alfred Diamont, "Democratizing the Workplace: The Myth and Reality of Mitbestimmung in the Federal Republic of Germany", *Worker Self-Management in Industry: The West European Experience*, edited by G. David Garson (New York: Praeger, 1977), pp. 44, 45.

71. Carnoy and Shearer, *op. cit.*, pp. 252, 253.

72. *Ibid,* pp. 257, 258.

73. Bullock Report, *op. cit.*, p. 109.

74. Martin Slater, "Worker Councils in Italy: Past Development and Future Prospects", in Garson, *op. cit.*, p. 197.

75. *Ibid,* p. 198.

76. Carnoy and Shearer, *op. cit.*, pp. 261-263.

77. *Ibid,* p. 135.

78. Thomas C. Hayes, "At G.M.'s Buick Unit, Workers and Bosses Get Ahead by Getting Along", *New York Times*, July 5, 1981. See also Irving Bluestone, "Work Humanization in Practice: What Can Labor Do?" in *A Matter of Dignity: Inquiries into the Humanization of Work*, ed. W.J. Heisler and John W. Houck (Notre Dame, Ind.: University of Notre Dame Press, 1977), pp. 165-178.

79. Paul S. Goodman, "Realities of Improving the Quality of Work Life", *Proceedings of the Industrial Relations Research Association*, Madison, Wisconsin, 1980, pp. 489-493.

80. Douglas Soutar, "Trends Foreseen for Collective Bargaining in the '80s", *Proceedings of the Conference: Are Changes Ahead in Labor Relations?*, Notre Dame, Indiana, June 12, 1981, pp. 4, 5.

81. Carnoy and Shearer, *op. cit.*, pp. 265, 266.

82. *Ibid*, p. 134.

83. *Ibid*

84. Steve Lohr, "New in Japan, The Manless Factory", *New York Times*, December 13, 1981.

85. Kathleen Molony, "Selective Paternalism", *The Nation*, February 13, 1982, pp. 184, 185.

86. Lohr, *op. cit.*

87. John Holusha, "Layoffs Are Just One U.A.W. Problem", *New York Times*, January 24, 1982.

88. "Unionists Warned New Technology Coming Fast", *Newsletter*, School of Labor and Industrial Relations, Michigan State University, Detroit, Fall Quarter, 1981, p. 1.

89. H. Jack Geiger, "Illusion of Survival", *The Final Epidemic*, Educational Foundation for Nuclear Science, Chicago, 1981, p. 173.

90. *Laborem Exercens*, Para. 11, Dimensions of the Conflict.

91. Para. 10, Work and Society: Family and Nation.

92. Autumn 1980 Urban Family Budgets and Comparative Indexes For Selected Urban Areas, The Bureau of Labor Statistics of the U. S. Department of Labor, Washington, D.C.: April 22, 1981, p. 2.

93. U. S. Department of Commerce, 1982.

94. *Solidarity, op. cit.*, p. 4.

95. *Ibid*

96. A. H. Raskin, "The Cooperative Economy", *New York Times*, February 14, 1982.

97. *Laborem Exercens*, Para. 14, Work and Ownership.

98. A. N. Kahn, "Who Is A Servant?", *The Australian Law Journal*, Vol. 53, December, 1979, p. 832.

99. *Index to Legal Periodicals*, September 1979 – August 1980, The H. W. Wilson Company, New York, 1980, p. 311.

CHAPTER 12

Co-Creation and Corporate Capitalism: The Problem of Bureaucracy

by Elmer W. Johnson

RECENTLY IN A DIALOGUE WITH THE RELIGIOUS ETHICIST, JAMES M. GUSTAFSON, on the ethical resources which religion can bring to business corporate leadership and governance, I argued that

> . . . the development of modern managerial capitalism has given rise to important ethical concerns. As a result of two contemporaneous and interrelated evolutions over the last 100 years or so, one organizational and the other technological, most working members of our society earn their living today as employees of large-scale schemes of cooperation. These schemes of cooperation have vastly increased our economic productivity. This has come about through two chief means: an extensive differentiation of tasks, or specialization of labor; and a highly pyramidal, hierarchical structure of management. Relatively few people have been given the authority to direct and coordinate the work life of the masses of workers.

> While such cooperative schemes of work life have been thrust upon us, we have nevertheless continued to spout the Western ideals of invidualism: competition in the marketplace, private property, personal initiative, and so forth. Let's call them the competitive virtues. We kneel in reverence before Adam Smith and John Stuart Mill, but we wonder increasingly whether the individualist tradition is adequate.[1]

It is with this perception of corporate capitalism that I read John Paul II's encyclical, *Laborem Exercens*, and will make some analysis and suggestions which, hopefully, would insure authentic progress by humans and society and would replace the antagonism and alienation of labor and management with a more cooperative spirit.

Pope John Paul II begins his encyclical with the wish "to devote this document . . . to man in the vast context of the reality of work".[2] He talks about the "new developments in technological, economic and political conditions which . . . will influence the world of work and production" in the remainder of this century and beyond. These new conditions, he says, "will require a reordering and adjustment of the structures of the modern economy and of the distribution of work."

These new developments include automation, rising costs of energy and raw materials, environmental degradation and political upheaval in the world. While it is not for the Church to analyze scientifically the societal consequences of these changes, it must examine the fresh fears and threats posed by these changes to the dignity and rights of workers and provide general guidance so as to ensure authentic progress by man and society.

What are these fresh fears and threats? The principal new danger referred to in the encyclical is that technology "can cease to be man's ally and become almost his enemy . . . , taking away all personal satisfaction and the incentive to creativity and responsibility, . . . when, through exalting the machine, it reduces man to the status of its slave"[3]. A second threat is not so new: the antinomy between labor and capital that originated not merely in the philosophy and economic theories of the eighteenth century, but rather in the whole of the economic and social practices of the time. The great error of these theories and practices was to treat man as nothing more than a factor of production. But this great historical error of primitive capitalism and liberalism can nevertheless be repeated in other circumstances of time and place. One of the calls of the encyclical is to overcome this unnatural opposition between labor and capital.[4]

A third threat is the tendency in our time toward systems of "excessive bureaucratic centralization, which makes the worker feel that he is just a cog in a huge machine moved from above, that he is . . . a mere production instrument rather than a true subject of work with an initiative of his own."[5]

What guidance does the Church offer to those persons and societies which acknowledge these threats and wish to avoid or minimize them? Pope John Paul II begins by stressing the sacramental venture of work. That is, hard work under appropriate conditions is required by God for the good of man. In work man realizes his potential as a moral agent, "a subjective being capable of acting in a planned and rational way, capable of deciding about himself and with a tendency to self-realization."[6] Through work man grows in virtue. Work is one of God's principal mechanisms for the formation of character.[7] In addition to this personal dimension, work is a condition to family life and the entire social order. Through work man is educated for community, and the nation or society is the "social incarnation of the work of all generations."[8]

A number of principles follow from these fundamental truths: (a) the priority of labor over capital; (b) the principle that the "right to private property is subordinated to the right to common use, to the fact that goods are meant for everyone;"[9] (c) the principle of the just wage; (d) the obligation of society to provide unemployment benefits; (e) the rights of employees to various social benefits such as health care, safe work conditions, vacations, pensions, and so forth; and (f) the right of union membership.

Scattered throughout the encyclical are various concrete suggestions for changes in institutional structures that would be responsive to the dangers outlined in the encyclical and in furtherance of the values and principles summarized therein. Among these suggestions is the idea of "associating labor with ownership of capital, as far as possible, and by producing a wide range of intermediate bodies with economic, social and cultural purposes."[10] Another is the proposal for "sharing by the workers in the management and/or profits of business."

Technology and Progress

Pope John Paul II is not alone in his concerns over the new threats to worker well-being as the 20th century draws to a close. In the March-April 1982 issue of *Harvard Business Review*, Robert Wuthnow, a sociologist at Princeton University, wrote an article entitled "The Moral Crisis in American Capitalism," in which he argues that the morality of the market is being eroded by the forces of technology. He sets out three moral assumptions that have undergirded the market system: (1) the Horatio Alger assumption that the market is an engine for shaping moral character and providing the dynamics of self-esteem; (2) the Milton Friedman assumption that the market is a bulwark against over-reaching government and that it ensures our personal freedoms and autonomy; and (3) the economist assumption that there are objective economic laws governing the market system over which we have no control. This last assumption, he says, has performed a salutary, safety-valve function similar to that of the existence of a devil in religion, permitting us to excuse ourselves from some of the consequences of our actions.

These assumptions, which have sustained our belief in our own goodness and decency, are now being undermined by our growing dependence on technology. For one thing, says Wuthnow, in a technological society it is difficult for the individual in his work life to believe that his effort makes any discernible difference, and so the sphere of his meaningful activity becomes restricted to the realms of family, leisure and voluntary association. Second, technology has so affected the production, consumption and pricing of goods that we no longer sense that these functions reflect the individual preferences of free, autonomous individuals. Third, as planning agencies assume more control of the economy, our leaders can no longer fall back on the objective laws of the market for relief from moral responsibility.

What do these developments portend? We will have to restructure the organization of work itself so that individuals find personal gratification, not so much from making choices in the market place as from making contributions to technological projects. The forces of the market and of technology will make for considerable tension in our life for some time to come, the reason being that the market is a decentralist, individualist principle of organization, whereas technology requires collective planning and centralized administration. Wuthnow concludes that, while a new moral code slowly takes shape, we must strive to maintain a delicate balance between "the freedom underguarding moral responsibility and our perception of unchangeable forces in the external world." That is, man requires sufficient freedom to develop his moral and rational capacities, but he cannot stand too much.

I referred earlier to three principal threats outlined in the encyclical:

the exaltation of machine over man; the continuing adversary relationship between management and labor; and bureaucratic centralization. The remainder of this paper focuses almost entirely on the last of these threats. As to the first problem, I defer to the industrial psychologists and other appropriate experts. As to the second, I have previously addressed the problems of the adversary society in the context of corporate leadership, both at this University (in a dialogue with James Gustafson) and elsewhere.[11] However, some of the proposals that I later develop in response to the problem of bureaucracy are, I believe, responsive as well to the adversarial problem.

Let me turn, then, to the problem of excessive bureaucracy. Technological revolution logically leads to organizational revolution, and the large corporation (as well as large government) is the ultimate result. The large corporation substantially reduces the area of individual market activity. One of the chief reasons that large corporations grow larger is to eliminate continual market exchange. It is apparently cheaper to pay employees to obey commands than to negotiate contracts with independent enterprise units to produce and sell the required goods and services. In the early 1800's, four out of five Americans were self-employed; the number is now less than one in ten.

> An unplanned revolution has been brought about by men who, without making a political issue out of their dimly perceived intentions, drew most of the work force out of small farming and small enterprise into the authority relations of the modern bureaucratic enterprise. It is a revolution that in industrialized systems has fundamentally changed the work patterns and other forms of human interdependence for most of the gainfully employed. Not a revolution pursued for egalitarian, democratic, or other humane motives, its motives are profit and power, and it succeeds for no more lofty reason than efficiency. But it is no less a revolution for that. It has altered politico-economic organization more than the French, the Bolshevik, or Mao's revolution. And it has established a new order in the U.S.S.R. and China no less than in the West.[12]

As Lindblom notes, the world has finally become an integrated whole—

> . . . not in language or government or culture but in coordination of work and use of the world's resources. In each inhabited continent, millions of people performed services for, and received

benefits from, a large number of people in every other continent. Accordingly, in about 1900 for the first time in history millions of the world's inhabitants—the Western Europeans and North Americans—left illiteracy, plague, and famine behind them. Whatever may be said about colonialism and imperialism and the continued suffering of those millions left out of the new order, this first global integration represented a new level and complexity of social organization.[13]

Over the last 20 years, thanks to the modern jet, international telephone communications and computer technology, we have witnessed the emergence of global corporations, which now account for perhaps 15% of world gross product.

We have been reading lately about the internationalization of work and the movement of jobs from America to foreign countries. The global corporation has become ever more adept at what is commonly called the "rationalization of its plants and operations," setting up operations in whatever corner of the world its particular needs for labor and resources and supplies can be met most cheaply. Management control and coordination of this vast network of operations is said to require comprehensive hierarchy and authority.

What is the nature of this pyramidal authority and hierarchy that we call bureaucracy? According to Max Weber, its characteristics are as follows:

> (1) the regular activities required for the purposes of the organization are distributed in a fixed way as official duties. The clear-cut division of labor makes it possible to employ only specialized experts in each particular possible position and to make every one of them responsible for the effective performance of his duties.

> (2) The organization of offices follows the principle of hierarchy; that is, each lower office is under the control and supervision of a higher one. Every official in this administrative hierarchy is accountable to his superior for his subordinates' decisions and actions. Authority flows "down" this chain-of-command; accountability flows "upward."

> (3) Operations are governed by a consistent system of abstract rules that are applied to individual cases. This formalistic system is designed to assure uniformity of performance. Explicit rules and regulations define the responsibility of each member of the organization and the relationships between them.

(4) The ideal official conducts his office in a spirit of formalistic impersonality. The exclusion of personal considerations from official business is a prerequisite for impartiality as well as for efficiency.

(5) Employment is based on technical qualifications and is protected against arbitrary dismissal. It constitutes a career.

(6) Experience tends universally to show that the purely bureaucratic type of administrative organization is, from a purely technical point of view, capable of attaining the highest degree of efficiency.[14]

While technology has made possible the global corporation, the question remains whether its emergence in its present form is due almost entirely to the inexorable logic of modern technology or is also attributable in large part to a defect in the managerial soul. That is, has the global corporation, with its high degree of centralization of management control, risen to its position of dominance in our economic life based on efficiency grounds? Or is this dominance partly explained by the presence of a strong element of managerial insensitivity and stupidity and perhaps managerial greed for power? Does the threat to worker well-being really stem from the erosion of the moral assumptions underlying the market system, namely the loss of a sense of market freedom, combined with a declining belief in limiting, objective economic laws? (It is curious that Erich Fromm, in *Escape From Freedom*,[15] argued just the opposite: that life in market societies compels people to bear an intolerable burden of decision-making.)

I have come to the following conclusions with respect to these questions. First, there are compelling efficiency reasons that largely explain the existence and dominance of the global corporation. Second, these large-scale schemes of social cooperation undoubtedly require extensive hierarchies of authority and privilege. The organization of the Roman Catholic Church is eloquent testimony to this point; and in this regard, the encyclical's reference to proposals for sharing by workers in management has a somewhat hollow ring. Third, many corporations (mainly those that are not subject to the rigors of international competition) are larger than efficiency considerations would dictate, and this is due to institutional rigidities that have calcified the joints of our market-oriented system. Fourth, by reason of ignorance and insensitivity and other human faults, we have not yet begun to deal wisely with the matter of how management hierarchies should be structured so as best to promote the spiritual ends of work. I believe that our problems of worker alienation and anomie have much more to do with the way authority is organized in the workplace than with the erosion of the market's moral code.

Cleaning Away the Underbrush

The remainder of this paper constitutes my attempt at wisdom in this arena, and while the global corporation, to which I have referred, best dramatizes the dangers with which *Laborem Exercens* is concerned, my remarks will be applicable to any corporation or organization that employs a sizeable number of people, say 1,000 or more. But before I turn to my agenda of concrete proposals, I would like first to discuss and dismiss a few perennial proposals from other quarters—proposals that I believe have little or no merit. In fact the never-ending discussion of these proposals often serves to divert our attention from the real issues.

1. *Worker Co-Ownership*. One idea is that workers should own a major portion of the voting equity capital of the corporation. In this way, it is argued, workers can have some influence in the selection of management and they can better control their own destiny. Further, it is asserted that they will have greater incentive to put forth their best work effort, so that everyone is better off as a result of worker co-ownership.

The chief fallacy lies in assuming that ownership of the equity capital has a great deal to do with management control and influence. Marx made this same assumption at a time when it was a correct one, and on that assumption he predicted a polarization between capital and labor that would ultimately spell revolution and the death of capitalism. What in fact happened is quite different: namely, a gradual evolution in which control of the enterprise has come to depend on educated skills, not ownership of capital. This evolution occurred side by side with the ever-increasing size of corporations and the need for more hierarchical schemes of organization. Adam Smith's principle of division (or rather specialization) of labor was simply being played out to its logical conclusion. The management of human resources and capital assets for the production of goods and services, it turns out, calls for quite different skills than does the investment function.

If I am right in this analysis, then worker co-ownership would result in a tragic and costly confusion of roles. It would be subversive of the hierarchy of talent necessary and appropriate to the effective operation of the large corporation. As to the incentive aspect, there are far simpler and more direct means of creating incentives for worker satisfaction and productivity.

2. *Worker Participation in Management.* This proposal calls for worker representation on boards of directors and management committees. The idea is that if worker representatives were able to participate in the decision-making process at the highest policy levels, the adversary atmosphere would tend to be replaced by one of cooperation.

As in the case of the first proposal, I believe that this idea is unsound because it does not take seriously the hierarchy and specialization of talent required for the effective management of the large corporation. I believe it is possible to devise means of corporate governance that will (a) help ensure that only the best qualified persons rise to positions of top authority, (b) hold these persons accountable for the responsible exercise of that authority, and (c) substantially reduce the adverse effects of bureaucratization.

3. *Worker Sharing of the Profits.* Another idea for dealing with the problem of worker alienation is to enable workers to share in corporate profits. If profit-sharing makes sense for management personnel, why not for the workers? Wouldn't this proposal lead to a greater spirit of cooperation between management and labor and a greater desire on both their parts to work for the common good?

This proposal has some merit. Perhaps the best argument for the proposal is one that has nothing to do with worker alienation: that is, if a substantial portion of worker compensation depends on corporate profits, the corporation will be more likely to survive in bad times, and corporations will not as likely be left with the unfortunate alternative of massive layoffs. But there are problems. First, whereas top management has broad responsibility for overall results of operations and it is therefore fair to base part of their compensation on these results, workers in a particular plant or division would be unfairly penalized if despite the successful results in their area, the rest of the corporation incurred a loss. It would seem better to tie their incentive compensation to the results of their particular operation. Second, we must be mindful that equity capital has a cost. Management can hire new equity capital but only if there is a reasonable prospect of a fair return. Any profit-sharing scheme for workers or managment should come into play only after a minimum return has been earned for stockholders.

Some Concrete Proposals

Let me now turn to some suggestions for institutional change that I believe would further the human and social ends enunciated in *Laborem Exercens.*

1. Market Efficiency and Size. Pius XI, in *Quadragesimo Anno* (1931) articulated the principle of subsidiarity:

> . . . [It] is an injustice and at the same time a grave evil and a disturbance of right order, to transfer to the larger and higher collectivity functions which can be performed and provided for by lesser and subordinate bodies. . . .

While the Pope was focusing on governmental bodies, the same principle, I believe, applies to business corporations. There is reason to believe that there is far too much "big business" in our country than can be justified on efficiency grounds, to say nothing of considerations of social desirability.

If we were to take seriously the human and social ends of work enunciated in *Laborem Exercens*, we would, at the very minimum, remove two features of our tax code that now encourage large corporations to grow by plowing back most of their earnings in ways that are inconsistent with market efficiency signals. The first of these features is the capital gains tax (especially in combination with the tax-free reorganization provisions of the Internal Revenue Code), which tends to block the flow of capital out of less rewarding into more rewarding investments. The second is the double taxation of dividend income, which tends to result in the retention and reinvestment of corporate earnings in lines of business that are less profitable than others in which stockholders would prefer to invest if corporate earnings could be distributed without such a heavy penalty.

There has been growing support in recent years for a fundamental reform in our tax system from a tax on income to a tax on spending. There are many forceful arguments for a consumption-type tax, including those relating to efficiency, fairness and capital formation. But one of the incidental benefits of such reform would be to eliminate the double-taxation of dividend income. As a consequence, there would be strong pressure on corporate managers to distribute the bulk of corporate earnings to stockholders as dividends, and stockholders would be heavily penalized if they did not re-invest the dividends in productive capital. Thus it would remove the powerful built-in bias toward empire-building. Instead, corporate managers would have to appeal to investors for new capital by spelling out the merits of their new capital projects. Such a discipline would impose much greater constraints on size than now exist.

2. *Decentralism Within the Corporation.* I shall never forget discussing with William G. Karnes, on his retirement after twenty-five years as chief executive officer of Beatrice Foods, the company's almost unparalleled compound rate of growth in earnings per share over the period of his long tenure. He told me that by far the most important reason for this growth was a strong policy of decentralism combined with a policy of never entering a new line of business unless it could be staffed with top-quality management. "And you must feel it in your gut every day you go to work," he said, "because there are always powerful temptations and tendencies toward centralization."

Why did he feel so strongly on this point? Because one will not acquire and keep top-quality managers if he strips them of authority and initiative. Because managers will not grow and flourish as human beings if they cannot make major decisions and assume substantial risks. Because managers who are carefully controlled and limited by headquarters will tend to engage in the same practices respecting their subordinates. And as the atmosphere of bureaucratic stultification ultimately pervades the entire organization, the energies of managers and workers alike will be sapped, and product quality and innovation, as well as profits, will deteriorate.

What form does a decentralist management hierarchy take? How does the chief executive officer spend his time? Simply put, the parent company staff is lean, and it functions as a full-time board of directors overseeing but not running the diverse operations of the company. If there are twenty divisional presidents, the chief executive officer will likely devote the major portion of his time to the few that are having problems at any particular time. The division heads will be given a loose rein as long as they are doing well and will be judged only after the fact. Thus the executive staff of a five- to ten-billion dollar conglomerate may number no more than thirty or forty persons at the parent level, consisting of the top executive officers and the financial and legal staffs.

On the positive side, the decentralist manager understands that the corporate ethos is established at the top. While I do not accept the validity of trickle-down justice, I am a born-again believer in trickle-down leadership. In this regard, the top officers, while spending the bulk of their time on the problem operations, will also be mindful of a quite distinct responsibility: namely, the need for their personal involvement in creating and maintaining a sense of community among all the personnel. As I have written elsewhere:

> . . . that the leader is an inspirer of others within the organization. He brings about solidarity and fellow-feeling among the key personnel. He assists younger executives in realizing their full potential. The leader has a vision of the common good of the organization. Not only has he devoted his efforts to articulating and working toward that common good, but it has become dramatically apparent to other members of the organization that his vision is a noble one, that there is a real passion in his commitment to this vision, and that he really cares for the members of the organization. The leader with this kind of vision and fidelity and caring has the fiber and strength that enable him to face up to tough problems and make decisions under pressure, to make constructive criticisms of young executives in a kindly manner, and to assist older executives in preparing the way (and making way) for the next generation of leadership.[16]

Much of this will consist of the many informal relationships and friendships that spring up rather spontaneously and that enhance the level of mutual trust, respect and confidence throughout the organization. But this function will also include the thoughtful, sometimes unexpected gestures by way of recognizing personnel on the occasion of promotions, retirements and other important events.

3. *Compensation and Promotion Policy.* The source of inspiration for the decentralist manager is his compelling vision of a just community in which each employee and officer has the opportunity to realize his full potential as a purposeful, moral agent in rich interaction with his fellow workers. He is driven and exhilarated by this vision. Accordingly, he cannot subscribe to the "giraffe" principle of compensation, in which one or a few top officers tower above all others in income. He will shun perquisites that cannot be clearly justified by the corporate interest. The giraffe in compensation and "perks" is without moral authority to build a community of highly productive workers.

A second principle is that of a meritocracy. Unfortunately, it is difficult or impossible to implement in the case of workers under union representation. Yet, all of us need to be held accountable on an individual basis. Every worker should have an annual merit review, and his compensation change should be based on his own development in terms of competence, teamwork and productivity, and, at the middle and upper management levels, on judgment and leadership qualities as well. This is not to say that a significant part of his total compensation should not also depend on the overall results of operations of the corporation or his particular division.

Merit review is important not only for compensation purposes but also for promotion decisions. Without a good merit review system, employees will have no confidence that they can grow in responsibility as they develop their skills. Merit review is indispensable if employees are not to feel like cogs in a vast machine.

In the corporation whose directors share the values and principles of *Laborem Exercens*, there will be a third principle of compensation. This principle, which looks to the long-term good of the corporation and its constituencies, will require that a very sizeable portion of the incentive or bonus compensation payable to executives and perhaps all employees with respect to any particular year of service be based on the financial performance of the corporation or their specific divisions over the ensuing five years or so. There are at least two rationales for this principle. The first is that the best measure of the value of officers' and employees' performance is that of how well their judgments and the quality of their work enhance the corporate goodwill, as reflected in future earnings over a sustained period. The second is that managers and workers should be made to think of themselves as temporary stewards and custodians of the corporate workbench, and the compensation system should induce them in their daily work lives to concern themselves with the legacy they will leave their successors.

4. Open Communications and Mutual Consultation. What institutional changes are appropriate to ensure that managers will think of employees as human beings, the quality of whose work life is important to their moral and rational development in community? One of the chief problems with hierarchy is that those at or near the top tend to lose touch with those at or near the bottom. Employee relations are institutionalized in such a manner that lower echelon employees never have access to upper echelon executives. This is also true at the board level. Directors often hear only from the top few officers and are insulated from the rest of the organization. The danger is not only one of morale; there is also the danger of misinformation.

I believe that it is possible to deal with these dangers without undermining the effectiveness of the managerial hierarchy. As to the board of directors, its most important function, by far, is the selection and monitoring of top management and seeing to orderly successions in top management. In order to perform this function well, the board needs to hear periodically from a number of key executives. For example, at least once a year the vice-president of research and development should appear at a board meeting and report and be questioned as to his scope of operations, his division's most important opportunities and challenges and its most serious problems. While the chief executive may sometimes be tempted to be selective on the information he brings to the board's attention, the vice-president will have to report on his particular problems: perhaps a serious product defect that is not being solved. As important, where the board hears directly from a different key executive at each monthly meeting, there will be a salutary effect on officer morale.

As to the communications gap between upper echelon managers and lower echelon employees, the same principle should apply. The employees should be encouraged to establish Japanese-style quality control circles in which they can identify problems and develop proposed solutions. Senior officers should meet periodically with a few of the more responsible and respected employees in each area of the Company's operations. The mere fact that these sporadic meetings take place will help ensure that middle management personnel are being responsive to legitimate grievances. These sessions can and must be conducted in a manner that does not undermine the authority of middle management personnel, and accordingly, these personnel should be present at such meetings.

A Final Note: Justice between Generations

Laborem Exercens notes a number of injustices in the organization of our work lives, but it does not mention what I believe is one of the more serious violations of economic justice in our time: namely, the collusion over the last two decades between legislators (both liberal and conservative) and the older adult population, both workers and retirees, in breach of their inter-generational responsibilities. The breach consists of the erection of a complex of income security and welfare programs—programs that for the most part are not based on need and that now impose an intolerable, largely unfunded, obligation on the younger generations.

It is as if twenty of my partners and I, who are presently in control of my law firm, were to award ourselves handsome, indexed retirement contracts that would eat up half the earnings of the next generation of hard-working partners. The analogy breaks down, of course, because the younger partners upon learning of the swindle would soon leave the firm and set up their own law practice. It is not that easy for our children and grandchildren to leave the United States.

This is not the place to consider and propose solutions responsive to this critical problem. Suffice it to say that the kinds of institutional changes in work life that have been discussed in this paper fail to respond to the profound problem of inter-generational injustice that has been inflicted on younger workers and on those who have not yet reached working age.

NOTES

1. James M. Gustafson and Elmer W. Johnson, "The Corporate Leader and the Ethical Resources of Religion: A Dialogue," in *The Judeo-Christian Vision and the Modern Corporation*, ed. Oliver F. Williams, C.S.C. and John W. Houck (Notre Dame, Ind.: University of Notre Dame Press, 1982), p. 306.

2. *Laborem Exercens*, Para. 1. All citations are to the text published by the United States Catholic Conference: Publication No. 825, Office of Publishing Services. To reduce the number of footnotes referring to the encyclical, one note below occasionally covers sequential citations from the same paragraph.

3. Para. 5.
4. Para. 13.
5. Para. 15.
6. Para. 6.
7. Para. 9.
8. Para. 10.
9. Para. 14.
10. Ibid.
11. See Gustafson and Johnson, *The Judeo-Christian Vision and the Modern Corporation*, pp. 321-325.
12. Charles E. Lindblom, *Politics and Markets: The World's Political-Economic System* (New York: Harper & Row, 1978), pp. 28-29.
13. Ibid., pp. 36-37.
14. W.J. Heisler, "Worker Alienation: 1900-1975," in *A Matter of Dignity: Inquiries into the Humanization of Work*, ed. W.J. Heisler and John W. Houck (Notre Dame, Ind.: University of Notre Dame Press, 1977), pp. 70-71.

15. Erich Fromm, *Escape From Freedom* (New York: Farrar and Rinehart, 1941).

16. See Gustafson and Johnson, *The Judeo-Christian Vision and the Modern Corporation*, pp. 312-313. See also Oliver F. Williams C.S.C. and John W. Houck, *Full Value* (New York: Harper & Row, 1978), chap. 3.

Contributors

FATHER ERNEST BARTELL, C.S.C. is Executive Director of the Helen Kellogg Institute for International Studies of the University of Notre Dame. He also serves as Overseas Mission Coordinator for the Priests of Holy Cross, Indiana Province (C.S.C.). He has been the Director for the Fund for the Improvement of Post Secondary Education of the U.S. Department of Health, Education and Welfare, and president of Stonehill College. Father Bartell earned a Ph.D. in economics from Princeton University. His published works include *Economic Problems of Nonpublic Schools; Metropolitan II: An Econometric Study of Potential and Realized Demand for Higher Education in the Boston Metropolitan Area;* and *Costs and Benefits of Catholic Elementary and Secondary Schools.*

FATHER MARK JAMES FITZGERALD, C.S.C. is professor emeritus, department of economics, and was its director of industrial relations studies, University of Notre Dame. In 1957, he was president of the Catholic Economics Association, and was vice-president of the Catholic Association for International Peace. For two decades, he has been an active arbitrator in industrial relations and has convened a national conference on contemporary themes in labor-management relations. Father Fitzgerald received his A.B., Notre Dame; M.B.A., Harvard University; and Ph.D., University of Chicago. He is the author of *Britain Views Our Industrial Relations* and *The Common Market's Labor Programs.*

DENIS GOULET holds the William and Dorothy O'Neill chair in Education for Justice at the University of Notre Dame. He did his undergraduate and graduate studies at the Catholic University of America and received his doctorate in political science from the University of Sao Paulo, Brazil. He has worked as a factory hand in France and Spain and shared the life of two nomadic tribes in Algeria. He has filled visiting professorships at universities in France, Canada, and the United States, and has been engaged in worldwide research on value conflict in technology transfer at the Overseas Development Council, Washington, D.C. Besides articles, reviews and monographs, he has published: *A New Moral Order: Development Ethics and Liberation Theology; A Cruel Choice: A New Concept in the Theory of Development; The Uncertain Promise: Value Conflicts in Technology Transfer; Survival with Integrity: Sarvodaya at the Crossroads;* and *Mexico: Development Strategies for the Future.*

STANLEY MARTIN HAUERWAS, professor of theology at the University of Notre Dame, is an ethicist who is concerned primarily with the basic methodological issues in theological ethics. In particular, he has stressed the importance of character and virtue for understanding the moral life. In this connection he has also developed the implications of narrative as a crucial concept for understanding Christian ethics. He has also published on such issues as situation ethics, abortion, euthanasia, the care of the retarded, and political ethics. His publications include *Vision and Virtue: Essays in Christian Ethical Reflection; Character and the Christian Life: A Study in Theological Ethics; Truthfulness and Tragedy;* and *A Community of Character: Toward a Constructive Christian Social Ethic.*

FATHER J. BRYAN HEHIR, for the last decade, has been the director, Office of International Justice and Peace, United States Catholic Conference, Washington, D.C., and visiting lecturer in Social Ethics, St. John's Seminary, Brighton, Massachusetts. He has been a member of the Vatican Delegation to the United Nations' General Assembly, 1973, and the United Nations' Special Session on Disarmament, 1978. He took degrees from St. John's

Seminary, Brighton, Massachusetts, and his doctorate in Applied Theology, from Harvard Divinity School. A frequent contributor to journals, he is on the editorial board, *Worldview*, and a columnist for *Commonweal*.

JOHN W. HOUCK is professor of management at the University of Notre Dame. A former Ford and Danforth Fellow, he has earned both a liberal arts and a J.D. degree from Notre Dame, an M.B.A. from the University of North Carolina at Chapel Hill, and a master of laws from Harvard. He has lectured and conducted workshops on the role of religious and humane values in business at several universities and management groups. In 1983, he is a Luce Foundation Lecturer on "Religion and the Social Crisis," Wake Forest University. In addition to articles and reviews, he has published: *Academic Freedom and the Catholic University; Outdoor Advertising: History and Regulation; A Matter of Dignity: Inquires into the Humanization of Work;* and with Oliver F. Williams, C.S.C., *Full Value: Cases in Christian Business Ethics* and *The Judeo-Christian Vision and the Modern Corporation.*

FATHER DAVID HOLLENBACH, S.J. is associate professor of Theological Ethics at Weston School of Theology, Cambridge, Massachusetts. He earned his Ph.D. at the Yale University Divinity School. Father Hollenbach is the author of *Claims in Conflict: Retrieving and Renewing the Catholic Human Rights Tradition.* He recently reported on and participated in a conference sponsored by the Bread for the World Education Fund and the Weston School of Theology under the title, "The Churches, the Bible, and the Politics of Justice."

ELMER W. JOHNSON is general counsel and group executive—public affairs, General Motors Corporation, and a limited partner in the Kirkland and Ellis law firm in Chicago. His undergraduate degree is from Yale University and his law degree from the University of Chicago. He specializes in the areas of banking, corporation, and securities law and was a lecturer in these subjects at the Law School, University of Chicago. In addition he has been a guest professor at Colorado College, a lecturer at Yale University, and in both the Divinity and Business Schools, University of Chicago. He has been a consultant to major multinational corporations in regard to their codes of conduct. He is a member of the executive committee, board of trustees, University of Chicago. He is co-author of the volume, *Can the Market Sustain an Ethic?*

SISTER ANDREA LEE, I.H.M. is the dean of Continuing Education at Marygrove College, Detroit, Michigan. A specialist in Educational Administration, Sister earned her Ph.D. at Pennsylvania State University. Sister Andrea is a member of the National Steering Committee of the Religious Commission on E.R.A. She is also a past president of the National Coalition of American Nuns.

PROFESSOR GEORGE C. LODGE, a graduate of Harvard College, has been a member of the Harvard Business School Faculty since 1963. He teaches *Business, Government and the International Economy* in the MBA Program and related courses in the School's executive programs. He is a member of the board of trustees of the Carnegie Endowment for International Peace, of the World Peace Foundation, and of the Robert F. Kennedy Memorial; a member of the Council on Foreign Relations and the Newcomen Society of North America. He serves as educational consultant to several large corporations, including IBM, AT&T, Gulf Oil Corporation, and Allied Chemical. He is the author of numerous articles and books, including *Spearheads of Democracy; Engines of Change: United States Interests and Revolution in Latin America;* and *The New American Ideology.*

SISTER AMATA MILLER, I.H.M. is the financial vice president of the I.H.M. Sisters of Monroe, Michigan. Educated in economics, Sister Amata has a Ph.D. from the University of California at Berkeley. Sister is a member of the Board of Directors of NETWORK, the first registered Catholic social activism lobby.

"Established in 1971, NETWORK has been organized in 245 congressional districts and has a membership of about 5,000 persons. NETWORK is committed to affect issues 'that afflict the poor and powerless,' and works toward this goal by lobbying, educating for a political ministry, and bringing to its efforts a 'feminine perspective.' "

BERNARD MURCHLAND is a professor of Philosophy at Ohio Wesleyan University and Director of the Antaeus Center for the Study of Society and Education. He was born in Canada and is now a naturalized American citizen. He holds a BA from the University of Moncton, a degree in theology from the University of Montreal, and the Ph.D. from the State University of New York at Buffalo. Among his books are: *The Age of Alienation; The New Iconoclasm; The Meaning of the Death of God; The French Existentialists in Politics; The Dream of Christian Socialism;* and the forthcoming *Humanism and Capitalism.* His writings on education have appeared in *Change, The Chronicle of Higher Education, The Christian Science Monitor,* the *Wall Street Journal, Worldview, Commonweal, Thought* and elsewhere.

MICHAEL NOVAK is resident scholar at the American Enterprise Institute, Washington, D.C. He has received degrees from Stonehill College, the Gregorian, and Harvard University. He has been an advisor in national political campaigns, and was chief of the United States Delegation to the Human Rights Commission in Geneva. Among his books are: *A Theology for Radical Politics; Ascent of the Mountain, Flight of the Dove; Belief and Unbelief; The Experience of Nothingness; The Rise of the Unmeltable Ethnics; The Guns of Lattimer;* and *The Spirit of Democratic Capitalism.*

JOSEPH A. PICHLER is executive vice president of the Dillon Companies, Inc. of Hutchinson, Kansas. Until June 1980, he was the Dean of the Business School of the University of Kansas. A 1961 graduate of the College of Business Administration of the University of Notre Dame, Mr. Pichler earned an M.B.A. and a Ph.D. from the University of Chicago. He is on the Board of Directors of Cities Service Corporation, The Dillon Companies, Inc., and Benedictine College. He also serves as a member of the National Board of Consultants for the National Endowment for the Humanities. Mr. Pichler has published numerous articles. His books include: *Inequality: The Poor and the Rich in America;* and *Ethics, Free Enterprise, and Public Policy.*

FATHER OLIVER F. WILLIAMS is adjunct associate professor of management, University of Notre Dame, and a member of the Congregation of Holy Cross (C.S.C.). After undergraduate work in engineering and graduate studies in divinity at Notre Dame, he received his Ph.D. in theology from Vanderbilt University. He has been president of the Association for Professional Education for Ministry, director of the Master of Divinity program at Notre Dame, and research fellow at the Graduate School of Business Administration, Stanford University. He is a fellow of the Society for Values in Higher Education and of the Case Study Institute. In addition to articles and reviews, he is a contributer to *Christian Theology: A Case Method Approach,* coauthor of *Full Value: Cases in Christian Business Ethics,* and coeditor of *The Judeo-Christian Vision and the Modern Business Corporation.*

Index